D0085185

Ambivalent Conspirators

Ambivalent Conspirators

JOHN BROWN, THE SECRET SIX, AND A THEORY OF SLAVE VIOLENCE

Jeffery Rossbach

University of Pennsylvania Press
PHILADELPHIA 1982

This work was published with the support of the Haney Foundation.

Copyright © 1982 by the University of Pennsylvania Press
All rights reserved

Library of Congress Cataloging in Publication Data

Rossbach, Jeffery S., 1944–
    Ambivalent conspirators.

    Bibliography: p.
    Includes index.
    1. Brown, John, 1800-1859. 2. Harpers Ferry (W. Va.)
—John Brown's Raid, 1859. 3. Abolitionists—United
States—Attitudes. 4. Slavery—United States—
Insurrections, etc. I. Title.
E451.R75 1982   973.6'8   82–60303
ISBN 0–8122–7859–3

Printed in the United States of America

E
451
.R75
1982
c.1

BB

To the Rossbach–Szustecki family

UWEC McIntyre Library

DISCARDED

APR X X 1983

EAU CLAIRE, WI

Contents

Acknowledgments

Somehow Those Damn Research Boxes Kept Following Me.

I BECAME INTERESTED in the question of why individuals seek violent means to affect political change about ten years ago when I was a graduate student in history at the University of Massachusetts. At the suggestion of Stephen B. Oates, I began my investigation by examining the motives of the Secret Six, and in 1974 I presented my findings as a dissertation. After I had earned my degree, I left Amherst and moved throughout New England. For the first few years, each time I packed I enthusiastically loaded my research boxes, believing that I'd eventually settle somewhere and use the time that a university teaching position so generously provides to expand my manuscript into a book. So much for that dream. I soon realized that if I ever did write the book, it would have to be at night and on weekends, when there is enough time to collect one's thoughts and wrestle with that devilish process called writing. But flesh is weak and my good intentions never did lead to off-hour scholarly pursuits. I also found that, as I kept moving, loading boxes seemed more like lugging boxes; and I decided that while books, albums, and cooking utensils were worth the candle, dusty note containers were not. I mean, how much gear can a VW be expected to accommodate? The question was murderously simple: How do I get rid of them? The answer wasn't as easy. I finally decided to abandon them in an apartment I was about to vacate, almost convincing myself that the six-pack I customarily leave in the refrigerator for the apartment's new occupants would adequately compensate them for the time they spent solving my problem. But, of course, I could never bring myself to actually part with the boxes; my house continued to be their house. Then, about three years ago, I arrived in Tallahassee to work as an editor for the Black Abolitionist Papers Project and, thankfully, to return to the study of history. I could have sworn the boxes sighed. They were dusted off and reopened, and with the encouragement and support of the project's editor, C. Peter Ripley, I used their contents and additional research and reading to revise my original work. The project provided a working context for my labors; nights and weekends provided the hours.

Unfortunately, slightly magical boxes may prod the author's conscience, but they do not lift pens, tap typewriter keys, or print books. People do that, and I'd like to take this opportunity to thank the individuals who helped make this study possible. I am indebted to the staffs of those research libraries where materials about John Brown and the Secret Six are held. The institutions include: The Library of Congress, the Boston Public Library, the Massachusetts Historical Society, the Houghton Library at Harvard University, the Kansas State Historical Society, the Atlanta University Library, the Sterling and Beinecke Libraries at Yale University, the Cornell University Library, the Syracuse University Library, the New York Historical Society, the Huntington Library, the Columbia University Library, and the Concord Free Public Library. I am especially grateful to Marty Shaw of Harvard University, John Aldin of the Boston Public Library, and Marcia Moss of the Concord Free Public Library for the attention they devoted to my project. Each suggested additional sources of information about the Six and each cheered me onward. For many personal reasons, Concord, Massachusetts, holds a special place in my affections; my research there provided me with an additional opportunity to reflect on the many gifts I'd received during previous visits.

As I said earlier, Stephen B. Oates suggested that I might find some of my answers about political violence by looking at the Six. Steve also directed my dissertation, shared his John Brown research, and gave me the benefit of his great talent as a writer and critic. More than anyone I've met, Steve understands the process of writing and is able to communicate that understanding to those who work with him. Without his counsel, this book would not have been written.

One of the points I hoped to make by bringing up those dusty research boxes is that, for me, writing about history is immeasurably facilitated by working in an environment that nurtures the realization of its value. I was fortunate to be hired as an editor at the Black Abolitionist Papers Project and once again to encounter people who possess the same enthusiasm for history. Both Pete Ripley and Joe Richardson of the Florida State University History Department encouraged me to revise my manuscript and gave me the benefit of their criticism. The work has been very much improved through their efforts.

Part of the reason those boxes were never left behind had to do with my conviction that the Six's story was worth telling. Another person who also believed that was Malcolm Call, associate director at the University of Pennsylvania Press. It is difficult for me to express how much I appreciate his friendship and continued support. I can only hope that you have the good luck to meet him and hear his extraordinary laugh. And if you get the chance, ask him to say, "When are you going to finish that manuscript?" As I completed the book, I realized that many of the ideas which influenced my presentation were formed during my graduate study at the University of Massachusetts. My days at the university were exciting because I worked with challenging and knowledgeable teachers like Richard Levy, Jack Tager, Paul Boyer, Steve Nissenbaum, and Leonard Richards; and I had a chance to listen to the crackling conversation that more often than not resulted from their exchanges with graduate students like Bill Kapelle, Betty Mitchell, Dennis McNally, and Jack Murphy. Thank you, all.

Only now do I realize the gulf that exists between completing the final sentence of a last chapter and seeing a book in print. I'd never have made the trek without the assistance of Janet Greenwood, who copyedited the manuscript, and Jean Stolarski and Muriel Stuart, who typed it. Debra Susie and Roy E. Finkenbine are friends and associates at the Black Abolitionist Papers Project. While I made final preparations on the manuscript, they endured my repetitious complaints and punctured my pretensions with their humor.

I could not close my acknowledgments without saying a word about three people who did not give me professional advice but who did provide a great deal of care while I wrote the book. Josephine and John Arcanti made a small-town boy feel at home in Boston. They shared their table and, more important, their sense of how to live well. I raise my glass and say—*salute!* Judy Harding is a friend who will always remain family. She knew the book would be published when I didn't.

Ambivalent Conspirators

Introduction

A FEW DAYS AFTER New Year's in 1857 on a windy, bitter cold afternoon in Boston, a somber-faced man named John Brown appeared at the offices of the Massachusetts Kansas Committee. The gray-haired, fifty-six-year-old abolitionist had recently returned from the Kansas Territory, where for over a year he had helped lead the struggle against slavery. Brown believed that armed force had to be used to prevent a proslavery takeover in Kansas, and he had come east seeking funds to further free-state military efforts. After introducing himself and presenting his references, he was welcomed by the committee's newly appointed secretary, young Franklin Benjamin Sanborn. Their meeting began a three-year relationship, during which Sanborn and five prominent abolitionists—Theodore Parker, Samuel Gridley Howe, Thomas Wentworth Higginson, Gerrit Smith, and George Luther Stearns—would not only help Brown collect funds for Kansas, but would also form a secret committee to subsidize his Harpers Ferry raid. By March 1858, these six men had become engaged in a conspiracy to provide the cash, arms, and equipment for Brown's violent thrust at slavery. They supported Brown's plan to "make a dash" south, incite a slave uprising, and retreat into the mountains of Virginia, where a fortress would be established and other similar attacks prepared.

When Brown's assault aborted in the fall of 1859, all of the committeemen except Higginson destroyed documents linking them to the scheme. Yet enough information survives to suggest a number of conclusions about their activity. The Six learned of Brown's plan in late

February and early March of 1858. They were able to overcome their initial doubts about it during the next year, and by late spring of 1859, they had raised nearly $4,000 in money, guns, and supplies for the proposed attack. The raid had originally been scheduled for the summer of 1858, but the group postponed it when a disgruntled associate of Brown's, Hugh Forbes, threatened to reveal the conspiracy to influential political leaders in Washington, D.C. Though all of the committee members did not know all of the details of the attack (for instance, they were shocked when Brown was trapped inside the Harpers Ferry arsenal, since he had assured them that his primary objective was to strike the arsenal quickly and capture the weapons housed there), at least four —Sanborn, Stearns, Smith, and Higginson—certainly knew when, where, and how Brown intended to start his violent work. Ten days before the October assault, Sanborn, Stearns, and Lewis Hayden, a leader of Boston's black community (who was not a formal member of the secret group but undoubtedly had intimate knowledge of its proceedings), stayed awake all night outlining the proposal to Francis Merriam, a young man who soon afterward joined Brown's insurrectionary cadre. In short, the factual record of the conspiracy can be accurately reconstructed despite the destruction of some sources.[1]

A number of excellent studies which examine abolitionist attitudes toward violence have appeared in the past few years, and these works have served as a starting point for my research. However, no study has thoroughly investigated why these six nominally pacifist abolitionists decided to support slave violence at Harpers Ferry. The reasons for this omission vary. Works treating the conspiracy in the context of Civil War causality have submerged the episode in the larger debate about how John Brown's raid contributed to hostilities. Most biographical studies of Brown and the individual committeemen have concentrated

---

1. Oswald Garrison Villard, *John Brown, 1800–1859: A Biography Fifty Years After* (Boston, 1910), pp. 271–591; Stephen B. Oates, *To Purge This Land with Blood: A Biography of John Brown* (New York, 1970), pp. 181–353; Otto J. Scott, *The Secret Six: John Brown and the Abolitionist Movement* (New York, 1980), pp. 1–323. Scott's work is the most recent narrative presentation of the conspiracy. It is based primarily on secondary sources and does not substantively examine the question of motive.

on the role one person played in the affair. Essays that examine Brown's relationship with group members have frequently been conditioned by efforts in the first two categories. Another serious impediment to analysis of motive results from the historiographical struggle surrounding the examination of antislavery reform. Brown's relationship with the Secret Six is obscured by what Stanley Elkins once described as the "persistent rhythm" of rightness and wrongness which frequently characterizes the treatment of abolitionism.[2]

Although this historiographical debate inhibits the investigation of committeemen's reasons for trying to instigate a slave revolt, an interpretive point on which conservative and revisionist historians agree has further clouded those reasons. Scholars from both schools portray Brown as a man who dominated the members of the group

2. Stanley M. Elkins, *Slavery: A Problem in American Institutional and Intellectual Life,* 2d ed. (Chicago, 1968), pp. 1–26. Elkins's entire introduction is a model for historiographical analysis. For examinations which do look at the class values of abolitionists, see Leonard L. Richards, *Gentlemen of Property and Standing: Anti-Abolition Mobs in Jacksonian America* (New York, 1970); Gerald Sorin, *The New York Abolitionists: A Case Study in Political Radicalism* (Westport, 1971); William H. Pease and Jane H. Pease, *Bound with Them in Chains: A Biographical History of the Antislavery Movement* (New York, 1972); George Fredrickson's introduction to Hinton Rowan Helper, *The Impending Crisis of the South* (Cambridge, Mass., 1968).

To date, the most revealing examinations of abolitionist attitudes toward the use of violent means have appeared in Lawrence J. Friedman, "Antebellum American Abolitionism and the Problem of Violent Means," *The Psychohistory Review* 9 (Fall 1980): 23–58; John Demos, "The Antislavery Movement and the Problem of Violent Means," *New England Quarterly* 37 (December 1964): 501–26; William H. and Jane H. Pease, "Confrontation and Abolition in the 1850s," *Journal of American History* 58 (March 1972): 923–37; Lewis Perry, *Radical Abolitionism: Anarchy and the Government of God in Antislavery Thought* (Ithaca, 1973); Bertram Wyatt-Brown, "John Brown, Weatherman and the Psychology of Antinomian Violence," *Soundings* 58 (Winter 1975): 425–41; Carleton Mabee, *Black Freedom: The Nonviolent Abolitionists from 1830 through the Civil War* (New York, 1970); Ron Walters, *The Antislavery Appeal: American Abolitionism after 1830* (Baltimore, 1976). Other works include James Brewer Stewart, "Peaceful Hopes and Violent Experiences: The Evolution of Reforming and Radical, 1831–1837," *Civil War History* 17 (December 1971): 293–309; Merle E. Curti, "Non-Resistance in New England," *New England Quarterly* 2 (January 1919): 34–57; Sylvan S. Tomkins, "The Psychology of Commitment: The Constructive Role of Violence and Suffering for the Individual and His Society," in *The Antislavery Vanguard,* ed. Martin Duberman (Princeton, 1965), pp. 419–51.

with his personality and "awed" them into supporting him with "deluded visions" of "widespread insurrection." He is depicted as a mysterious and unfathomable individual who could "electrify," "magnetize," and "hypnotize" committeemen with his charismatic presence and persuasive rhetoric. He is also seen as a person whose religious, political, and social values were so different from those of the men in the Boston-based group that he was regarded as a kind of fervently admired curiosity. This view inhibits a careful assessment of the committeemen's behavior because it disregards their thoughts and feelings when they were not in contact with Brown; it ignores the importance of their own long-standing relationship and tries to squeeze the evolving interaction of seven individuals into a static framework. The men who formed the Secret Committee of Six had been friends for some time before they met Brown, and they had engaged in continuing discussions about the nature of slavery, the ways to end it, and its effect on the slave personality. Brown's ideas about using violent means to destroy the institution and his powerful religious appeal to force impressed the Six but did not overwhelm them with its originality. Nor did Brown's occasional attempts at isolating individual committeemen from the others in the group sever the bonds of loyalty, trust, and open communication which had characterized their relations.[3]

---

3. J. C. Furnas, *The Road to Harpers Ferry* (New York, 1959), pp. 327, 330–31, 334; Allan Nevins, *The Prologue to Civil War, 1859–1861*, vol. 2 of *The Emergence of Lincoln* (New York, 1950), p. 21; Furnas, *Harpers Ferry*, pp. 335–36, 339, 344–47, 349–52, 354, 365–67, 329–30, 378; Villard, *Brown*, pp. 274–321, 333, 271–72, 588–89; Henry Steele Commager, *Theodore Parker, Yankee Crusader*, 1st paperback ed. (Boston, 1960), pp. 250–51, 253; Harold Schwartz, *Samuel Gridley Howe: Social Reformer, 1801–1876* (Cambridge, Mass., 1956), pp. 223, 238–39, 248, 219–21; Frank Preston Stearns, *The Life and Public Services of George Luther Stearns* (Philadelphia, 1907), p. 129; C. Vann Woodward, "John Brown's Private War," in *The Burden of Southern History* (New York, 1960), p. 51; Ralph V. Harlow, *Gerrit Smith, Philanthropist and Reformer* (New York, 1939), pp. 308, 363, 336–37. Commager's treatment of Parker is also illustrative of the ambivalence revisionists have generally displayed in examining the group's support of violent political methods—applauding the Six for their courageous moral stand against slavery yet backing away when it comes to certifying the conspirators' appeal to force. His assertion that Parker was hypnotized by Brown,

Another problem that has prevented a thorough examination of the committeemen's motives arises from revisionists' interpretations of Higher Law. These historians rightfully emphasize the abolitionists' moral contempt for slavery, and they correctly focus on one of the sources of that contempt—the belief that there was a natural law beyond men which condemned the peculiar institution. But in writing about the committee members, they have often interpreted the Six's commitment to Higher Law and their infatuation with Brown's personality as parallel causal agents which allowed the group to rationalize their appeal to violence. The difficulty with this approach is that it uncritically equates the sincere avowal of Higher Law principles with a willingness *to act* on those principles. I believe a look at group members' participation in both the Anthony Burns affair and the Kansas aid movement suggests that, with the exception of Thomas Wentworth Higginson, none of the conspirators was able to translate the sanction of Higher Law into a practical commitment to forceful means. Committee members found that the gulf between belief and action was too great to be bridged solely by an appeal to Higher Law principles. During their relationship with Brown, these men felt compelled to fashion a new rationale to justify their embrace of violent political methods. They formulated a theory for slave insurrection

---

whether meant literally or figuratively, serves to both attach the minister to and detach him from the conspiracy, because if Parker was under some sort of spell, it becomes uncertain whether he was responsible for his actions. And Commager adds to this uncertainty when he introduces a second mitigating factor to explain his subject's behavior. Commager ritualizes the conspiracy into a mere semiserious effort by Parker and his friends, suggesting that the Secret Six didn't really engage in violent insurrection but were merely playing a "game." The Six "enjoyed . . . the hatching of plots, the secret meetings, the code . . . the purchase of arms and the rodomontade, matching Southerners word for word" (p. 253). C. Vann Woodward concurs. He sees the secret committee's relationship with Brown as a "conspirational drama." Other biographers of committee members treat their subject's commitment to Brown and insurrection similarly. They use Brown's supposed power over their subject to portray the relationship in two ways, simultaneously revealing what seems to be their own personal distaste for the use of political violence as well as the historical conviction that their biographical subject was firmly committed to its use in 1859.

which sought to address the issue of slave life *after* insurrection, a theory which momentarily drove them beyond the threshold of conventional political behavior.[4]

Two historians, Stephen B. Oates in his biography of John Brown and Tilden Edelstein in his study of Thomas Wentworth Higginson, have reexamined the committee's attraction to violence. Oates presents a number of reasons why the Six financed Brown, noting especially their conviction that a successful slave revolt would alter white preconceptions of the slave's nature. Edelstein similarly argues that Higginson wanted Brown to destroy the belief that all slaves were as "submissive as Uncle Tom." This book indicates that there is yet another reason to examine group members' ideas about altering white racial images. The Secret Six were themselves imbued with romantic racialist notions of African capacities and believed, to one degree or another, that slaves were docile, pliant, and "little addicted to revenge." Any examination of the committeemen's motives must retrace the tortuous path each followed in attempting to square his own personal racial preconceptions with the instigation of slave violence. The group members' movement from romantic racialism to a budding faith in the ability of slaves to fight for their own freedom is linked to their involvement with "practical" abolitionism.[5]

More important, the committee members were *as much concerned with altering the slave's nature as they were with changing their own and white America's perception of that nature.* The Secret Six wanted slaves to be liberated, but they wanted that liberation to be governed by a

---

4. Commager, *Parker*, chap. 10; Harlow, *Smith*, pp. 289–90, 304–5, 336–37; Franklin Benjamin Sanborn, *Recollections of Seventy Years* (New York, 1909), 1: 49–50; Schwartz, *Howe*, pp. 165–66. Numerous historians have attributed Higher Law motivations to abolitionists.

5. Oates, *Brown*, p. 238; Tilden G. Edelstein, *Strange Enthusiasm: A Life of Thomas Wentworth Higginson* (New York, 1970), pp. 224–25; George Fredrickson, *The Black Image in the White Mind: The Debate on Afro-American Character and Destiny, 1817–1914* (New York, 1971). Fredrickson's analysis of abolitionist racialism in Chapters 5 and 6 is an important one. The question he poses in Footnote 47 of Chapter 5 about the paradox of Parker's romantic racialism in the abstract and the minister's militant egalitarianism on the question of racial policy helped spur this study.

particular social outlook. In their minds, slave violence would destroy an institution, undo white racial attitudes, *and* foster a specific set of values in the newly freed Afro-American. All of the committeemen felt that a willingness to fight for freedom was at the core of Anglo-American political, social, and economic life. By June 1859 they had concluded (and, for an instant, were able to leap beyond theory to subsidize a plan based upon that conclusion) that the act of insurrection would be the slave's first step toward assimilation of a value system that emphasized individualism and was synonymous with the North's superior (if not completely faultless) culture. Political violence would prepare exslaves for participation in the democratic, industrial marketplace.

Just as the Six's reasons for supporting a slave uprising evolved, so too did their evaluation of Brown's character and their confidence in his capacity to direct the Harpers Ferry raid. Although committee members never completely lost faith in Brown's competence, their willingness to finance insurrection was based more on a belief in violence's cathartic effect on the slave personality than it was on the assumption that Brown was the only man to lead the attack. Still, an examination of group members' collective and individual interaction with Brown shows a far more complex relationship than many scholars have so far realized. John Brown and the Secret Committee of Six were not incomprehensible to each other, not separated by an abyss of experience and conviction. They were not fuzzy representations in each other's eyes. Indeed, in the formative stage of their relationship and throughout the better part of that relationship, the six committeemen thought they knew John Brown very well, thought that the social values he recommended and personal virtues he embodied mirrored their own. The attitudes of Brown and the Six were shaped in the increasingly urban-oriented North by experiences which elicited a thirst for civic repute and professional achievement and by a culture which left each man's quest for place frenetic and anxiety-filled. Brown and the members of the Secret Six came to revere self-control, order, and circumspect ambition in themselves and their society; they demanded the self-conscious expression of those values as well. The three-year relationship between Brown and the Six was not based on his power to manipulate them (although he frequently tried to), but partially on the mutual confidence which develops among people who hold common social assumptions and personal aspirations.[6]

When these shared values are linked to the moral outrage each man felt for slavery and to the group's emerging theory about the effect of political violence on the slave's character, I believe the motives for the conspiracy become clearer. I am not suggesting that differences did not exist between Brown and committee members. Nor am I saying that Brown was without charismatic appeal. Brown's intense Old Testament Calvinism contrasted sharply with the Six's transcendental religious convictions. His reckless physical valor (a valor only equaled

6. Oates, *Brown*, pp. 233–34, 237; Edelstein, *Strange Enthusiasm*, pp. 216, 208. Oates and Edelstein also grapple with the whole issue of Brown's "hypnotic" power. Though Oates forwards a variation of the theme when he portrays Brown as an Old Testament Calvinist who impressed the Six with an "unbending conviction" in his providential instrumentality, he does not fully embrace the ascendancy theme, nor does he describe the Six as mere pawns. Edelstein goes further and finally pulls the plug on the theory of "electric" attraction. Sanborn, for instance, is seen as something more than Brown's orderly. Edelstein reveals the young committee secretary as an ambitious and calculating person who used Brown as much as Brown used him. Also, in May 1858, a period of crisis in the conspiracy, Edelstein has Higginson cooly watching the proceedings from the sideline and then "shrewdly baiting" Brown with his continued commitment to insurrection.

These two historians present a far more balanced picture of Brown than has emerged in previous historical writing. Edelstein, in particular, sees Brown as a man who depended as much on slyness as he did on his ability to inspire and as much on a businesslike manner as on his "spiritual power." When Brown made his first plea for support of the Harpers Ferry plan in March 1858, Edelstein shows how he "artfully played-off" his "key supporters" against each other.

A number of historians have attempted to examine John Brown's personal value system. An important interpretation comes from Ronald Story in a paper he read before the Department of History at the University of Massachusetts entitled "John Brown and the Injuries of Class," Spring 1973, pp. 1–15. See also Ronald Story, "Black, Brown and Blood: The Hourglass Pattern," *Reviews in American History* 3 (June 1975): 213–18; Stephen B. Oates, "John Brown and His Judges: A Critique of the Historical Literature," *Civil War History* 17 (March 1971): 5–23; Louis Ruchames, ed., *A John Brown Reader* (New York, 1960); Richard O. Boyer, *The Legend of John Brown: A Biography and A History* (New York, 1973); Jules Abels, *Man on Fire: John Brown and the Cause of Liberty* (New York, 1971).

by that of Higginson) impressed all of the committee members and reminded them of the limitations they placed on their own abolitionist activity. Brown made personal sacrifices—including the ultimate sacrifice at Harpers Ferry—which inspired the group and pointed out their estimable, but certainly more limited, contributions to the movement. And the conspirators were also separated by success. Brown failed in the marketplace, while the Six prospered there and received society's accolades. Yet the observation of Brown's life and the lives of each committeeman leaves one with the impression that all of the conspirators were much more united by the beliefs gained from their struggles for achievement than they were separated by their varying resolution of those struggles. Most significant, in dealing with Brown, the Six encountered a man whose failure had sharpened his sensitivity to the marketplace's rhetorical demands and deepened his heartfelt commitment to its values. Furthermore, the Six recognized, as their rationale for insurrection grew and superseded all other motives, that Brown's system (their *own* system) was the model which had to be presented to slaves, whose nature, they believed, would be altered by participation in a bloody uprising.

CHAPTER 1

Anthony Burns
and Ambivalent Violence

DEPUTY MARSHAL ASA BUTMAN paced nervously as he waited on the sidewalk across the street from Coffin Pitt's clothing store. Arresting a fugitive slave in Boston was never easy; attempting it during Anniversary Week when hundreds of delegates were in town for the Antislavery and Women's Rights Conventions compounded the problem. Butman kept himself well hidden. He periodically checked the time and glanced down Brattle Street to see if his men were properly positioned. It had been a mild May day, but as the sun set and nearby church bells struck five, a chill breeze began to stir.

Moments after five, Coffin Pitts and Anthony Burns, a black man Pitts had recently hired, stepped out of the store offices and into the street. The two men had a brief conversation; then Pitts headed toward the corner of Brattle and Court Streets, Burns in the opposite direction. Butman panicked. Every day for a week Burns had accompanied his employer, and the deputy marshal had positioned his men accordingly. Now the suspected fugitive was walking away from the trap set for him. It looked as if a day of waiting and a week of investigating had been wasted. Suddenly Burns stopped, turned around, and ran to catch Pitts. Butman jumped from his hiding place, signaled his men, and hurried across the street with stiff-legged strides. When he reached Burns, the deputy marshall identified himself and announced that the black man was wanted in connection with a robbery investigation. Before Burns could protest, Butman's deputies lifted him off his feet, held him horizontally above the ground in their outstretched hands, and rushed to the Court House. Once inside the building, the suspected fugitive was carried up three flights of stairs and taken to the jury room, where he was bound hand and foot and placed in a chair.[1]

About twenty minutes later the door of the jury room opened, and Butman accompanied Virginia slaveowner Charles F. Suttle and his hiring agent, William Brent, inside. Obscuring Burns's view of the others in the room, Suttle faced Burns and asked him why he had run away. "I fell asleep on board the vessel where I worked, and before I woke up, she set sail and carried me off," Burns replied.

"Haven't I always treated you well, Tony?"

"You have always given me twelve and a half cents once a year," Burns said.

In the silence that followed this exchange, Butman blurted out, "Well, that's the man, is it?"

"Yes," replied Suttle. A moment later he and Brent left the room.[2]

After they left Burns faced Butman and asked why he had lied about wanting him in connection with a robbery. Butman smiled and replied that he was "afraid of the mob." Burns turned away from his captor. He knew there would be a hearing to certify his identity. Then he would be shipped back to Virginia. He anticipated harsh treatment and realized his ordeal had begun when the taunts of guards outside his cell prevented him from sleeping. They kept reminding him that Thomas Sims, a fugitive slave captured in Boston two years earlier, had occupied the same cell before being sent back to slavery. Ironically, if Burns had even a slight chance for freedom, it was because of the Sims rendition. The failure to stop Sims's return had stimulated Boston's abolitionist community to develop better methods for dealing with slave arrests. By early evening, the Boston Vigilance Committee was

1. Charles Emery Stevens, *Anthony Burns: A History* (Boston, 1856), pp. 15–17; Samuel Shapiro, "The Rendition of Anthony Burns," *Journal of Negro History* 44 (January 1959): 34–35, 40–41; David R. Maginnes, "The Case of the Court House Rioters in the Rendition of Fugitive Slave Anthony Burns, 1854," *Journal of Negro History* 61 (January 1971): 31–43; William H. Pease and Jane H. Pease, *The Fugitive Slave Law and Anthony Burns: A Problem in Law Enforcement* (Philadelphia, 1975), pp. 28–33.

2. Stevens, *Burns,* pp. 18–19.

aware of Burns's plight and had begun efforts to prevent his return to Virginia.[3]

At nine o'clock on the morning of May 25, 1854, Commissioner Edward Loring convened the rendition hearing of Anthony Burns. Famed novelist and Vigilance Committee lawyer Richard Henry Dana, Jr., was at the fugitive's side from the beginning of the hearing, hoping to defend Burns. But after a night in jail, further reflection on what awaited him in Virginia, and an understanding of Fugitive Slave Law provisions, the captive felt defense counsel was "no use." He was certain to "fare worse" if he resisted rendition. A short time after his refusal, Dana was joined by two other committee members, Charles M. Ellis and Theodore Parker, the well-known Unitarian minister. Parker conferred with Burns and explained his appointment as minister-at-large for the Boston Vigilance Committee. He pressed Burns to accept counsel, but the fugitive refused to reconsider his decision. Burns said he wanted to go back to Virginia "as easy as I can," but Parker wouldn't yield. It was only "fear" which gave Burns such a "sad presentment" of his fate, and no harm would be done by making a defense. Still Burns hesitated as Loring began the proceedings by summoning William Brent to give testimony. Then, just as Brent began to discuss the conversation that had taken place between Suttle and Burns in the jury room on the previous day, Dana interrupted. He notified the commissioner that Burns had accepted counsel and strenuously objected to Brent's testifying before a proper defense could be prepared. Suttle's attorney, Seth Thomas, was enraged—the law precluded a defense. Thomas was certain that "the only object of those who sought delay was for public purposes of their own." Pandemonium broke loose in the courtroom, and Loring repeatedly gaveled order. When calm was restored, he asked the fugitive to approach the bench. What was his decision? Would he accept a defense? Burns glanced over his shoulder at Suttle and Brent, then at Parker and Dana. Finally he turned to Loring and announced his desire for counsel.

3. Ibid., pp. 19–21.

Loring called for order, postponed the hearing until Saturday, May 27, and dismissed the court.[4]

Parker was elated as he left the building and went home to await the Vigilance Committee meeting scheduled for two o'clock that afternoon. He felt great satisfaction at having convinced Burns to make a defense. After the humiliation of the Sims affair, Parker had repeatedly predicted that Boston would become easy prey to federal authorities if slave "kidnappings" were not resisted. A powerful reaction to Burns's arrest would prove that Boston would not bow to unjust laws and would "fight manfully" for the freedom of slaves. It was time "to push and be active . . . call meetings, bring out men . . . agitate, agitate." Parker had been "waiting a long time for some event to occur which would blow so loud a horn it should waken the North." Seth Thomas was correct; Anthony Burns would serve "public purposes." If Burns's "defense" was handled properly, the black man from Virginia might have his freedom. But whether Burns was freed or sent back, Parker knew the incident could sound a "starting horn" for a new wave of antislavery sentiment.[5]

Theodore Parker was born in the town of Lexington on August 10, 1810, the eleventh child of John Parker, a taciturn farmer-mechanic, and his wife, Hannah. Parker belonged to the sixth generation of his family born on Massachusetts soil, and he reveled in the fact that his grandfather had led the Minutemen on Lexington Common that fateful day in April 1775. Though he spent long hours working on his father's small farm, Parker did receive sufficient training at the local

4. Richard Henry Dana, Jr., Journal, May 25, 1854, Massachusetts Historical Society, Boston, Mass.; Shapiro, "Rendition," p. 37; Stevens, Burns, pp. 24–26; Theodore Parker, The Collected Works of Theodore Parker, ed. Francis P. Cobbe, "The New Crime Against Humanity" (London, 1863–1874), 6: 55–57 (hereafter to be cited as Works [Cobbe edition]).

5. Ibid., "The Condition of America," 5: 318, 326; "The Three Chief Safeguards of Society," 8: 55–58; Parker to William H. Seward, May 19, 1854, Parker Letters, Harvard-Andover Theological Library, Harvard University, Cambridge, Mass.; Theodore Parker, The Life and Correspondence of Theodore Parker, ed. John Weiss (Boston, 1864), 2: 206–7 (hereafter to be cited as Parker, Correspondence).

academy under the tutelage of his lifelong friend Caleb Stetson to qualify as a schoolteacher. Between the ages of eighteen and twenty-three, he held a number of posts in the Boston area and, in spite of meager financial resources, managed to attend Harvard as a nonresident student. In 1834, at the urging of Rev. Convers Francis, Parker enrolled at Harvard Divinity School—a place he later came to regard as one great "embalming institution." By 1837 he was ministering to a modest congregation of shopkeepers and farmers in the small town of West Roxbury, adjacent to Boston. That same year he also married Lydia Cabot, whom he had met a few years earlier while living in Watertown.

During his stay in West Roxbury, Parker carefully attended to the needs of his congregation, but he gave equal time to the world of scholarship which had beguiled him since his Harvard days. He read voraciously and eclectically, cosponsored the *Dial,* a magazine devoted to transcendental thought, and frequently visited Brook Farm, the experimental transcendentalist community begun by his good friend George Ripley. Parker's reading and religious reflection soon put him at odds with conventional Unitarian theology. He believed that men must know themselves directly and not merely through the church or social convention. What is more, he was convinced that Ralph Waldo Emerson's view of religion as innate to human nature was correct. The price for his beliefs was religious ostracism by Unitarian clergymen in the Boston area. He further estranged himself from orthodox opinion and, at the same time, became a leading transcendentalist spokesman, when he summarized his position in a series of five lectures, "Discourses on Religion," presented at the Masonic Temple in Boston during the winter of 1841/42.

In the wake of the debate and criticism which engulfed him after the "Discourses," Parker left Boston in the fall of 1843 and toured Europe for a year with Lydia. When he returned home, he was installed as pastor of the Twenty-eighth Congregational Society, a good-sized parish of people with diverse social backgrounds which had been organized during his absence by a group of his most ardent supporters. The Parkers moved to Exeter Street in Boston, where they renewed their friendship with the Howes (begun the previous year in Rome), and Parker started giving sermons from the rostrum of the Music Hall, a large building downtown which was rented by his congregation.

Throughout the late 1840s, Theodore Parker continued his scholarly studies, lectured on the lyceum circuit, and edited the *Massachusetts Quarterly Review*. The essays he wrote for this periodical reveal an evolving concern with the role of the scholar-minister in American society. Parker was certain such men should "represent the highest facts of human consciousness to people"; they must expose evil, encourage reform, and help build a new and more perfect society. There was an "infinite worthiness" in man, and the scholar-minister must remove the impediments to the expression of that worthiness. Parker took this injunction literally and became active in a variety of reform efforts. By 1846, however, one reform movement, abolitionism, increasingly dominated his actions. As early as 1832 Parker had been made aware of antislavery activity by Lydia Maria Child, the sister of Convers Francis and a leader of the movement from its inception. Parker delivered a "Sermon on Slavery" to his Roxbury congregation in 1841, but it was not until 1846 that he made his first public speech against the institution at a Faneuil Hall protest meeting held after the rendition of the fugitive slave Joe. Parker was not a pacifist. Indeed, he believed that "all the great charters of humanity are *writ in blood* and must continue to be for some centuries." He was, however, outraged by the Mexican war because he saw it as the unbridled expression of the slavocracy's control of American government. Slavery's immorality and the defense of it by men who ran American political institutions infuriated him and fixed his attention more and more on the abolition of what he came to regard as man's greatest sin against man.[6]

Though Parker came late to the antislavery movement, he devoted himself wholeheartedly to the cause. The minister studied Roman slave codes, pored over census statistics, examined the economic indices of

6. Commager, *Parker,* pp. 7–198; Michael Fellman, "Theodore Parker and the Abolitionist Role in the 1850's," *Journal of American History* 61 (December 1974): 666–84.

slavery, and read tracts which condemned the institution as well as those which justified it. He listened to the stories of fugitive slaves living in Boston and consulted with black leaders like William C. Nell, Lewis Hayden, Frederick Douglass, and William Wells Brown. By 1850, Parker had relegated all other concerns to a secondary status. Abolition became his primary religious duty—absorbing his passion and serving as a way to bring morality to an imperfect but perfectible world.[7]

Parker did not confine his activity to study or sermons. He knew that men and women in the movement must act, as well as speak, in accordance with their beliefs. After the new Fugitive Slave Law was passed in 1850, he was instrumental in forming the Boston Vigilance Committee, an organization dedicated to preventing the return of slaves who fled to the city. During October of that year when fugitive slaves William and Ellen Craft were threatened with "kidnapping," Parker led a group of sixty vigilantes to the hotel where marshals charged with arresting the Crafts were staying. Without any physical violence, the group successfully intimidated the officers, drove them from the city, and protected the Crafts' freedom.[8]

Then, in April 1852, Parker took an active part in the attempt to prevent the rendition of Thomas Sims. But he and other committee members never did settle on a specific plan, and they listened only skeptically as a young firebrand minister from Worcester, Thomas Wentworth Higginson, called for an attack on the Court House to free Sims. Their indecision forced them to witness Sims's return to slavery.[9]

Theodore Parker based his abolitionist efforts on a foundation of Higher Law. There was an infinite law existing before all time and stored in the intuitive recesses of man's soul which justified resistance to the great moral crime of slavery. Higher Law negated any and every man-made measure designed to preserve and perpetuate the institution of slavery. It impelled antislavery men to "help fugitives" and to "seek

7. Commager, *Parker*, pp. 193, 201–2.
8. Ibid., pp. 140, 199, 214.
9. Ibid., pp. 220–22.

and save what is lost." Although Parker believed in Higher Law, he had problems in applying the theory. By late May 1854, the minister still had not determined the bounds or form of his own personal resistance to the "crime" of fugitive slave renditions. He was uncertain as to whether forcible means should be used in defense of black liberty. Theoretically men were justified in using such means, but the distance between theory and practice was great, and it was one which Parker had not fully traversed.[10]

In 1850 the minister informed President Fillmore that he was "not a man of violence." He had tremendous respect for the "sacredness" of life. If he resisted efforts to enforce the Fugitive Slave Law, it would be "as gently as I know how but with such strength as I command." He vowed to serve as "head . . . foot or . . . hand to any body of serious and earnest men who will go with me with no weapons." In early 1851, when free blacks in Boston led by Lewis Hayden rescued a fugitive slave named Shadrach, Parker called it the "most noble deed done in Boston since the destruction of tea in 1773." However, he still shied away from personally committing himself to the use of force. He would "not . . . use force to rescue a man with. But go unarmed when there is a chance of success."[11]

By 1853, Parker's views had shifted slightly. The nature of that shift is suggested by the lecture Parker earlier gave to William Craft when he spoke to Craft about the obligations of a husband. Parker suggested that if Craft was attacked and there was an attempt to force him back into slavery, he had "a natural right to resist the man to death." Though Parker indicated Craft might refuse to exercise the right for himself, "his wife was dependent upon him for protection and it was his duty to protect her." It was a duty Craft "could not decline." Even in this admonition the minister was cautious. He warned against hatred and vengeful emotions—hating the man one struck "would not leave action without sin." This warning, when coupled with future actions, suggests that, by May 1854, Parker still

10. Ibid., chap. 10; Parker, *Correspondence,* 2: 95; Theodore Parker, *The Boston Kidnapping* (1852; reprint ed., New York, 1969), pp. 2–3.

11. Parker, *Correspondence,* 1: 102–3.

had not resolved his personal debate about participating in forcible resistance to law.[12]

It is quite possible that Parker was apprehensive as he prepared placards advertising the date and time of the Burns hearing. Surely forcible resistance would be demanded by some of the membership when the Vigilance Committee met that afternoon. How would he respond?

Some two hundred members of the Boston Vigilance Committee met in Faneuil Hall that humid Thursday afternoon, and soon two plans commanded their attention. Twenty men spoke ardently for the forcible rescue of Burns from the Court House, but the vast majority of the committee took a "wait and see" position, claiming they didn't want to move until Commissioner Loring made his decision. Then, if Burns was to be returned, they could jam the streets, create a melee, and spirit the fugitive away. Logic supported the majority position. After all, it would be very difficult to force entry into a strong, stone Court House which was sure to be filled with armed deputies. And even if the attack succeeded, it was quite possible that Burns would have been hidden and would not be found during the brief possession of the building. By eight o'clock that evening, the majority plan was formally adopted. In addition, a public meeting was called for Friday night, May 26, in Faneuil Hall, and a detail of men was sent to watch the Court House. If there was any attempt to remove the black captive, these committeemen would provide a warning. Proper planning and organization would prevent a repetition of the Sims affair.[13]

After the meeting adjourned, the advocates of forcible rescue and some of those in doubt, such as Parker, remained in the hall and continued to discuss the feasibility of their plan. Parker, Wendell Phillips, Samuel Gridley Howe, Austin Bearse, and William Kemp eventually formed an executive committee for the group. They de-

12. Ibid., 1: 99–101.

13. Stevens, *Burns*, pp. 29–32; Ann Weston to (?), May 30, 1854, in M. B. Stern, "Trial of Anthony Burns," *Proceedings of the Massachusetts Historical Society* 44 (1910–11): 326 (hereafter this article will be cited as "Burns Trial").

cided to reconvene on Friday afternoon and again debate the plan. Though Parker had not committed himself to the plan, his membership on the executive committee indicates his continued willingness to entertain the idea of using force. His experience with the Crafts, Sims, and now Burns, coupled with the intensity of his commitment to antislavery reform and the logic of his Higher Law doctrines, demanded that he consider the use of violent methods as a legitimate form of resistance. Parker's personal debate was also strongly affected by the militance of his young protégé, Thomas Wentworth Higginson, minister of the Worcester Free Church.[14]

Like Parker, Higginson came from a family that traced its ancestry back to the first families of the Massachusetts Bay Colony. He was the son of Stephen and Louisa Higginson. Stephen Higginson came from a highly successful merchant family but had experienced personal economic misfortune during the War of 1812 because of bad investments and his own mismanagement. He eventually took a position as treasurer of Harvard College but continued to be plagued by a poor organizational sense and the inability to handle accounts properly. Stephen Higginson never did regain the affluence of his early years and died soon after his youngest son, Thomas Wentworth, was ten years old. It was up to Thomas's mother, Louisa, to rally the family fortunes and provide for the children's education. She did a creditable job. In 1837 her prodding, Thomas's hard work, and family connections paved the way for his entry into college. He was only thirteen.[15]

While at Harvard the grade-conscious young man distinguished himself. He was elected to Phi Beta Kappa, graduated near the top of his class, and seemed destined for great achievements. There was only one problem: Higginson was uncertain about what career he should apply his intelligence and energy toward. After graduation, the gangling six-footer spent three years marking time as an unfulfilled schoolteacher and trying to decide in which direction he should move.

14. Stevens, *Burns,* p. 32; Samuel May, Jr., to Higginson, May 25, 1854, Higginson-Burns Collection, Boston Public Library, Boston, Mass.; Edelstein, *Strange Enthusiasm,* pp. 7–17.

15. Ibid., pp. 18–52.

Finally, in 1844, he enrolled in Harvard Divinity School, prompted less by his own desire than by the urging of family (particularly his mother) and friends. They wanted him to begin satisfying the promise of his undergraduate days.[16]

Higginson's own uncertainty about a career as minister and the boring, rationalistic Unitarian theology taught at Harvard combined to alienate him from his studies. He concluded that as a minister he couldn't really be a "leader of men," and so he left school at the end of his first year. He soon reconsidered his decision, however, after listening to Theodore Parker's address to that year's graduating class. The young scholar was astounded by the effect Parker's ideas had upon his listeners. Parker's radical theology and the reputation he had built as a minister fused Higginson's personal need to be "a leader of men" with religious, romantic, and reform elements. He went back to Harvard Divinity School and distinguished himself by graduating at the top of his class. Fittingly, when Higginson gave the graduation address in 1847 on "The Clergy and Reform," Parker sat in the audience and marveled at the speaker.[17]

Despite his commitment to religious life, Higginson's doubts about a ministerial career occasionally surfaced over the next nine years in an abated form. He questioned whether such a career was "worthwhile" or would give him "position and influence." Higginson's confidence in his decision to become a minister was also severely challenged by his first congregation in Newburyport. Here he pumped for antislavery reform among men who made their living trading with cotton-planting slave owners. Then he further upset members by exchanging pulpits with Parker, a man shunned by virtually all established Unitarian ministers in the Boston area.[18]

While at Newburyport, Higginson did earn a considerable reputation among Massachusetts reformers. He was active in the Free Soil campaign of 1848, and by the time he was forced to resign from his

16. Ibid., pp. 56, 66; Higginson to Louisa Higginson, November 30, 1852, Higginson Collection, Houghton Library, Harvard University, Cambridge, Mass.

17. Edelstein, *Strange Enthusiasm*, pp. 66 – 68.

18. Ibid., pp. 68–82.

pastorate in 1850, he was well enough known to do a brief tour on the lecture circuit.[19]

Like Parker, Higginson saw the enactment of the Fugitive Slave Law as contrary to the dictates of Higher Law. He suggested that the men and women of Massachusetts "disobey it" and show their "good citizenship" by "taking the legal consequences." His address "The Crisis Now Coming," written during the attempt to arrest William and Ellen Craft, advanced a more militant position than that of his mentor. Although he claimed to "abhor bloodshed," Higginson found it difficult to "say when a man must stop in defending his inalienable rights." To Higginson, the Shadrach rescue was not merely "a noble deed," because the "issue of manliness" was too keenly involved. There wasn't anyone of any "real manliness" who did not in his "secret soul respect these colored men of Boston."[20]

During the Sims affair, Higginson put greater distance between himself and Parker on the issue of forcible resistance. In a Vigilance Committee meeting he held the audience "spellbound" with an eloquent plea for rejection of the law. Wendell Phillips thought Higginson had brought the group to the "eve of Revolution." And Parker realized the intensity of Higginson's convictions when the young minister planned with Austin Bearse to rescue Sims from the frigate *Acorn.* The two men wanted to try a pirate-like attack on the boat which was taking Sims back to Virginia. Nor did Parker miss the impact Higginson was making on many antislavery leaders by advocating such tactics.[21]

Thomas Sims's rendition upset Higginson greatly. He was bitter about the committee's failure to develop and execute a rescue plan and he was angered by "disorderly" meetings, where each man advanced his "own theory." A fugitive slave arrest was an occasion which "required the utmost promptness and decision." It also required men

19. Ibid., pp. 84–109.

20. Ibid., pp. 130–31; Howard N. Meyer, *Colonel of the Black Regiment: The Life of Thomas Wentworth Higginson* (New York, 1967), pp. 69–72 (hereafter to be cited as *Black Regiment*).

21. Edelstein, *Strange Enthusiasm*, pp. 112–18; Meyer, *Black Regiment*, pp. 69–72.

to scrap "fixed rules" and "strive to do what seems best without reference to others." If commitment to Higher Law meant commitment to "bloodshed," Thomas Wentworth Higginson was ready to take the step.[22]

A month before the Sims rendition, in March 1852, Higginson began work as minister of the Worcester Free Church, a congregation organized on principles similar to those which governed Parker's religious society. In fact, Parker had argued for Higginson to take the position. At first, Higginson was reticent, but he finally decided to accept the post and soon enjoyed a warm relationship with the men and women of his congregation. On Thursday, May 25, 1854, while preparing his sermon for that week, Higginson was notified of Burns's capture and the Vigilance Committee public gathering scheduled for Friday evening. By early Friday morning he was on a train headed for Boston. As he rode to Boston, Higginson must have reflected on the Sims arrest two years earlier and wondered if the committee would still be plagued by "great want of preparation" for their "revolutionary work." Like himself, they had been brought up to respect law. It had taken the "whole experience" of the Sims case to educate his mind "in the attitude of revolution." He wondered how others had been affected by the episode. For Higginson, it had been "strange to find oneself outside established institutions, to be obliged to lower one's voice and conceal one's purposes, to see law and order, police and military on the wrong side." Had Parker, Phillips, Howe, and the others been affected in the same way? Did they really understand the necessity of using force? Were they as ready as he was to prevent Burns's return by any means? He wondered.[23]

Higginson arrived in Boston shortly before noon and soon learned of the afternoon executive committee meeting called the previous

---

22. Memo on Sims, Higginson–Burns Collection, Boston Public Library, Boston, Mass.

23. Higginson to Parker, June 24, 1852; Parker to Higginson, June 25, 1852; Higginson–Huntington Collection, Huntington Library, San Marino, Calif.; Memo on Sims, Higginson–Burns Collection, Boston Public Library; Samuel May, Jr., to Higginson, May 25, 1854, in Stern, "Burns Trial," p. 324.

evening. He attended the meeting, asked that his Worcester friend Martin Stowell's name be added to its membership, and hinted that Stowell was coming to Boston with men who were willing to attempt a forcible rescue. But because Higginson could not give any details about the plan before consulting with Stowell and because the executive committee had not fully developed any plan of its own, the meeting was adjourned until a few minutes before the eight o'clock assembly at Faneuil Hall. If Stowell did have a plan, it could be discussed at that time.[24]

Around six o'clock Higginson went to the train station. There he met Stowell and the few men he had brought with him from Worcester. Stowell immediately outlined his scheme. He wanted to attack the Court House in two stages. First Higginson, Stowell, and his men would storm the building's doors. After the initial charge, they would be reinforced by the large crowd slated to attend that evening's gathering. A great deal depended on the speakers who were addressing the assembly. It was up to one of them to incite the crowd and send them rushing to the Court House. Stowell realized the precariousness of the plan, realized how important it was for Higginson and himself to coordinate their efforts with those of the speakers, and he knew that the timing would be delicate. It was absolutely necessary that the Faneuil Hall crowd arrive moments after the first stage of the attack began. But Stowell was sure it could be done. Higginson thought so too.[25]

The two men hurried to meet with the executive committee members and outline their proposal. When they unveiled the plan, Austin Bearse immediately rejected it. William Kemp liked it but claimed he couldn't help because he wasn't scheduled to speak. Phillips was scheduled to address the assembly but couldn't be found because he was busy with last-minute preparations for the gathering. Only Parker and Howe, both of whom were to speak, could assist. These two men listened incredulously as Stowell and Higginson discussed the planned

24. Burns Narrative, Higginson-Burns Collection, Boston Public Library.
25. Ibid.

rescue effort. Howe and Parker weren't sure of the scheme's chances and seem to have been a bit confused about their own role in it, but neither vetoed the plan. As a result, Higginson and Stowell left the anteroom meeting believing they could depend on one of the two (most likely Parker) to send the crowd rushing to Court Square. Higginson and Stowell were further heartened by Lewis Hayden's promise to send ten blacks to assist in the first stage of the attack. Minutes after they left the hall, the two Worcester men strolled around Court Square, checking to see that everything was ready for the assault. As they did, Samuel Sewall introduced George Russell to the large assemblage at Faneuil Hall. After Russell welcomed the audience, Samuel Gridley Howe stood up to read the resolves of the meeting.[26]

Samuel Gridley Howe was born in 1801, the second son of Patricia Gridley and Joseph Neals Howe. The Howes were descended from one of Boston's first families, and Samuel Gridley's grandfather was reputed to have been one of the "Indians" at the Boston Tea Party. Young Howe was educated at the Latin School in Boston and then attended Brown University because his family held Jeffersonian-Republican convictions and believed that Harvard was too much of a Federalist domain. Federalist domain or not, Howe did eventually attend Harvard, entering the Medical School soon after completing his undergraduate work at Brown. He received his medical degree in 1824.

During his three-year stay at Harvard, Howe, like so many other Americans, became enthralled by the news of Greece's struggle for independence. When he finished his medical training, he traveled to the Mediterranean country to enlist in the revolutionary army as a soldier and surgeon. Howe served as a doctor in the army for over three years and learned a great deal about medicine, though he quickly lost his idealistic assumptions about the nature of the struggle. Still, his belief in the Greek cause did not completely wane, and when the

26. Ibid.; Samuel Gridley Howe, *The Letters and Journals of Samuel Gridley Howe,* ed. Laura Richards (Boston, 1906), 2: 268–69 (hereafter to be cited as Howe, *Journals*); Edelstein, *Strange Enthusiasm,* pp. 155–57; "Burns and Butman," [newspaper clipping], Higginson Collection, Houghton Library.

revolutionary government requested him to raise relief funds in America, he eagerly complied. Between February and July 1828, he toured and lectured throughout the United States, raising substantial sums for Greece and finding time to collect the impressions of his experience in a work entitled *An Historical Sketch of the Greek Revolution.* He went back to Greece at the end of July and in the next year and a half directed various reconstruction projects. He then traveled in Europe for a year and returned to Boston in 1831.

In September, Howe was hired as director of the New England Asylum for the Blind by Dr. John A. Fisher, who asked him to go back to Europe to study the newest teaching techniques and to recruit the necessary staff. Howe was particularly impressed by French instruction methods and spent time in Paris familiarizing himself with them. While there, he also interested himself in relief efforts organized to assist Polish exiles who had been forced to flee their homeland in the wake of a Russian invasion. He even journeyed to East Prussia (a key point on the Polish escape route) to examine Polish difficulties firsthand, but he was detained in prison for three weeks by Prussian authorities and then sent back to Paris.

Howe returned to Boston in July 1832. In the years that followed, his work with the blind (and eventually the blind-deaf) was so successful that he received financial assistance from the Massachusetts legislature, enrolled students from all over New England, and happily occupied the home of Colonel Thomas H. Perkins, which was donated as the institution's first permanent residence.

In 1843 the doctor married twenty-four-year-old Julia Ward, the gifted daughter of a well-to-do New York businessman. Shortly after their marriage, the couple sailed for Europe on a yearlong vacation. During the winter of 1843 the Howes settled in Rome, where they met and became friendly with Theodore and Lydia Parker. In the spring of 1844 Julia Howe gave birth to the first of six children.

During the mid-1840s Howe continued his work with the blind and assisted Horace Mann's campaign to reform public education in Massachusetts. But, increasingly, his attention turned to the issue of slavery. The doctor's earliest writing on the subject, a "Letter on Slavery," had appeared in the *New England Magazine* in 1833. At the time he argued that the future of the Union depended on the country's ability to solve the problem of man's property in man, but he characterized Garrisonian calls for immediate emancipation as "the greatest enemy of blacks and whites." His views changed markedly in the 1840s when his numerous encounters with slavery's brutality (he was particularly shocked by a slave prison in New Orleans) were coupled with what he believed to be a Slave Power conspiracy to annex Texas. He joined Parker and other leading antislavery advocates at a public meeting in Faneuil Hall during 1846 to protest the rendition of the fugitive slave Joe and to call for an immediate end to slavery. That fall he ran for office on the antislavery Conscience Whig ticket. He was defeated; however, the effort proved to be only the first of many political abolition activities which he would undertake in the next few years. In 1848 he supported the Free Soil Party and, two years later, worked for Charles Sumner's election to the United States Senate. Howe never stopped believing in a political response to the slavocracy's control of American government, but the machinations that surrounded Sumner's candidacy and the seemingly endless string of defeats for political antislavery in the late 1840s prompted misgivings about the efficacy of political means. These misgivings were fueled by passage of the Fugitive Slave Law in 1850, an act which led him to join with Parker and others to form the Boston Vigilance Committee and which signaled the beginning of a nine-year quest to find alternative means to resist the encroachments of slavery.[27]

The doctor smiled warmly and acknowledged the applause that greeted him as he stepped to the rostrum. Actually, Howe was quite tense as he prepared to introduce the resolutions. He realized the implications of his meeting with Higginson and Stowell moments earlier. Yes, he believed in Higher Law and knew that unjust laws must be resisted, but, like Parker, he had always stopped short of personally participating in acts of political violence. Why had he assented to the Higginson-Stowell plan? It could mean bloodshed.

27. Harold Schwartz, "Fugitive Slave Days in Boston," *New England Quarterly* 27 (June 1954): 191–212; Schwartz, *Howe,* pp. 2–193.

Only half concentrating on the resolves, Howe's mind must have been flooded with memories of past fugitive slave rescue efforts when he had vainly wrestled with the question of forcible resistance.

"Resistance to tyrants is obedience to God. . . ." Eight years before, Howe had stood in Faneuil Hall and addressed a gathering of abolitionists on the necessity of preventing the rendition of fugitive slaves. At the beginning of his speech, he assured the audience that he did not propose to "move the public mind to any expression of indignation —much less acts of violence." Yet during the speech he could not contain his anger and said law should "not prevent" the "outrage" of kidnapped slaves. Despite such anger, Howe did not take the final step. In his conclusion, he veered away from the outright suggestion of violent resistance by claiming that renditions could be prevented if citizens fixed their "eyes upon him [the slave hunter]" and didn't take them off until "he leaves our borders without his prey."[28]

Throughout the early 1850s Howe had continued to struggle with the idea of using violent means and had continued to believe that strict adherence to law could do great harm to men. When Horace Mann asked him what he thought of legislation prohibiting corporations from employing people for more than ten hours a day, Howe replied heatedly that he was against the proposal. Law emasculated men. It prevented them from protecting themselves and blinded them to their own responsibilities. But this distrust of law and his recurring contention that nothing should become law that could not "answer the eternal principles of right" did not help him resolve the debate inherent in his first speech against the Fugitive Slave Law. For all his conviction about the transcendence of Higher Law, the evil of the Slave Power, and the justice of protecting escaped slaves, he still could not accept bloodshed in the resistance to unjust laws. He could not bring himself to participate in "practical" abolition.[29]

28. Stevens, *Burns,* pp. 33–34; Samuel Gridley Howe, "Address on the Prevention of Kidnapping," September 24, 1846, pp. 4–5, Widener Library, Harvard University, Cambridge, Mass.

29. Howe to Horace Mann, February 18, 1851; October 21, 1852; Howe to Charles Sumner, December 5, 1851, Howe Collection, Houghton Library, Harvard Univer-

Now as he pronounced the words of the last resolution and sat down, Howe knew his approval of the Higginson-Stowell plan meant very little. He would do nothing to incite the crowd because, in spite of his theories, he could not abet violence. He was horrified by the thought of what might happen in Court Square.

The next speaker was Wendell Phillips. He rose, stepped to the rostrum, and was greeted by an enormous ovation. Phillips knew nothing of the rescue plan. He spoke temperately and made only the unspecific suggestion that people turn out on Saturday morning to show that Anthony Burns had "no master but his God."[30]

At Court Square, Thomas Wentworth Higginson heard the roar go up from Faneuil Hall. He realized the ovation must be for Phillips, since he was scheduled as the first major speaker. Higginson reasoned that it would be best to delay the attack until it was Parker's turn to speak. Phillips had not been informed of the plan, and there was no way to be certain that Howe or Parker had approached him before he gave his speech. The ovation that greeted Parker would cue their attack. Higginson and Stowell drew the men together, passed out a dozen hand axes, readied the huge wooden beam they were going to use as a battering ram against the Court House doors, and waited patiently. At that moment Lewis Hayden appeared with ten blacks. Everything was going as scheduled. It was all up to Parker. He must trigger the emotions of the crowd and send them to the Court House. Higginson was confident. If anyone knew how to arouse an assembly, it was Theodore Parker.[31]

After Phillips's speech Parker stepped nervously to the rostrum.

---

sity, Cambridge, Mass.; Howe, *Journals,* 2: 385; Howe's reaction to the Daniel Drayton episode also suggests the ambivalence he felt about putting his belief into practice. Samuel Gridley Howe, *Slavery at Washington: A Narrative of the Heroic Adventures of Drayton, An American Trader* (London, 1848), p. 5.

30. Stevens, *Burns,* pp. 38–39.

31. Burns Narrative, Higginson-Burns Collection, Boston Public Library; Receipt for Handaxes, May 26, 1854, Higginson Collection, Houghton Library; Shapiro, "Burns Rendition," pp. 38–39; Edelstein, *Strange Enthusiasm,* pp. 155–57; Thomas Wentworth Higginson, *Cheerful Yesterdays* (Boston, 1896), pp. 148–50 (hereafter to be cited as *Yesterdays*).

Higginson's revelations a few minutes earlier had been startling and a bit confusing, but Parker was aware of the scene about to be enacted in Court Square. What is more, he knew the importance of his role in the scheme. He was the only major speaker with prior knowledge of the planned attack. It was up to him to incite the crowd and send them rushing toward the square. When Higginson revealed the plan, Parker had been certain he could assist. Now that certainty faded, as his persistent doubts about using forcible means returned.

Parker started his speech auspiciously with a taunt, addressing the asseembly as his "fellow subjects of Virginia." Shouts of "No!" "No!" greeted his words. After these inflammatory words, Parker referred to the Sims capture and claimed that "if Boston had spoken then, we should not have been here tonight." Yes, the people of Boston were "vassals" of Virginia, and federal authorities were so confident of this that they had not bothered to chain the Court House. They had no fear of Burns being rescued. Boston's submissive behavior would allow the police to carry Burns off "in a cab." Again, the crowd roared back: "No!" "They can't do it!" "Let's see them try!" Parker exhibited a masterful control of the assembly. Actually, this was the only kind of violence he really understood. It was a vicarious form, purely rhetorical, rising out of the mix of his own incendiary words and the crowd's emotions. First, he built the crowd's confidence by invoking Higher Law. Then he advised them of the power of public opinion, claiming there was only one law—"slave law"—and it was everywhere. Next, he spoke to them of "another law," one that was in their "hands and arms," one which they could put into effect whenever they saw fit. Parker challenged the crowd and shoved them toward violence. He was a "peace man" but realized "there is a means and there is an end, liberty is the end, sometimes peace is not the means toward it." Parker seemed to be condoning violence, seemed to be resolving his own personal debate over participating in forcible resistance. As he spoke, he fed and was fed by the rampaging emotions of the crowd. They were ready to charge the Court House, and he was ready to send them.[32]

32. Stevens, *Burns,* pp. 39, 289–95.

Yet in the very next moment his power, control, and commitment drained away like fine sand from a tightly clenched fist. When he asked the crowd what they planned to do about Burns and they replied, "Shoot!" "Shoot!" Parker was stunned. Words caught in his throat. In an instant he realized his desire for action was far less intense than his fear of bloodshed. He could not send the crowd to Court Square. He must restrain them. "There are ways of managing this without shooting anybody," he yelled. "These men who have kidnapped a man in Boston are cowards . . . if we stand up there resolutely and declare that this man shall not go out of the city of Boston *without shooting a gun,* then he won't go back." In his next sentence he forfeited any chance of forcible rescue that evening. "Now I am going to propose that when you adjourn, it be to meet in Court Square at nine o'clock." Parker had abandoned Stowell and Higginson. But before he could carry his own motion, cries rang out. "Let's go tonight!" "Let's pay a visit to the slave-catchers at Revere House." Desperately trying to prevent an exodus to Court Square, Parker seized upon the last suggestion and tried to send the crowd to the Revere House. "Do you suppose to go to Revere House tonight?" "Then show your hands." After counting those who supported the measure, Parker claimed it was "not a vote" and again suggested meeting in Court Square at nine in the morning. Again his motion was met by screams of "Tonight!" "Tonight!" Parker paused for a moment, then hesitantly called for a vote. Half the assembly wanted to go to the Court House that evening. What could he do now? Shouts of "To the Court House!" echoed around the hall. Parker was at the mercy of the crowd he had dominated only moments before.[33]

Sensing Parker's plight, Wendell Phillips leaped to the rostrum and yelled out, "If I thought it could be done tonight I would go first. I am ready to trample any statute or any man under my foot to do it. But wait until daytime. . . . It is in your power to lock up every avenue so the man cannot be carried off." Moments after he uttered these words and the crowd seemed to settle down, a man burst into the hall.

33. Ibid.

He screamed incoherently about an attack on the Court House. Everyone shoved and pushed for the doors of the hall.[34]

When Higginson heard the ovation that greeted Parker and the clamor caused by his introductory remarks, he felt sure the crowd would soon converge on Court Square. It was time to attack. On Higginson's signal, several men extinguished street lamps and darkened the square. Then, with Higginson manning a large battering ram, the small cadre moved toward the center entry of the west side of the Court House. Burns was in a room two floors above this entry. As the minister moved through the square and up the steps toward the doors, he recalled the words he had spoken that afternoon. Some attempt to rescue Burns should be made; if it weren't, "future cases would occur with less traces of manly feeling." Once up to the door, Higginson and the black man who stood opposite him guided the thrusts of the battering ram. Standing behind those who were manning the beam, other members of the group shouted and hurled rocks through the windows of the building. A few of the attackers slashed away at the doors with hand axes. In the midst of this furor, Higginson glanced furtively into the square. He wondered what was keeping the crowd from Faneuil Hall.[35]

Fifty "special" guards recruited by United States Marshal Freeman pressed against the inside of the Court House doors, trying to prevent them from giving way. But repeated thrusts of the battering ram buckled the door paneling. A few of the "specials" stepped back from the door, drew sabres and firearms, and prepared to repel any attacker who managed to get inside the building. Higginson and his black cohort were the first to squeeze through the small passageway in the paneling. Once in the building, they grappled with some of the deputies. In the melee, shots rang out, Deputy James Batchelder was mortally wounded, and a flashing cutlass dug into Higginson's chin. At the same time, Higginson realized that only he and his black friend were

34. Ibid.
35. Burns Narrative, Higginson-Burns Collection, Boston Public Library; Stevens, *Burns,* pp. 42–44.

fighting; the rest of the attackers had already retreated. He drew back and shouted at his fleeing comrades, "You cowards, will you desert us now?" He was bleeding profusely and moved slowly down the steps. At that moment, the crowd from Faneuil Hall arrived only to see the battered Court House doors slammed shut. Amid the confusion of milling people, Higginson staggered haltingly away from the square. Within hours he was on a train headed back to Worcester.[36]

It has been argued that Theodore Parker was one of antislavery's most renowned "moral agitators." Indeed he was, and so was Samuel Gridley Howe. Throughout the early 1850s, both men claimed the right to "nullify the laws of slavery" because they were contrary to the edicts of Higher Law. Unfortunately, it has also been assumed that both men's fugitive slave activities implied their willingness not only to theorize the violent overthrow of slavery but to act on those theories. A careful examination of the Burns affair and both men's roles in it suggests a different conclusion: Neither man had committed himself to anything but theory. Both Parker and Howe were prey to great tension and ambivalence. Before they could make a practical commitment to political violence, they would have to understand that although Higher Law provided a powerful rationale for using force, it alone was not sufficient to carry them beyond the threshold of conventional political action. A stronger stimulus was needed to over-power their aversion to bloodshed.[37]

Thomas Wentworth Higginson arrived in Worcester deeply dis-heartened by the attack's apparent failure. However, he soon revised his opinion of the effort as he gauged the public excitement caused by the attempt. He heard the "wildest things" proposed by men who formerly had little or no antislavery sentiment, and he learned about the power of concerted popular feeling. What to do with this power,

36. Higginson, *Yesterdays*, pp. 148–50; Stevens, *Burns*, pp. 42–44; Edelstein, *Strange Enthusiasm*, pp. 156–57.
37. Commager, *Parker*, p. 211.

however, was a new question as mystifying as the exhilaration he had felt in breaking down the Court House doors. In any case, he was now "thankful for what had been done," considered the whole effort the "greatest step in antislavery which Massachusetts had ever taken," and was "ready to do my share again."[38]

A few days later, Samuel May, Jr., wrote a letter which dampened Higginson's enthusiasm. May notified the young minister that a warrant had been sworn for his arrest. What upset Higginson more, however, was May's implication concerning Parker's conduct during the episode. According to May, "Friday night had a chance of success but the Court Square movement right in the face and eyes of Faneuil Hall advice was ill-advised and so failed when with perfect harmony it might have succeeded." As other information filtered into Worcester about Parker's speech, Higginson understood why the crowd had arrived late.[39]

Samuel Girdley Howe was equally disappointed by the outcome of the rescue attempt. He shared responsibility with Parker for failing to send the crowd to aid Higginson and guiltily watched the rendition proceedings unfold. First, there were rumors of another rescue attempt. Then, Dana's plea for postponement was followed by an attempt to purchase Burns's freedom. Finally, with soldiers stationed at all windows, crowds milling in Court Square, and women abolitionists led by Lydia Parker standing vigil outside the Court House, the hearings opened on Monday, May 29, at nine in the morning. Dana conducted a brilliant defense, but his efforts were futile. Suttle, Brent, and Thomas certified Anthony Burns's identity and proved ownership. Commissioner Edward Loring defined his responsibility in the case as "ministerial" and not "judicial" and asserted that he was not empowered to preside over a jury trial aimed at testing the validity of the Fugitive Slave Law. As long as proof of identity and ownership had been

38. Higginson to Mary Higginson, May 26, 1854; Higginson to Samuel May, Jr., May 28, 1854, in Stern, "Burns Trial," pp. 323, 325.

39. Samuel May, Jr., to Higginson, May 30, 1854, Higginson-Burns Collection, Boston Public Library.

established, Loring said he had no choice but to turn Burns over to Suttle for shipment back to Virginia.[40]

On June 2 thousands of men, women, and children thronged the streets of Boston to watch Anthony Burns march from the Court House to the wharf for transportation to Virginia. The march was scheduled to begin at eleven o'clock but was delayed three hours while hundreds of soldiers attempted to clear streets and prevent any further effort to free the slave. Cavalry patrols drove citizens back onto sidewalks. Police suggested businessmen close their stores for the day. Militiamen locked arms and held back the crowd. Once these "path-clearing" efforts had succeeded, Burns was surrounded by a column of 125 special deputies and 140 United States troops and marched to the wharf.[41]

Standing at the edge of the crowd on one of the streets en route, Samuel Gridley Howe watched the troops pass with Burns in their midst. He saw black-edged flags, unions down, hanging everywhere. A coffin inscribed with the words *Funeral of Liberty* hung from a window opposite the old state house. Howe was overwhelmed with anger and self-recrimination, disturbed at having glibly theorized about the necessity of using force and then having failed to execute his theories. Howe may have remembered a suggestion he made to Charles Sumner only a few weeks earlier. At that time he claimed that force might be "the only means . . . to save the perishing." Now, the full implication of his inability to act was clear: Burns was being

40. In fact, Burns signed an affidavit to the effect that Suttle had not been a hard master. But when he was informed that the statement would affect his hearing, he seized the statement and tore it up. Stevens, *Burns,* pp. 127, 62, 71–79; Samuel May, Jr., to Higginson, May 29, 1854, in Stern, "Burns Trial," p. 325; Shapiro, "Burns Rendition," p. 40; Stanley W. Campbell, *The Slave Catchers: Enforcement of the Fugitive Slave Law, 1850–1860* (New York, 1968), pp. 124–32; Shapiro, "Burns Rendition," pp. 40–43; Stevens, *Burns,* pp. 96, 100–108; Samuel May, Jr., to Higginson, May 31, 1854, Higginson-Burns Collection, Boston Public Library; Stevens, *Burns,* pp. 115–23.

41. Stevens, *Burns,* pp. 127–34, Appendix G., Appendix H.; Campbell, *Slave Catchers,* p. 130; Samuel May, Jr., to Higginson, June 2, 1854, Higginson-Burns Collection, Boston Public Library; Stevens, *Burns,* pp. 137–50; Shapiro, "Burns Rendition," pp. 45–49.

shipped back to slavery. Howe "wept for sorrow, shame and indignation."[42]

Again and again the physician asked himself why he and so many others had not resisted the rendition and tried to tell himself that if it had not been for "citizen soldiery and armed citizen police, the *people* would have routed the United States troops and rescued poor Burns." Ultimately, he concluded that it was "the *fetish* of law which disarmed and emasculated" himself and the rest of Boston's citizenry. Higginson was correct. It was difficult to find oneself on the wrong side of established institutions when one had been raised to respect those institutions. He had not been radicalized by the Sims affair and was unwilling to "burst down a door."[43]

In his self-anger, Howe was struck by a vivid image which eventually helped him to break through the crippling "fetish" for law. The image was that of "a comely colored girl of eighteen" who happened to be standing near him as Anthony Burns passed. She stood watching the column with "clenched fists . . . flashing eyes and tears streaming down her cheeks, the picture of indignant despair." When he noticed how upset the girl was, Howe tried to comfort her. He told her not to cry; Burns wouldn't be hurt. Immediately, the black girl turned to him and screamed: "Hurt! I cry for shame he will not kill himself. Oh why is he not man enough to kill himself!" Howe was stunned by the vehemence of her words. By 1858, a personal debate about the issue of black manhood and a belief that slave violence would demonstrate that manhood would allow Samuel Gridley Howe to resolve briefly the paralyzing tension which existed within him between the theory and practice of political force. It would help carry him and others beyond convention.[44]

The Burns rendition is a significant episode in the chronicle of the antislavery movement. It is especially important for understanding the

42. Howe to Charles Sumner, December 28, 1851; February 16, 1854; Howe to Horace Mann, June 18, 1854, Howe Collection, Houghton Library.
43. Howe to Parker, June 1854; Howe to Horace Mann, June 18, 1854, ibid.
44. Howe to Horace Mann, June 18, 1854, ibid.

attitudes of Howe, Parker, and Higginson about political violence, and it provides a context for their later activities in the movement. The failures of Howe and Parker accentuated their personal struggles to resolve the discrepancy between their political theory and its practice. Higginson's participation in the assault caused him to move rapidly down the road of practical abolition.

Yet, in spite of his commitment to violent means, Higginson was still a novice when it came to using the public sentiment his attack produced, and in this respect he learned much from Howe and Parker, who did know what to do. Neither Howe nor Parker could bring themselves to use forcible means, but both knew how to milk the emotion stirred by the Burns affair. When it came to exploiting the "martyrdom" of Anthony Burns, both men were experts. Both knew how to win converts to the antislavery faith, and their activities in the aftermath of rendition are as important for understanding their future commitment to John Brown and slave violence as is their failure to forcibly resist the Fugitive Slave Law.

Parker used his Sunday sermons as a device to relieve himself of responsibility for the Burns failure and to whip up popular anger about the rendition. In his May 28 discourse, given only two days after Higginson's attack, he spoke of such attempts as "wholly without use." Then he deftly sidestepped blame for the crowd's failure to reinforce Higginson by praising Wendell Phillips who, according to Parker, had "hardly restrained the multitude from going and by violence storming the Court House."[45]

The Sunday after Burns was returned, Parker was less circumspect with his remarks. He incited his audience by speaking with disdain about Massachusetts's failure to act. "We deserve all we have suffered. We are the scorn and contempt of the South. They are our masters and treat us like slaves. It is ourselves who made the yoke." Parker wondered aloud if men would always come to a rendition "with only

45. Parker, *Works* (Cobbe edition), "Lesson for the Day" [a sermon given on May 28, 1854], 6: 44–49.

the arms God gave," then claimed to want "no rashness," only calm, considerate action.[46]

While Sunday sermons had their effect, other techniques were necessary to maintain aroused antislavery sentiment. After the rendition Howe wrote to Parker with a suggestion. Confessing his feelings of "disgrace," Howe thought one way to redeem the honor of the "degraded community" of Boston would be to remove Commissioner Edward Loring from his position as judge of probate. Parker received the idea with enthusiasm. He had already initiated the process of discrediting Loring by suggesting that it was the commissioner who was responsible for Deputy James Batchelder's death. Nothing could be done about Loring's federal appointment, but in his state position as judge of probate, he could be recalled. Such a tactic would certainly sustain antislavery sentiment and, at the same time, shift attention from antislavery violence and the failure to prevent rendition. By making Commissioner Loring a symbol of the institution of slavery, the institution could be personalized, and Loring's removal would signal an antislavery triumph. Loring's ordeal became another lesson in the continuing struggle to win the public mind of the North. Undoubtedly Parker remembered the words he spoke in the aftermath of the Sims rendition when seeking to settle responsibility for Sims's return. The minister wished "it was some single man . . . some official of the City . . . so we could make him a scapegoat of public indignation."[47]

46. Ibid., "New Crime Against Humanity," [a sermon given on June 5, 1854], 6: 75–77, 105–7.

47. Howe, *Journals,* 2: 268–269; Parker, *Works* (Cobbe edition), "Lesson for the Day," 6: 50; Austin Bearse, *Reminiscences of Fugitive Slave Days in Boston* (Boston, 1880), pp. 12–13, 31–32. A comment made by Ann Phillips during the Burns trial suggests strongly the nature of this "scapegoat" effort. One of the charges made against Loring was that he had not allowed counsel proper access to the defendant. Yet Ann Phillips notes in a letter to Ann Weston that "Commissioner Loring was behaving very admirably as far as giving time and all that went. Wendell [Phillips] has free entry as the slave's agent." Ann Phillips to Ann Weston, May 25, 1854, in Stern, "Burns Trial," p. 302; Irving H. Bartlett, *Wendell Phillips, Brahmin Radical* (Boston, 1961), pp. 54, 115. Bartlett presents an excellent analysis of Phillips's theory about the use of public opinion.

The effort to make Loring a scapegoat commenced on July 4 at an abolitionist picnic in Framingham, where a petition was circulated calling for Loring's removal. By early February 1855, the effort had partially succeeded. Loring's appointment as permanent lecturer at Harvard Law School was defeated, and in late February the House of Representatives began hearings on the removal petition. Loring was accused of conducting the examination of Burns unfairly, hurrying the proceedings, and not maintaining free access to court for the prisoner's counsel. Loring defended himself by protesting that he had handled the proceedings impartially and by reminding the legislative committee that his duties as commissioner were not incompatible with those he rendered as judge of probate. If they were, why hadn't objections been raised when he was appointed commissioner? Despite his plea, Loring's position was in jeopardy when the hearings were recessed in late March. But he was soon to receive support from an unexpected source.[48]

Richard Henry Dana, Jr., was disturbed by the attempt to remove Loring. He had hoped the whole Burns episode was behind him because it had been a painful experience. Now he had to rekindle those unpleasant memories in order to testify in Loring's behalf. While Dana condemned the commissioner's decision as morally wrong, he defended Loring's actions on the basis of the legal principles involved. Dana argued determinedly for the independence of the judiciary. If Loring were removed, judicial independence would receive a severe blow. Dana did not believe Loring was guilty of official misconduct. In fact, Loring had encouraged Burns to make a defense and had posponed the hearings long enough for counsel to make adequate preparation. The commissioner had demanded that Phillips and others be allowed free access to court and had cooperated with efforts to purchase Burns's freedom. Dana's defense of Loring was temporarily effective. The legislature voted for removal; however, Governor Gardner vetoed the measure, and it took three more years before abolitionists succeeded with their campaign.[49]

48. Stevens, *Burns,* pp. 223–31.
49. Shapiro, "Burns Rendition," pp. 46–47; Charles Sumner to Richard Henry Dana, Jr., June 4, 1954, Dana Journal, Massachusetts Historical Society; Stevens,

Theodore Parker was furious with Dana. He was certain the lawyer's influence had destroyed the removal effort. This, coupled with Dana's condemnation of Higginson's Court House attack, led the minister to claim he had long "despised" Dana's scruples against violence and was "disgusted [when] Dana withdrew fr[om] the Vig[ilance] Committee because of contempt for the use of force." Considering his own role in the affair, Parker's criticism was tainted, yet his vehemence is significant because it shows the importance he placed on the removal tactic and the intensity of his own personal debate about the use of forceful methods.[50]

Higginson was not active in the Loring removal effort, and his own sermons were more statements of his new level of awareness than purposeful antislavery devices. The minister claimed that he had "lost the dream" of America as a land of peace and order and now believed that slavery could only be ended by "physical force." The law was simply on the "wrong side." Though he did not discourage "peaceful instrumentalities," he knew the Burns episode signaled the beginning of "a revolution." Higginson believed that the forthcoming crisis would repair a "deeper disease" in American life than even the institution of slavery. Mid-nineteenth-century society had become "selfish" and "timid," afraid to risk physical injury in order to achieve liberty and virtue. Hearts and minds "untrained" by "physical habits" lost their strength and conviction; they declined and became a source of slavery and an impediment to man's progress.[51]

Burns, pp. 237–39. After losing the verdict, Dana left the Court House and walked to his home in Cambridge. On his way there he was attacked by two men who were angered by his defense of Burns. The lawyer was beaten and then knocked unconscious by the blow of a lead pipe. It took him weeks to recover full health. Ironically, during the course of his recuperation, Dana received a letter from Charles Sumner which asserted that "the blow [would] tell on slavery more than on you" (ibid., pp. 242–43).

50. Shapiro, "Burns Rendition," pp. 39, 43; Richard Henry Dana, Jr., Journal, May 27, 1854, Massachusetts Historical Society; Theodore Parker, Scrapbook, March 18, 1851, Parker Collection, Boston Public Library, Boston, Mass.

51. Thomas Wentworth Higginson, "Massachusetts in Mourning" [a sermon given June 2, 1854], Higginson Collection, Houghton Library; Edelstein, *Strange Enthusiasm,* pp. 162–64.

Within a short time, however, Higginson's lack of sophistication in exploiting the Burns incident was remedied, and his introspection was replaced by a fascination with antislavery maneuvering in the Loring affair and a concern about the impending trial for his part in the Court House break-in. His worry about legal proceedings was brief because he discovered that the state's only witness was unsure of his testimony. The certainty of acquittal, coupled with an emerging understanding of the ways of managing popular opinion, persuaded him that a trial might serve the same tactical purpose as the efforts against Loring— it could be an "additional stimulus" to antislavery sentiment.

Because the others arrested in connection with the attempt were "obscure men," Higginson hoped his new-found reputation would make his indictment a lesson. He relished arrest and considered the possibility of pleading guilty and requesting acquittal on moral grounds. But he dropped such notions once he received expert legal advice and started listening to Wendell Phillips, whose theories on popular opinion governed even Howe and Parker. Phillips was still smarting from the Faneuil Hall episode when he wrote to Higginson a few weeks later. He was upset that he had not been "given a chance to help . . . instead of making a fool of myself." Phillips advised Higginson (in rather cynical terms, given Burns's rendition) that he must plead not guilty because "the opportunity of preaching to that jury is one of the things you fought for perhaps the most important object." Phillips's view was restated by Albert Browne, a youth who had been arrested, questioned, and released in connection with the rescue attempt. He told Higginson that "agitation on the subject is good for the cause. Keep his inequity [Burns's rendition] . . . before the public [and] it cannot fail of producing a good effect. God knows I feel for Burns but I am sure it is a thousand times better for our cause that he . . . was sent back." In the future Higginson would make excellent use of these "lessons."[52]

52. Higginson to Louisa Higginson, May 31, 1854, Higginson-Burns Collection, Boston Public Library; William H. Channing to Higginson, June 1, 1854; Wendell Phillips to Higginson, June 14, 1854; Albert Browne, Jr., to Higginson, June 14, 1854, ibid.

By the end of the summer of 1854, the state had been unable to gather enough evidence to bring those arrested in connection with the attack to trial. Only Martin Stowell seemed in any serious trouble. In November, after a number of postponements, some new names, including those of Parker and Phillips, were halfheartedly added to the list of people to be indicted. When this occurred, the slight strains already existing between Higginson and Parker became intensified. Parker wanted to make a stout defense, but by late fall, almost six months after his own indictment was handed down, Higginson was impatient to conclude the affair. He had been threatened with trial for too long and was in no mood to carry the farce any further by arguing the unconstitutionality of the Fugitive Slave Law. The main legal fight should be "on the evidence," and Higginson outlined his position to Parker in concise terms slightly tinged with antagonism. He wanted to "go for victory" if he pleaded not guilty. Yet, "there must be nothing unfair and no compromise in my opinions." He wanted "to combine a *successful* defense with an *honorable* one." Higginson jabbed subtly at the colleague who had abandoned him that humid evening in May. The next time they quarreled over broken commitments, Higginson would be less delicate.[53]

In April 1855, charges were dropped against all people indicted in connection with the Burns rescue effort, and Parker was dismayed. He claimed he "should have liked the occasion for a speech" and, never one to lose an opportunity to agitate the antislavery cause, he eventu-

53. Martin Stowell to Higginson, June 7, July 16, 1854, ibid. Stowell's behavior during the whole affair impressed Higginson. Yet it is interesting to speculate why Martin Stowell remained so tight-lipped and seemingly protective. Some thirty years after the rescue attempt, Thomas Drew suggested that Stowell, by his own admission, had fired the shot that killed James Batchelder (Thomas Drew to Higginson, April 16, 1888, ibid.). Parker, *Correspondence,* 1: 140, 146–50; Higginson to Parker, December 11, 27, 1854, January 17 and February 12, 1855, Higginson-Burns Collection, Boston Public Library. The whole question of antagonism between Higginson and Parker after the attempt has received little attention. It is significant, however, because it aids our understanding of the comments and assertions each man made during the three years of negotiations with John Brown. Higginson to Louisa Higginson, May 31, 1854; Higginson to Samuel May, Jr., October 11, 1855; Samuel May, Jr., to Higginson, October 11, 12, 15, 1885, ibid.

ally published an elaborate defense of his role in the proceedings which avoided any analysis of his actions before the Faneuil Hall crowd.[54]

Regardless of the personal animosities or philosophical tensions that arose over the Burns "kidnapping," William H. Channing, nephew of the noted Unitarian minister, was pleased with the results of the incident, and he wrote Higginson about his feelings. According to Channing, events like the Burns arrest would "raise higher the growing desire to break our yoke by *awakening the consciousness of the power to do it.*" Channing was certain the fullness of this sense of "power" could be managed in a "single season." Given the right events and the proper use of those events by abolitionists, men could be awakened from "their drunken dreams of gain and ease." Channing had another idea in case men weren't "awakened" by events like the Burns episode. He advised Higginson that "the next thing to do is *guerrilla war* at every chance. They shall not sleep whether they pull down their caps or not." News from Kansas must have pleased Channing greatly.[55]

54. Parker, *Correspondence,* 1: 140, 146–50.
55. William H. Channing to Higginson, July 4, 1855, Higginson-Burns Collection, Boston Public Library.

CHAPTER 2

The Massachusetts Kansas Committee: Sanborn, Stearns, and System

O N   M A Y   3 0 ,   1 8 5 4 , in the midst of the Burns hearings, President Pierce signed the Kansas-Nebraska Act into law. News of the signing prompted Theodore Parker to suggest that the Burns episode had been merely a diversionary tactic contrived by the Slave Power for the purpose of turning Boston's attention away from efforts to institute slavery north of the Missouri Compromise line. Parker, like so many other antislavery men, had opposed the Stephen Douglas-sponsored measure from the day it was introduced in the Senate. He felt it made fradulent use of the popular sovereignty issue to expand slavery into the territories.[1]

In the next two years, the Kansas-Nebraska Act and the attendant problems of proslavery Missouri "border ruffianism," inept federal territorial office appointments, and ballot-stuffed election victories stimulated a new wave of antislavery protest and became the keynote of northern political activity. Harriet Beecher Stowe organized 3,050 New England preachers to sign a petition condemning the Kansas-Nebraska measure. William Lloyd Garrison denounced the act at an Independence Day picnic and then torched copies of the Fugitive Slave Law, the Burns decision, and the United States Constitution. At least partially aided by reaction to the Kansas-Nebraska Act, Know-Nothingism swept into office in Massachusetts. Popular indignation also benefited antislavery men in their attempts to enact personal liberty laws designed to protect fugitive slaves. Sermons were preached and protest

1. Commager, *Parker,* p. 232; Parker, *Works* (Cobbe edition), "The Nebraska Question," 5: 280–96.

meetings organized to prevent Kansas from becoming the newest bastion of slavery.[2]

But by March 1855, antislavery men and women saw that it would take more than angry words or political rallies to prevent a proslavery takeover in Kansas, and they started to finance free-state settlement of the territory. A number of relief committees were set up throughout the North (particularly in Massachusetts) for the purpose of collecting funds and supplies to assist people who were emigrating to the territory. The committees were nonprofit models of Eli Thayer's Massachusetts Emigrant Aid Society. Their purpose was to provide free-state Kansas emigrants with enough food, clothing, homesteading supplies, and money to insure successful settlement. Antislavery reformers hoped to prevent slavery in Kansas by fostering the growth of a population willing to vote the institution down when it came time to prepare a constitution for statehood.[3]

One individual who was active with the Middlesex County Kansas Committee in the late fall of 1855 was Franklin Benjamin Sanborn, a recent Harvard graduate and son of Aaron Sanborn, town clerk of Hampton Falls, New Hampshire. Aaron Sanborn understood the value of proper religious and educational training for his children. He made sure that they were thoroughly familiar with the Bible and received as much public schooling as Hampton Falls had to offer. Because young Frank excelled in his studies, Aaron Sanborn was persuaded to pay J. G. Hoyt to prepare him for college. Hoyt, a Dartmouth graduate and an "ardent antislavery man," began tutoring Frank in 1850 and within a year was sufficiently impressed to suggest further studies at Phillips Exeter Academy, where young Sanborn could receive rigorous training in the classics. At Phillips Exeter, Sanborn continued to excel. He passed Harvard's stiff classics admission examination and, by July

2. Godfrey T. Anderson, "The Slavery Issue as a Factor in Massachusetts Politics, from the Compromise of 1850 to the Outbreak of Civil War" (Ph.D. diss., University of Chicago, 1944), pp. 75–159; William G. Bean, "Party Transformation in Massachusetts with Special Reference to the Antecedants of Republicanism, 1848–1860" (Ph.D. diss., Harvard University, 1922).

3. Horace Andrews, Jr., "Kansas Crusade: Eli Thayer and the New England Emigrant Aid Company," *New England Quarterly* 35 (December 1962): 498.

1852, entered the college as a member of the sophomore class.[4]

During his tutelage by Hoyt, Sanborn was impressed by the Dartmouth graduate's commitment to antislavery. After a few months in Cambridge, where he regularly read the *National Era* and the *New York Tribune* and sometimes attended abolitionist lectures, the young college student proudly proclaimed his own engagement with the movement. He was certain slavery was wrong and that "some of the North were governed by a minority small in numbers but powerful in wealth and influence." This minority was composed of "slaveholders and their commercial allies at the North and West." Slavery must be destroyed in order for the "mass of people" to be free from this "dominating aristocracy."[5]

Despite such strong views about the Slave Power, occasional attendance at antislavery lectures, and routine abolitionist reading, young Sanborn had relatively little time to devote to the movement while at college; there were too many other things to do. During his years at Harvard, Sanborn attended Unitarian services, took long walks out to Concord in hopes of meeting Emerson or Thoreau, and constantly worried about what career he would pursue once he graduated. In early July 1853, he and his friend Edwin Morton listened intently as Emerson addressed himself to a question of vital importance to each of them. They wondered "whether literature in America could be a young man's occupation and bread winner." Sanborn also worked very hard at his studies, earned excellent grades, and became editor of the school paper. He won an election bid to Phi Beta Kappa but declined the offer because he felt the society to be an "unjustifiable intellectual aristocracy."[6]

While at Harvard, Sanborn became a disciple of Theodore Parker.

4. Ronald Story, "Class Development and Cultural Institutions in Boston, 1800–1870: Harvard, The Athenaeum, and the Lowell Institute" (Ph.D. diss., University of Wisconsin, 1970), pp. 128–34; Sanborn, *Recollections*, 1: 13–14, 28; 2: 302, 261.

5. Ibid., 1: 30–31, 45.

6. Ibid., 1: 19; 2: 315, 324–25. For the class implications of Sanborn's contacts with Boston and Concord society, see Story, "Class Development," p. 154; Mary Crocker Newbold, "Franklin Benjamin Sanborn, 1831–1917: The Unknown Concord Transcendentalist" (Honors essay, Harvard University, 1970), pp. 4–5.

He first heard Parker when the minister gave his famous Fast-Day sermon on April 19, 1852, after Thomas Sims had been returned to slavery. Sanborn was amazed by Parker's political wisdom, religious fervor, and intense abolitionism. In time, the young scholar was granted permission to forego Sunday services in the college chapel for Parker's preaching at the Music Hall. As a senior, Sanborn presented a series of lectures on Parker's writings before fellow members of the Hasty Pudding Club.[7]

The majority of Frank Sanborn's college days, however, were dominated by his relationship with the beautiful and frail Ariana Walker. He first met Ariana in 1850 while visiting a cousin and was charmed by her grace. After a few more meetings, Sanborn was certain of his love for Ariana. For her part, Ariana liked Frank because he thought "more wholly for himself" than anyone she had ever met, but she wasn't really attracted to the dark-haired young man. She liked him for his "intellectual and spiritual nature" but "not *himself*," and she claimed she was "never interested in one where feeling was so little personal."[8]

Sanborn could hardly be as dispassionate. He hoped to nurture their friendship and win the love of the woman whose feelings were "so little personal." The young man cast their relationship in typically nineteenth-century terms. He believed Ariana could be a guiding force in his life; an infallible source of advice and comfort. Actually, there does seem to be some justification for his view. Ariana was two years older than Sanborn, exceptionally intelligent, and possessed an uncanny ability to analyze the people around her. She often amused herself by predicting people's actions. In addition, Ariana was quite helpful to Frank during moments of indecision. He repeatedly unburdened himself to her, and she calmed him with wise counsel. She always claimed his success was "sure" as long as he bent his "whole energies" to whatever he hoped to achieve. It was Ariana who encouraged Sanborn to attend Harvard and devote his college years to "severe study." When Sanborn wondered aloud what he could do with his Harvard

7. Sanborn, *Recollections*, 1: 45–46; 2: 315.
8. Ibid., 2: 268–72.

education, it was Ariana who suggested that while he was at college, it was the discipline of education he wanted and "not to be fitted for any particular profession."[9]

Slowly Ariana began to love the friend she so often counseled, and during the early spring of 1854 as Frank finished his junior year, they announced their engagement. The relationship had grown from one in which Ariana had "no personal feelings" into something much deeper. Frail Ariana Walker became fascinated with the handsome young man, who was like a "kind of book in which I like well to read." When she turned to her journal to "review" the "book," a loving, perceptive, and highly revealing character profile emerged.[10]

Ariana knew of Frank's weaknesses, knew that he worried about everyone "overrating" him. She knew that the young scholar viewed himself as "quick" but "confused," and totally lacking in "strictness and steadiness." She understood the paradoxes of his character as well. Frank valued his "independence" highly and thought of himself as "capable of living alone and . . . *apart* from all others," yet in his "innermost soul," he looked for "some *authority* upon which to lean" and was "influenced more than he is aware by those whose opinion he reflects." Sanborn was a man of many "noble aspirations, yet unsatisfied." He was constantly "seeking, seeking, grasping in the dark." The young man wanted a *"definite* end for which to strive heartily," and he believed that if he had such an end, "success" would be sure. Ariana had confidence in Frank because he had "much executive power," though she realized he often "executed better than he planned." Ariana Walker loved Frank Sanborn because he had "great pride," was "gentle" in spite of a certain coldness, and had "strong passions." She also loved him because he was a man whose nature would not allow him to find rest, a man who regarded "struggle" as a "native element" and who "must have a great motive for which to strive."[11]

In the summer of 1854, Ariana Walker became seriously ill. She had

9. Ibid., 2: 274–75, 282–87, 289–91, 307.
10. Ibid., 2: 289–91, 307.
11. Ibid., 2: 275–80.

battled recurring, short-lived "nervous attacks" almost every year after 1846, when she first contracted "a painful lameness" which kept her from walking freely. But previously she had always recovered her health. Now, in the humid weeks of June and July, her condition continued to deteriorate, and her periods of debilitation lengthened. Shattered and disconsolate, Sanborn turned to Parker for comfort. He told the minister that Ariana had "the marks of . . . a settled consumption" and that, unless some change for the better took place, she could not survive another year. He found it difficult to accept that only a few months before it had seemed that he and Ariana "should live together the life to which we have long looked forward." Ariana meant so much to him, was "so woven in [his] being," that he couldn't "think of life without her." He wondered what would become of himself in "so great a desolation." He wondered what work he could put his hand to, "what study I could pursue, what pleasure I could feel in anything."[12]

In spite of her illness, Frank and Ariana decided to marry. Eight days later, on August 28, 1854, the sickly young woman died. Sanborn was devastated. In the midst of his grief, he again turned to Theodore Parker and asked that a short note be read in Ariana's memory before the minister's congregation. He went on to say that he felt sure "God had some great work" for him to do, or "he never would have given me such a wealth of love." In the near future, Sanborn would meet a powerful authoritarian personality who had a "definite end" in mind and believed that he had been given a "great work" to do by God.[13]

Sanborn was too upset to continue his studies during the fall semester. By December 1854, however, he had recovered sufficiently to return to Cambridge and begin the last year of work for his degree. The somber young scholar applied himself diligently throughout the spring and summer of 1855 and completed his courses by late August. He was certain his success that year could be attributed to "less worldly

12. Ibid., 2: 289–91; Sanborn to Parker, July 27, 1854, Sanborn Collection, Concord Free Public Library, Concord, Mass.
13. Sanborn to Parker, September 11, 1854, ibid.

ambition than before . . . and a greater ability to work." After all, it was the "work of two" he was finishing.[14]

The Harvard senior was given an added incentive to complete his studies by Emerson and other Concord residents. The sage of transcendentalism had become so impressed with Sanborn in previous encounters that he now offered the young man a position as schoolteacher in Concord. The idea appealed to Sanborn; so in the early spring of 1855, he and his older sister, Sarah, moved to Concord and started developing an educational program for the coming school year. The young New Hampshire native made acquaintances rapidly and in the process was induced to join the Middlesex County Kansas Committee.[15]

Membership on the committee proved to be an important step in Sanborn's abolitionist career. Within the next year he gradually turned away from teaching and spent more time on Kansas aid work. He was soon appointed secretary and put in charge of directing committee affairs. The ambitious young man looking for a "great work" to do was an extremely effective organizer. As Ariana suggested, he had "much executive power." Sanborn scheduled lectures, managed fund-raising campaigns, and searched desperately for news from Kansas, so he could keep fellow committee members well informed. It was an ideal position for young Sanborn, providing him with a meaningful purpose in life, a new circle of friends, and some influential associations. He was beginning to understand Ariana's advice that he not worry about a career, and he was thankful for her suggestion that he concern himself with the "discipline of education." Harvard course work could never have prepared him for the effort in which he was now engaged. It was "discipline" and "organization" that made for successful management of committee business.[16]

The beating of Charles Sumner on the floor of the United States Senate chamber by the South Carolinian Preston Brooks in late May 1856, followed in rapid succession by a Missouri "border ruffian"

14. Sanborn to Parker, September 24, 1854, December 13, 1854, ibid.
15. Sanborn, *Recollections,* 1: 51; 2: 328; Newbold, "Sanborn," pp. 9–12.
16. Sanborn to Parker, June 10, 1856, Sanborn Collection, Concord Free Public Library.

attack on the free-state town of Lawrence and the killing of five antislavery men on Pottawatomie Creek, increased Sanborn's desire to do something for Kansas. The young secretary was so overcome with the thought of Kansas as a battleground of freedom that he debated giving up his organizational activity and going to the territory to fight. "Armed settlers" were desperately needed, and Sanborn seriously believed he should be one of them, though he soon abandoned such notions.[17]

In August 1856, Sanborn was asked to visit the territory for the Middlesex County Kansas Committee and to find out whether funds and supplies collected by the committee were arriving at their proper destination. At the same time he was to investigate how the materials were being used and what settlers would need in the future. It was the perfect opportunity to test his enthusiasm for "armed settlement." But once out west, Sanborn was made aware of the substantial difference between organizing settlement and actually living and fighting in Kansas. Like Howe and Parker during the Burns episode, Sanborn realized the distance between theory and practice in the abolitionist campaign against slavery. The young secretary scrupulously avoided entering the strife-torn area and, with a twinge of defensiveness in his words, claimed to his sister Sarah that his trip was "only to inspect the emigrant route through Iowa in order that it might be kept open for men, arms, and ammunition." When offered a revolver for protection by Samuel Gridley Howe who was on a similar inspection tour for the newly formed Massachusetts Kansas Committee, Sanborn took the gun reluctantly, saying he did "not expect to run any risk." Although he felt he should "go into Kansas" and use the weapon, he knew his own inability to do so and hoped it was "for the best" that he did not go. Sanborn was awed by the romance of "Western Life," awed by the courage and heroism of armed settlers, and he wished that he possessed the leadership qualities of men like James Lane, Charles Robinson, and John Brown, whose exploits in defense of the free-state cause were making them minor legends. But the trip had taught him

17. Ibid.

a lesson: His forte was "executive power," not "armed settlement."[18]

Upon his return to Massachusetts, Sanborn spoke of Kansas as the "most practical form in which the struggle for freedom has ever presented itself"—one that would "justify any exertion." More and more the "fight for freedom" in Kansas and his urge "to do something" merged. His own sense of "success" and his feeling of accomplishment were bound up with his participation in the Kansas aid movement. Providing aid for the territory became his "career" and, by early fall of 1856, Sanborn had entrusted his Concord school to Sarah. He then launched himself into committee work on a full-time basis.[19]

His rationale for this decision is contained in two letters to Theodore Parker. Both provide a revealing view of his motivation and values. Sanborn claimed that he was concerned because the aid movement had suffered from "the want of men . . . devoted wholly to it." The movement depended too much on "transient excitement and activity" and needed someone who could give it "system and perpetual order." Sanborn thought that even his "inexperienced labors" were "great" when compared to those of many others who professed interest in the movement. Kansas (and, by implication, abolitionism) needed men who would make it "their study and business." Until that happened, antislavery men had "no right to hope for any good." When Parker mildly objected to Sanborn's decision, the former schoolmaster reaffirmed his position and replied: "I see in almost every person traces of indecision which is fatal to any good settlement of the difficulty. Instead of coming out and facing the real evil we are all . . . held back . . . for some personal reason." Sanborn was "determined . . . to cut through all these meshes and do thoroughly what I have been so long talking about." It was a telling rebuttal from one who knew nothing of Parker's hesitation during the Burns rescue attempt. Sanborn saw himself as an example, a person who would convince friends to leave "business and pleasure" and work "wholly for the cause." His efforts

18. Sanborn, *Recollections,* 1: 68; Sanborn to (?), August 14, 1856, Sanborn Collection, Concord Free Public Library.

19. Sanborn to Parker, November 28, 1856, ibid.

would prompt men to "attach more importance to the movement." Sanborn claimed he couldn't expect such a commitment from others unless he was willing to make it "as soon as any," and he was "really ready to give up everything."[20]

Such assertions were highly idealistic, if not wholly accurate. Certainly Sanborn believed in the moral necessity of ending slavery, but he also had personal needs to fulfill that were not part of the same goal. By the fall of 1856, the young man saw that his committee activity could be an important vehicle by which to obtain a "place" in Boston society. Indeed, he was unfair to condemn men for being "held back" from work for the cause because of "personal reasons." All his instincts told him that his own self-interest would best be served by joining the movement on a full-time basis. His need to free Kansas and secure a position harmonized. Sanborn could advocate leaving "business and pleasure" and working "wholly for the cause" because his own self-interest and the free-state triumph in Kansas were one. As he said to Parker at the end of his second letter, it was not a violent step to leave teaching for a few months because there was always a chance his "place" might prove to be "an important one." If his efforts didn't work out, he could always "abandon" them and "take some other place —if I can get it."[21]

The "place" Sanborn referred to in his letter to Parker was the position of secretary of the Massachusetts Kansas Committee. The job had been offered to him in late September by George Luther Stearns, a Medford businessman serving as chairman of the committee. Stearns was encouraged by Sanborn's enthusiasm for the aid movement, impressed by the young man's effective fund-raising efforts, and eager for his firsthand knowledge of the Kansas situation. Most important, Stearns was pleased with Sanborn's awareness of the need for "system and order" in committee business. Since both men agreed that substantial portions of all funds gathered for Kansas should be used to purchase firearms for settlers, it was decided that Sanborn should join Stearns,

20. Ibid.
21. Ibid.

Howe, P. T. Jackson, and George Russell as a full-time committee member.[22]

At a June 3, 1856, public meeting, Massachusetts abolitionists had voted to raise funds for the free-state settlers of Kansas. The men selected to lead the statewide campaign were originally called the Faneuil Hall Committee. The committee was chaired by Samuel Gridley Howe (who was available for "any plan to beat down the Slave Power"), and it sought to combat the "systematic and extensive conspiracy" against freestaters in Kansas. By June 25, 1856, the group had been renamed the Massachusetts Kansas Committee, had acquired a new chairman, Stearns, and had proceeded to raise money with the avowed intention of going beyond what had already been done for settlers by way of supplies and funds. The committee's membership was convinced that guns were as important for Kansas as clothing and tools, and Stearns agreed. In the first four months of his tenure, he gave numerous speeches about the necessity of supplying Kansas settlers. He outlined what the settlers needed and raised $10,000 worth of supplies. Stearns was businesslike, organized, and very effective—never hesitating to use his influence throughout the state. Tinmen, plumbers, and other craftsmen who purchased goods from his lead-pipe factory were employed as a kind of fund-raising agency. Between August and December 1856, Stearns and his "agents" gathered $48,000 worth of equipment for the territory.[23]

George Luther Stearns and Frank Sanborn worked well together. The two men shared similar views and backgrounds. Each came from a family that traced its ancestry back to the first days of the

22. P. T. Jackson to S. W. Gifford, December 3, 1856, Records of the Massachusetts Kansas Committee, Massachusetts Historical Society, Boston, Mass.; Schwartz, *Howe*, pp. 205–6; "To the Public" [an advertisement for the Massachusetts Kansas Committee], Records of the Massachusetts Kansas Committee, Massachusetts Historical Society; Minutes of the Middlesex County Kansas Aid Committee, Septtember 20, 1856, Boyd B. Stutler Collection, Charleston, W.Va.

23. S. Beck to Howe, July 10, 1856, Howe Collection, Houghton Library; Frank Preston Stearns, *The Life and Public Services of George Luther Stearns* (Philadelphia, 1907), pp. 39, 118, 105, 126; Records of the Massachusetts Kansas Committee, Massachusetts Historical Society; Sanborn, *Recollections*, 1: 51–52.

Massachusetts Bay Colony. Each came from a family with modest economic resources, and each man had to exert great energy to fashion a niche for himself in Massachusetts society. This was particularly true of Stearns whose father, Luther Stearns, graduated from Harvard in 1791 and "quickly obtained a good reputation as an obstetrician." George never got to know his father well because in 1820 Luther Stearns died and left the responsibility of caring for the eleven-year-old boy, his brother Henry, and sister Elizabeth to Mary Hall Stearns, his wife of twenty-one years. Mary Hall Stearns undertook the task with strength. She was an inspiring person who not only saw to the needs of her family but became a "power in the community." The large, broad-shouldered woman walked with a cane, had the disposition of a justice of the peace, and faced the family's financial difficulties with courage. She was a staunch no-nonsense Calvinist, who refused to accept "optimistic theories" of religion and probably would have preferred to see her children dead rather than raised in "idle vicious courses." George saw such discipline as "severe and unreasonable," but his mother saw it as a necessity if she was to hold the family together. She was probably correct. Continual financial problems, sickness, and Elizabeth's death in 1828 strained the family bonds but never broke them.[24]

When George was sixteen, his mother sent him to Brattleboro, Vermont, where he trained for a career in business at his uncle's country store. Three and a half years later, in 1828, he returned to Boston and spent the next few years working as a ship's chandler, salesman, and bookkeeper. Then, in 1835, Stearns saw an opportunity to open his own business, the manufacture of linseed oil which was used extensively in shipbuilding. After borrowing money from relatives, mortgaging the family home (Mary Hall Stearns backed her son completely), and obtaining a loan of $10,000 from Medford businessman Deacon Train, he invested his funds in the necessary equipment. Because of careful management, Stearns soon prospered. In the first five years of production, the company's assets grew substantially, and

24. Stearns, *Life of Stearns*, pp. 13–17, 18–20, 24–27.

George Luther repaid all the obligations incurred when he started the enterprise.[25]

Shortly after repaying the last of these debts and rewarding himself with a vacation at some hot sulphur springs in Virginia, Stearns experienced personal tragedy. His wife of five years, Mary Train Stearns, died of a heart condition. For the next three years, the grief-stricken young businessman occupied himself with various community projects while working almost obsessively to improve his linseed oil business. Then, in the spring of 1843, he met the charming and head-strong Mary Preston, daughter of a Maine circuit court judge and cousin of the prominent abolitionist Lydia Maria Child. They were married that fall.[26]

Mary Preston Stearns had fixed ideas about her family's lifestyle, and, from the beginning of the marriage, friction developed between her and George Luther's mother. Their clashing personalities proved such an emotional drain for Stearns that, by 1845, he was building a palatial home on the south side of Medford in order to "look after his mother without having his wife see too much of her." Mary Preston Stearns was disturbed about more than a mother's influence over her son. She also disliked the long hours her husband worked, and she was not completely satisfied with the kind of business George Luther conducted. By 1845, Stearns had pooled capital from his linseed oil business and financed a venture in lead-pipe manufacture. To Mary's mind, "the lead-pipe manufacture" was "not a fine sounding profession." She often criticized her husband for refusing to adopt a more "stylish appearance." Socially ambitious, Mary was particularly annoyed at what she considered her husband's failure to "advance his own interests." Stearns seems to have been hurt by her criticism. Unlike his wife, he had endured economic hardships as a young man, knew the economic distance he had traveled, and was proud of his efforts. He attempted to blunt his wife's outbursts by defensively suggesting that, "considering all things," he had "done very well." People trusted him

25. Ibid., pp. 28–34, 36.
26. Ibid., p. 44.

because he had "no interests of my own to further." But Mary was not to be deterred. She was determined to achieve a name for her family in Massachusetts society or know the reason why not.[27]

Whether because of Mary's incessant promptings to advance his interests or because of his own personal desire to continue doing well, George Luther Stearns played a more active role in Massachusetts politics after remarrying. As early as 1840 he had supported formation of the Liberty Party, and it was rumored that he had been read out of a cousin's will because of his antislavery views. Until 1848, however, when he attended the Conscience Whig Convention in Worcester and "gave liberally" to the campaign, he was a novice. In 1850 he continued his political work by promoting Charles Sumner's candidacy for the United States Senate.[28]

Stearns's campaign activity was paralleled by his seemingly endless philanthropy. In 1848 he gave large sums of money to an Irish famine relief fund and rescued his father-in-law from bankruptcy when he was duped out of his judgeship. At about the same time he was working for Sumner, Stearns loaned money to shipbuilders and mechanics of Medford whose homes had been destroyed by fire. He and the ever-prodding Mary were part of a group of prominent Bostonians who hosted Louis Kossuth on his American tour. Stearns purchased a number of Kossuth's ten-dollar "freedom certificates" and raised a considerable sum in subscription for the Hungarian leader's entourage of exiles. Among this group was a young pianist named Zerahelyi. The young man's career had been destroyed by shattered nerves, a result of a six-month jail term he had served for being a member of Kossuth's army. Mary was captivated by his "pathetic expression," and her empathy translated into her husband's largesse. Several months after Kossuth left Boston, the young ex-pianist was still living at the Stearns mansion in Medford. At Mary's prompting, George Luther also raised a subscription for Kossuth's sister when she was deserted by her husband and left to care for three children. In 1858 Stearns gave Casimir,

27. Ibid., pp. 51, 54–56, 130.
28. Ibid., pp. 59, 81–83, 86.

one of her sons, a job in his factory's counting room only to find a short time later that the youth was stealing company funds. Such a discovery was upsetting but of minor significance because, by 1858, Stearns was consumed by his most important "philanthropic enterprise"—a venture he vaguely referred to as "the wool business" which was being promoted by a failed businessman who captivated Mary Preston Stearns every bit as much as the "pathetic" Zerahelyi.[29]

Ironically, Stearns's increased social and political activities, facilitated at least partially by his sense of economic security, were followed in 1853 by a personal economic disaster that nearly ruined him. During that year Stearns tried to corner the New England lead market. The attempt was ill conceived, badly managed, and cost the Medford businessman nearly all his capital. Desperate, Stearns made a last-ditch effort to save himself by borrowing from Peter Butler of Boston and Benjamin Collins of New York. Luckily, both men had confidence in Stearns and were willing to cover his debts. During the next three years, the would-be lead-pipe magnate worked strenuously, regained his financial fortunes, and reimbursed his benefactors.[30]

The trauma of economic misfortune, coupled with two incidents that occurred during his struggle to recoup his losses, seems to have further stimulated Stearns's philanthropy and at the same time to have intensified his abolitionism. Shortly after the passage of the Fugitive Slave Act in 1850, Stearns purchased a revolver and vowed that "no fugitive would be taken from his premises." Until 1853, however, the Medford businessman had taken no part in the resistance to the law. Then, in the fall of 1853, he was asked to shelter the runaway slave William Talbot. For six days Talbot was hidden in the basement of Stearns's Medford mansion, and when it was safe for the fugitive to leave, Stearns paid for his journey to Montreal. Conversations with Talbot deepened the manufacturer's awareness of slavery's brutality and strengthened his commitment to antislavery reform.[31]

The incident that confirmed Stearns's intention to devote himself to

29. Ibid., pp. 69, 71–74, 78.
30. Ibid., p. 91.
31. Ibid., pp. 41–42, 84, 88.

the antislavery movement was the caning of Charles Sumner by Preston Brooks. Stearns reacted angrily to news of the assault. He was sure it would "make a million abolitionists" and vowed "to do what one man can and devote my life and fortune to the cause." He did not take the vow lightly. In two weeks he had joined the Massachusetts Kansas Committee, and by the end of June 1856, was directing the committee's affairs.[32]

Stearns came to the movement with some definite theories about the nature and tactics of reform. For instance, he understood the need to cultivate popular opinion. Saddened by Sumner's beating, he was well aware that it could "make a million abolitionists" if it was properly exploited. As a businessman, he also knew his success had depended upon the ability to market his wares effectively, and he correctly assumed the same held true for abolitionism. Furthermore, Stearns was sure that the "idea of abolishing slavery in America by moral suasion" was a "delusion." He hoped the institution could be dismantled by political compromise but was willing to experiment with other methods. He never hesitated to use funds raised by the Massachusetts Kansas Committee for purchasing arms when other means of ending slavery seemed destined to fail. Then, too, Stearns had a keen sense of the disillusion that often plagued reformers and realized that no reform "could be made with the unanimous consent of the community." Anyone "who stepped forward must be ready to meet the fate of a reformer," must be ready to be disappointed by the public.[33]

The Medford businessman-turned-antislavery-activist frequently discussed his theories with Samuel Gridley Howe, the man he had replaced as chairman of the Massachusetts Kansas Committee. The two men first met in 1848 at the Conscience Whig Convention. Later they worked together for Sumner and cooperated with each other in Kossuth's behalf. Stearns was impressed by Howe's commitment to Kossuth and his willingness to "cheerfully make any sacrifices" to aid the Hungarian leader. When Charles Sumner asked Howe whether the

32. Ibid., p. 115.
33. Ibid., p. 49.

famous Hungarian exile was demanding more money than was reasonable, Howe replied that he was not at all disturbed that Kossuth's desire to fight for Hungary's freedom would cost too much. If a cause was "right," it could never cost too much. Howe agreed that wars were "bad" but suggested that "when the lower propensities are so active in a race they must occasionally be beaten down by muskets." Stearns marveled that Howe was not disturbed by Kossuth's exaggerated claims. The physician contended that Kossuth, "like all enthusiasts," overdid his claims and attempted "more than is possible to perform." But Howe felt it was necessary to indulge such exaggeration. Kossuth could "do much" for the cause of freedom and needed "a chance to try a struggle." If collecting funds or enduring overstatement was a way of "keeping" a great man like Kossuth, Howe was all for it.[34]

Howe and Stearns also shared a similar theory of education, one that would have an important effect on their future antislavery activity. Early in his career, Howe had pushed for the institutionalization of persons suffering from various mental or physical handicaps and, as the director of Perkins School for the Blind, he worked diligently to establish an institution which would prove the validity of that theory. His reputation in the Boston community owed much to the seeming success of these efforts. By the late 1840s, however, the physician began to have doubts about the effectiveness of institutional rehabilitation—experience had "lessened the enthusiasm" he had once felt for "such establishments."[35]

Howe now believed that the "leading principle" in treating those afflicted with a mental or physical handicap should be *separation and not congregation.* He called this his "theory of diffusion" and based it on the assumption that, although handicapped people did need special training at places like Perkins School, prolonged exposure to similarly handicapped persons could be detrimental to an individual's growth

34. Howe to Charles Sumner, December 26, 1851; April 1852, Howe Collection, Houghton Library.

35. Howe, *Journals,* "Report on State Beneficiaries," p. 13; Schwartz, *Howe,* pp. 271–72; Howe to Horace Mann, December 29, 1851; Howe to Charles Sumner, February 6, 1852, Howe Collection, Houghton Library.

and improvement. Isolation with similarly disabled peers could lead to deterioration. Howe began to push for increased exposure to "normal" persons. The blind, for example, should not stay at Perkins all the time but should "go among normal persons, adjust to a normal world, and not develop a separate class feeling." Howe favored boarding Perkins students out in the community and using the school only for teaching compensatory educational skills. The ideal to strive for was "normal existence among normal people"; one should learn by doing what "normal" people do.[36]

Stearns's work for the Medford Sunday School Association led him to a somewhat similar conclusion. As secretary of the association, he was concerned with the seeming failure of religious instruction: It had no effect on the children. He and other members of the group engaged in long debates over which form of instruction would best promote true "Christian living." His own conclusion was that religious instruction depended "too much on teaching theology, Scripture, History, etc." If Medford parents expected their children to learn what they themselves had only imperfectly mastered, then it was time for Sunday school teachers to start depending "more on themselves" and less on their "immediate preparation." A teacher could only legitimately enforce the portions of Christian truth he had realized in his own life, could only speak from "soul to soul." Stearns was looking for those people who applied the truths of Scripture to "everyday life." The "proper Christian teacher" had to be the "proper Christian disciple" —one who would "enforce percept by example." The Medford businessman wanted to conduct religious education on Sunday, as Howe conducted remedial education at Perkins, by exposing children to "normal persons" and to "living Christians."[37]

In 1858 both Howe and Stearns would be asked to subsidize the effort of a "living Christian" who hoped to lead a group of black men and women out of the oppressive and debilitating institution of slavery. This individual would premise his own work on the assumption

36. Ibid.
37. Stearns to Rev. R. G. Watterson, November 10, 1842, Stearns Letters, New York Historical Society, New York, N.Y.

that any "normal" person had a right and a duty to strike a violent blow for freedom and that slave insurrection was the first step in breaking down "class feeling" and inculcating "normal" values.

Besides sharing similar reform theories, Howe and Stearns seem to have had a genuine affection for each other. It was partially on the basis of their firm friendship that Stearns took over the reins of the Massachusetts Kansas Committee when Howe's poor physical and mental health prevented him from conducting the committee's affairs. Howe claimed to be "fairly broken down" in attempting to "pull the laboring oar" of the organization, and he was relieved when Stearns offered to shoulder the burden.[38]

38. Howe, *Journals,* pp. 417–19; Schwartz, *Howe,* pp. 197, 201, 205–6; Howe to Horace Mann, June 30, 1856, Howe Collection, Houghton Library; Howe to P. T. Jackson, November 22, 1856, Records of the Massachusetts Kansas Committee, Massachusetts Historical Society.

CHAPTER 3

Kansas Reflections

SAMUEL GRIDLEY HOWE was beset by an array of problems in the spring of 1856. He frequently argued with his wife, Julia, over family finances and her desire for a literary career. He was shocked by Sumner's beating and disturbed by his good friend's failure to respond properly to medical treatment. And, as always, the tension created by these problems affected his physical well-being and led him to fear impending death. However, more disturbing than these concerns—perhaps even a result of them—was a crisis of character that engulfed Howe. Seized by doubts, fears, and guilts, he became confused about who he was and where life was taking him. In a confidential letter to his close friend Horace Mann, Howe revealed the agony of this crisis. He claimed to be a "mistake, an abortion"; he insisted that his character was "a humbug" and described his reputation as undeserved because he had nothing more than "average benevolence." The latter years of his life had showed "a great selfishness" and "loss of the adventuresome spirit." He longed for a return to his youth when he had been governed by principle and was ignorant of what course was "profitable." Howe was worried about his manhood, worried about having no more than "ordinary courage." He admitted to Mann that he was sometimes afraid to board trolley cars and was forever concerned about "getting into danger, though able to appear decently cool." The doctor believed there was only one escape from his agony and only one way to recover confidence in himself. He needed another chance to prove himself, another chance to recapture the happiness of early life, when "health, a good course and clean conscience" were all that mattered. He was looking back to a time when he had been "unconscious of any purpose . . . called selfish." He longed for a simpler, more certain existence—one that wasn't filled with marital problems, financial concerns, and too many professional responsibilities. The same society that caused the "deeper disease" Higginson so loathed had placed exorbitant demands on Samuel Gridley Howe. He pined for the days of his imaginary past, when he hadn't been worried about what he ate or what he wore or "whether anybody knew about me."[1]

As his depression deepened in the summer of 1856, Howe looked to Kansas for a reprieve. He believed a reconnaissance mission there could help him recapture his lost confidence and rekindle his "adventuresome spirit." After sending Julia and the family to Newport, Rhode Island, Howe started west in mid-July, melodramatically viewing the venture as the "most dangerous" he had undertaken, but claiming he felt "bound to go." The Kansas mission seemed "a duty, the last of my life that I should ever be called to fulfill." Faced with the problem of alleviating a profound personal crisis, Howe (like Sanborn) proceeded to fuse his quest for relief with the free-state cause. In the name of seeing himself as something more than a "mistake" and "an abortion," he made Kansas into a fountain of youth, a retreat at which he might recapture the unselfish ways of the past and shed the cares of his urban, professional existence. Howe was confused, and he grasped for an ordering experience—something that could return a sense of himself to himself. In the end, the trip only served to deepen his guilt and fears.[2]

Howe never did enter Kansas and never did experience the happiness of a "good course." At Mount Tabor, Iowa, he learned of the critical condition of the free-state forces. Missouri border ruffians had pushed into northern Kansas and left only two ways to enter the territory. Howe could go into Kansas with a body of armed settlers, or he could go in alone on horseback. He claimed to have neither the time for the

1. Howe to Horace Mann, n.d., 1856, Howe Collection, Houghton Library.
2. Ibid.

first nor the energy for the second. Whatever his reasons, Howe's failure to enter the territory only added to his romantic view of the place and those men and women who were settling there. He imagined the Kansas struggle to be a reenactment of the English Civil War. He saw southerners as "all bad" and northerners as "good, God-fearing, temperate, and honest." Like Sanborn, however, Howe resigned himself to organizing, instead of joining, the "God-fearing." He still had a deep-seated fear of engaging in physical violence.[3]

The doctor spoke with as many settlers as he could, telling them what their "friends in the East" expected. They should maintain their "constitutional right to bear arms" and never lay those arms down while they had "strength to bear them." But Howe was still uncertain about subsidizing forceful means and unclear about what settlers should do with the arms they weren't supposed to lay down. The Boston physician suggested that when they found themselves opposed by federal troops, they should "stand still and insist on a *Free State,* still bearing arms." It was important, as well, that they preserve their image as law-abiding citizens, and he suggested they "ought not oppose the civil process in the uncertainty and disunion of counsel." If they did resist "the civil process," he was sure "mischief" would arise. Then, whether they were beaten or victorious, they would "stand wrong before the country."[4]

Howe was most upset with the actions of one of Kansas's foremost military leaders, James Lane, a lean and sinewy man of careless dress and raspy voice. Lane was a combination of "principle and opportunism" who had come to Kansas looking for the "main chance." He had organized a free-state militia and cooperated with Iowans in establishing the Lane Trail, through which settlers could move into Kansas and circumvent the Missouri blockade. Howe was not impressed by these credentials and felt Lane was guilty of "extreme indiscretion" when he visited Mount Tabor without remaining incognito. Howe believed Lane gave federal marshals in the area the idea that the emigrant train

<hr>

3. Schwartz, *Howe,* pp. 207, 208–11.

4. Ibid., pp. 209–11; Howe to Agents and Leaders of the Emigrant Train, August 1, 1856, Howe Collection, Massachusetts Historical Society, Boston, Mass.

leaving Tabor was a filibustering expedition, not a body of legitimate settlers. The doctor made Lane's departure from camp a condition for granting committee funds and supplies.[5]

Soon after Lane's departure in early August, Howe started back to Boston. Once home, he found that word of his visit to Kansas had spread quickly, and during late August and early September he was deluged with requests for funds by groups heading west. The fact that he had been able to open a channel of communication between the Massachusetts Kansas Committee and free-state settlers consoled him. He was also pleased at having been able to "hamstring the adventuresome Lane." Generally, however, his "mission," his quest to recapture his own "adventuresome spirit," had not turned out the way he had envisioned it. The doctor recognized that he had given in to his "fear of danger" by not going into Kansas and, in the process, had forfeited any chance to regain the happiness won by dedication to a good cause. It simply was not enough to do organizational work for free-state settlers. He was still ill, still filled with nagging doubts about his own character, still an "abortion." The trip had merely exacerbated Howe's self-recrimination. Again he had been forced to face the discrepancy between his theorizing about heroic, selfless behavior and the reality of his own abilities. He could advise people to maintain their constitutional right to bear arms, but he gave the advice ambivalently. He was lost, confused, and still looking for something "dangerous" to which he could commit himself. And the trip had done nothing to alleviate the difficulties between him and Julia; they continued to argue about family finances and her career. Howe's relationship with Sumner was also strained by his travel west. One of the reasons Howe had not journeyed to Washington to visit Sumner after the attack was the pending Kansas trip. When he returned to Boston, Howe feebly attempted to defend his behavior and tried to excuse his failure to stay by his friend's side in time of need. He wrote Sumner, saying "I now learn my presence

5. Howe to Horace Mann, July 27, 31, 1856, Howe Collection, Houghton Library; Wendell H. Stephenson, "The Political Career of James Lane," *Kansas State Historical Society Publications* 3 (1930): 74.

might have been pleasant and useful to you. I cannot reproach my-self, for when I would have gone I could not and when I could, it did not seem to us here that it was well for you to have any visitors." But Howe did reproach himself. He continued to look for a "good course," continued to look for something beyond the routine of his daily existence. In four months, he would find it in the form of a Kossuth-like hero named John Brown.[6]

During October 1855, before major hostilities had developed be-tween free-state and proslavery forces in Kansas and seven months after the State of Massachusetts finally dropped prosecution in the Burns case, Thomas Wentworth Higginson decided to take a vacation. His reform work, lectures, and Burns activities had exhausted him. The Worcester Free Church had also become a burden. The congregation flourished under his tutelage, but it demanded much of his time and energy. Another thing that put stress on Higginson was his wife's poor physical condition. Mary Channing Higginson had always been subject to chronic ill-health. In January 1853 she suffered an attack of "violent rheumatism." Whether this illness was a severe form of arthritis or an early symptom of muscular distrophy is un-clear, but throughout that spring she could barely walk. Though Higginson was upset, he did not restrict his reform activities. Indeed, he sought escape by avoiding the issue of his wife's health and spend-ing long periods of time on the lecture circuit. Their relationship became strained. Mary needed more and more attention but showed none of the "reverence" for her husband that he admittedly craved. Added to this was Mary's "undisguised repugnance of children and her husband's solicitousness." Finally by October 1855, in obvious discomfort with his marital situation and exhausted by the reform work that had helped him escape it, Higginson planned a trip to the semitropical island of Fayal in the Azores. After requesting David

6. Howe to Charles Sumner, May 28, August 23, September 16, 1856, Howe Collection, Houghton Library; Howe, *Journals,* p. 419; Schwartz, *Howe,* pp. 211–12.

Wasson (a friend of George Luther Stearns) to take over the responsibilities of the Free Church, Higginson and his wife set sail from
Boston harbor at the end of the month.[7]

A warm climate and relaxed daily routine refreshed the Massachusetts couple considerably and, by the spring of 1856, Higginson had
become impatient to return to his reform work. Before the Burns
episode, he had claimed to be "just waking up to Kansas-Nebraska"
and was ready to preach a sermon on it. Now, as news trickled into
the isolated island about the increased hostilities raging in Kansas, the
Worcester activist wanted to do more than sermonize.[8]

Immediately upon his return from Fayal in June, Higginson initiated efforts in Worcester to organize and supply people who
wanted to settle Kansas as a free state. These actions earned him an
agency with the Massachusetts Kansas Committee. When a group of
forty-seven Worcester men led by Calvin Cutter rejected instructions to enter Kansas by the land route through Iowa and were
"summarily disarmed" by a few Missourians, Higginson was asked
to investigate the incident. He jumped at the chance and headed
west in early July, certain he was living in a "great historic period"
and sure the future would "leave no true man unhonored." As he
traveled west, Higginson hoped people would understand the "emi-
nent need" to support free-state settlers and indulged himself by exaggerating his own contributions, convinced that if he had not organized the aid movement in Massachusetts, "nothing would have
been done." The Worcester activist still found it necessary to be
first among equals.[9]

In September 1856, he had a second chance to experience the conditions in Kansas. He contracted to write a series of articles on Kansas
for the *New York Tribune,* but he traveled west fearing his mission
would not be a very "manlike one." Unlike Howe, Higginson had

7. Edelstein, *Strange Enthusiasm,* pp. 177, 138, 151–52, 178.

8. Ibid., pp. 180–81, 186.

9. Ibid., pp. 180–85; Higginson to Louisa Higginson, June 26, 1856, Higginson
Collection, Houghton Library.

"only a sense of general danger" about entering Kansas and didn't think it would be enough of a test of his "manlike virtue." When he reached Chicago, Higginson was further disheartened to find that his itinerary called for him to be "employed more out of Kansas than in Kansas." He felt little consolation in the fact that the people he met in the city who had been in Kansas were "very glad" to see him and to know he was promoting the free-state cause.[10]

Like Howe, Higginson was impressed with those men and women who were settling Kansas—they were larger than life, romantic figures of heroic proportions. Ever since the rendition of Burns, Higginson claimed that he had been "looking for men." He found them in Kansas, and they proved that the "virtue of courage" had "not died out in the Anglo-American race." Like Howe and Stearns who understood and theorized about the influence of environment on personality, Higginson believed that the Anglo-American man needed only the proper "circumstances" to demonstrate his manliness. One day in Kansas made the "American Revolution more intelligible," and Higginson was sure that, if one could change "circumstances," one could change character —black or white.[11]

Higginson vehemently disagreed with Howe's view of James Lane, probably because the free-state leader went out of his way to patronize the minister. Lane appointed Higginson brigadier general of Kansas free-state forces "because of his past courage and ability," and also arranged for Higginson to join a group of twenty settlers traveling to Topeka. The journey was not all that Higginson expected. Some danger did exist, but the trip proved to be "discouragingly safe." He claimed the group feared "marching in without a decent excuse for firing at anything or anybody." Although he was intrigued with the

10. Higginson to Louisa Higginson, August 29, September 3, 1856, ibid.; Edelstein, *Strange Enthusiasm*, pp. 186–88.

11. Higginson to Louisa Higginson, September 18, 1856, Higginson Collection, Houghton Library; Thomas Wentworth Higginson, *A Ride through Kansas*, p. 14. This pamphlet first appeared in October 1856 as a series of articles in the *New York Tribune* under the signature "Worcester." It can be found in the Miscellaneous Pamphlets of Thomas Wentworth Higginson in the Higginson-Barney Collection, Houghton Library, Harvard University, Cambridge, Mass.

"wild manly looking riders around him," he was a bit disillusioned by the "dirty" life he was leading. "Death" for freedom was "all very fine," but when it came to "dirt for freedom," the sacrifice became "unexpectedly hard." Higginson didn't know how to romanticize dirt.[12]

One of the members of the group Higginson traveled with was James Redpath, a frenetic young journalist-adventurer who was also covering the Kansas struggle for Greeley's *Tribune.* The two men got along very well. They shared similar views on the moral evil of slavery, the necessity of arming free-state settlers, Lane's staunch defense of freedom, and the right to use violent means to preserve freedom. Redpath had been in Kansas a number of months and stimulated Higginson's curiosity about the place with a detailed discussion of free-state politics and leaders. He seemed to know all about men like Lane, Charles Robinson, and the mysterious John Brown. Higginson was impressed with Redpath's exceptional boldness. When both men were arrested and interrogated by John Geary, the newly appointed territorial governor, about the intentions of the settlers they were riding with, Redpath refused to be cowed and, instead, lashed out at Geary for attempting to conquer "the Free State cause by arresting Free State leaders." Higginson believed Geary intended to maintain peace in Kansas "at the price of obedience to a false legislature."[13]

Soon after his arrest and interrogation, Higginson was released and started back to Worcester. He was certain the brief pause in hostilities which settled upon Kansas after Geary's arrival was "only the prelude to a severer struggle." Both sides made preparation for renewed

12. Thomas Wentworth Higginson, *The Letters and Journals of Thomas Wentworth Higginson, 1846–1909,* ed. Mary Thacher Higginson (Boston, 1921), pp. 143–45 (hereafter to be cited as Higginson, *Journals*); Edelstein, *Strange Enthusiasm,* pp. 186–88; Higginson to Louisa Higginson, September 18, 1856, Higginson Collection, Houghton Library.

13. J. B. Pond, *The Eccentricities of Genius* (New York, 1900); Charles F. Hosmer, *The Life of James Redpath and the Development of the Modern Lyceum* (New York, 1926). These two works give a brief sketch of Redpath's early life. Higginson, *Journals,* p. 141.

fighting, and neither desired peace. Such a state of affairs further convinced Higginson that his theory about the effects of war on men was correct. "War," he claimed, "always educates men to itself, disciplines them, teaches them to bear its fatigue, anxiety and danger and actually enjoy them." War made men. Just as his own attack on the Court House had crystallized his own commitment to "practical abolition"; just as it had partially dispelled his own personal confusion about life goals and the means to achieve them, so too would violent confrontation discipline the men of Kansas. It would strip away their uncertainties about the immorality of slavery, and it would cure the "deeper disease" inflicted on them by American society. Righteous violence purified men and returned them to manliness and Anglo-American virtue. Yes, war made men, and men never stopped fighting until they achieved their goals. Because Kansas was not yet free, Higginson knew hostilities must continue.[14]

Upon his return to Worcester, the minister confessed that he had enjoyed himself while in the territory. In spite of the near state of siege that existed there (perhaps because of it), Higginson thought that things and people were "very real there." What was that reality? To Higginson, it was like "waking up some morning and stepping out on the Battle of Bunker Hill." Kansas was the reincarnation of eighteenth-century revolutionary America. It was a place of morality, courage, and freedom-loving simplicity. It was tradition and idealism freed from a "mainchance mentality." It was a place where discipline had replaced the chaos of his own society. Kansas was a place where people were dedicated to fighting for freedom and need not concern themselves with the anxiety of selecting a proper career. The people of Kansas were not only fighting to prevent the imposition of slavery, they were rejecting a mentality—one that enslaved four million black men and women and destroyed the "virtue" and "manliness" of revolutionary America.

Kansas was more than a battleground of freedom for Higginson and

14. Thomas Higginson, *A Ride through Kansas*, pp. 18, 22–23; Edelstein, *Strange Enthusiasm*, pp. 190–91.

Howe. It was a refuge—a vacuum apart from society—and, at the same time, a model for their society. In that imaginary vacuum, Higginson fared better than his Kansas committee colleague, Samuel Gridley Howe. While out on the plains of Kansas, Higginson experienced a sense of uplift. He enjoyed "sitting in a hotel and hearing men talk about me . . . while I know I have incurred the penalty of death for treason under the U.S. Laws and arming fugitives to Kansas." The men and women who were settling Kansas were indeed "fugitives." They were men and women seeking release from a "diseased" society. Once home, Higginson despaired at having left Kansas and its "fugitives." When he finally discharged his revolver and put it away in his trunk, there occurred "a curious reaction from the feeling with which I first loaded it. . . . It fully came home to me that all the tonic of life was ended and thence forward if any danger impended the proper thing would be to look meekly about for a policeman, it seemed as if all the vigor had suddenly gone out of me and a despicable effeminacy had set in." Kansas called forth a rugged individualist "vigor," while Worcester could only summon "despicable effeminacy."[15]

Higginson would soon meet a person who symbolized the "vigor" of Kansas—one who believed that white America could recapture the values of revolutionary days only when it saw the black man as man.

Like Howe and Higginson, Frank Sanborn was caught up in continuing self-analysis. In later years, he prefaced his autobiography with the creed which he believed had governed his life's work. Setting himself against the "main chance" psychology of the nineteenth century, Sanborn claimed never to have yearned for "great wealth" or to have sought "leadership or high place in the world." He maintained that whatever leadership he had acquired could be attributed to "character and not ambition." He was always filled with "contentment in station" though firmly resolved not to be "domineered over by others,

15. Higginson to Louisa Higginson, November 30, December 19, 1856, Higginson Collection, Houghton Library; Edelstein, *Strange Enthusiasm*, p. 195.

either individuals or classes." Yet Sanborn's activities as secretary of the Massachusetts Kansas Committee belie such assertions; they indicate that he vainly sought recognition among the intellectuals and reformers of Boston society. Indeed, Frank Sanborn was a very ambitious administrator, who repeatedly tried to widen the scope of his authority. Like Stearns, he was displeased with the haphazard organization of Kansas aid efforts and wanted to remedy the situation. He changed the committee's voucher system, demanded that many accounts be "explained," asked for careful itemization of all expenses, and constantly prodded agents to fulfill their obligations in these fiscal matters.[16]

During his tenure as secretary of the Middlesex County Committee, Sanborn learned that the amount of responsibility he acquired rose in direct proportion to the time he put into his committee work; to gain power in the bureaucracy, one had to become an indispensable bureaucrat. This was his first rule of operation as secretary of the Massachusetts Kansas Committee. Within a few weeks after joining the committee, his exertions earned him recognition and respect from fellow committee members. As a result, his opinions were more frequently solicited and receptively considered. This, in turn, led to Sanborn's increased self-confidence and assertiveness. In late December, he composed an article for the *Middlesex Journal* and boldly requested the Massachusetts legislature to appropriate $50,000 to $100,000 for relief of "our brethren" in Kansas. The state should place the sum in the hands of "a committee of good men" who would spend it only with "reliable information" about Kansas's needs. A large appropriation would encourage emigration, promote investment of capital, and prevent a proslavery takeover in the territory.[17]

Nevertheless, Sanborn's importance to the aid movement and to

16. Sanborn, *Recollections,* 1: 32–33; Sanborn to P. T. Jackson, January 13, 17, April 14, 1857, Records of the Massachusetts Kansas Committee; Sanborn to John Bertram, Esq., January 15, 1857, Sanborn-Brown Collection, Houghton Library, Harvard University, Cambridge, Mass.

17. Franklin Benjamin Sanborn, "State Aid for Kansas," *Middlesex Journal,* December 1856, in Sanborn Scrapbooks, 1, Boyd Stutler Collection.

Massachusetts abolitionism was established chiefly by his three-year relationship with the gray-haired, steely-eyed, fifty-six-year-old Kansas freedom fighter who, shortly after New Year's Day in 1857, walked into the committee offices on Bromfield Street in Boston. John Brown calmly introduced himself to Sanborn and then presented the young committeeman with reference letters from New York philanthropist Gerrit Smith, Kansas free-state leader Charles Robinson, and abolitionist-politician Salmon Chase. In measured tones, Brown told the secretary that he had recently returned from the territory after spending fifteen months fighting for the free-state cause. During that period he and his sons had skirmished with proslavery settlers in the so-called Wakarussa War, had played a major role in defeating Henry Clay Pate and his Missouri border ruffians at the Battle of Black Jack, and had fought along side James Lane at Ossawatomie. Brown remarked that his experiences had confirmed his belief in both the moral evil of slavery and the injunctions of retributive justice found in the Old Testament. Force was the only language proslavery men understood.

Brown came to Boston physically and mentally exhausted. He was out of money and harried by his family's desperate financial state—they were scraping a living out of a small, soil-poor farm in North Elba, New York. He was looking for supplies to continue his free-state activities and, most important, he was gently testing Massachusetts abolitionist attitudes on the use of violence to overthrow the institution of slavery. He told Sanborn that Gerrit Smith believed his chances of getting materials from the Massachusetts Kansas Committee were good and informed Sanborn that, before coming to Boston, he had stopped at Springfield, Massachusetts, where he had spoken to George Walker, Ariana's brother. Walker had suggested that Brown go straight to Sanborn for any information about obtaining free-state supplies.[18]

As Brown spoke, Sanborn carefully read the letters of introduction and was quite satisfied. Actually, the young secretary did not need

18. Sanborn, *Recollections,* 1: 80–81; Oates, *Brown,* p. 181; Brown to John Brown, Jr., January 1, 1857, Smith Collection, Syracuse University, Syracuse, N.Y.; Sanborn, *Recollections,* 1: 76.

testimony about Brown's heroism because he had been reading about the man's exploits for over a year. Abolitionist newspapers were filled with articles heralding the actions of this Bible-quoting freedom fighter. While in Kansas, Sanborn himself had listened to the settlers speak of the self-sacrificing colonist. Such stories reaffirmed Sanborn's own notions about the singularly courageous spirit of Kansas emigrants. When he had finished reading the letters, Sanborn was struck by the recollection of a note he had recently written to Thomas Wentworth Higginson. In it Sanborn replied to Higginson's call for the formation of an independent northern militia to assist Kansas freestaters. The committee secretary had assured Higginson that Kansas fighting and James Buchanan's election during that fall had shown him the need to do "something different." Submission to the Slave Power for another four years was out of the question, and Sanborn supported the militia idea. But until his meeting with Brown, Sanborn was unsure what "something different" was, in spite of his advocacy of Higginson's plan. Now, as the intense, imposing freedom fighter stood in front of him waiting for a response, the young secretary's instinct told him that John Brown was "something different" in a manly form.[19]

As soon as the two men began to discuss Kansas, Sanborn knew his instincts were correct. Often emphasizing his ideas with biblical quotations, Brown was a man who impressed one with his "seriousness of mood." He appeared hardened by his experiences in the "wild regions" of Kansas, and the young abolitionist admired the qualities of leadership these experiences seemed to have brought out. Brown knew what needed to be done to stop slavery in Kansas, and he knew how to do it. He was a man used to "directing other men" and not being "guided or trained by them." In addition, Sanborn, whose desire for his own family had been tragically disrupted by Ariana's death, was affected by Brown's reverence for family. Brown spoke sorrowfully about his son Frederick's death in Kansas, his other sons' imprisonment, and the

19. Sanborn to Higginson, November 6, 1857, Higginson-Kansas Collection, Kansas State Historical Society, Topeka, Kans.; Edelstein, *Strange Enthusiasm,* p. 193.

hardship his wife, Mary, had to endure because her men were off fighting for freedom. It was obvious to Sanborn that with such an acute sense of family, Brown more thoroughly understood the debilitating effects of slavery. In fact, after listening to Brown during this first discussion, Sanborn believed history would give the man a "proud place on her pages" and "posterity would pay homage to his heroism." Ironically, Sanborn would make a career out of seeing to it that "history" performed the task. In later years, promoting Brown's image and legend would be "something to do."[20]

For the next few days Brown and his young admirer talked about the Kansas struggle. Scrupulously avoiding any mention of his role in the Pottawatomie Massacre, Brown outlined his plans for a free-state defense. He spoke of organizing "every able bodied free-state man" into military companies and gathering the appropriate materials to supply these cadres. A cooperative effort could "inspire . . . confidence and courage" in men who would ordinarily be only "dead weight" on the hands of those who possessed "more fortitude and presence of mind." The leaders of these companies had to be men of "impeachable moral character . . . ardent devotion to . . . liberty, gentlemanly . . . demeanor, great practical industry and energy of character." Brown hardly needed to press such views on a young man whose ambition and industry had earned him a place with the Massachusetts Kansas Committee and who believed it was "character" that made for distinguished leadership. Sanborn also agreed with Brown's Higginson-like notions about the beneficial effects that military discipline had on weak men.[21]

Sanborn was equally impressed by Brown's unselfishness and organizational sense. All the man wanted was enough money to arm settlers and "the means for defraying" his "ordinary expenses." The request seemed reasonable to one who had advocated a huge legislative grant for Kansas and its defenders. Not surprisingly, the young secretary concurred with Brown's desire for a regularized payment schedule and

20. Sanborn, *Recollections*, 1: 76–79, 90–91, 120.
21. Oates, *Brown*, p. 184; Plan for the Defense of Kansas, Sanborn-Brown Collection, Houghton Library; Villard, *Brown*, p. 271.

a "fair and full account" of all expenditures. Brown's attitudes about the necessity of proper fiscal management mirrored what the efficiency-minded secretary had tried to implement as basic committee procedure. Like so many of Brown's past business associates, Sanborn was led to believe that the Kansas veteran understood the value of "system and perpetual order" in any financial aid program. Sanborn wrote to Higginson, explained that Brown needed $30,000, and asked the Worcester activist to come and meet the man. Simultaneously, the secretary sent notes to Garrison, Howe, Phillips, and other well-known Boston abolitionists, suggesting they meet Brown on January 5 at an informal reception to be held in Theodore Parker's home.[22]

John Brown was just as taken with Frank Sanborn, who was not only enthusiastic and organized, but was in an ideal position to help Brown make vital financial connections. The young committeeman understood the economic elements involved in resisting Slave Power encroachments and knew that men had to be willing to make anti-slavery activity their "business and study." Although Sanborn had very limited knowledge of what slavery was like, he was angered by the institution's debilitating effects on the black man, seemed ready to fight for a state appropriation to assist Kansas, and was more than willing to commit Massachusetts Kansas Committee funds to Brown's use. After a lifetime of experiences trying to get men to invest in his own ill-fated economic ventures, Brown quickly recognized young San-born's ambition and strong desire to succeed. This intensity, when joined with the young man's obvious inexperience and deferential attitude toward anyone willing to actually fight for freedom, made Brown think he would be more manageable than other committee members. In the ensuing weeks and months, Brown tried to exploit that manageability. Like Ariana Walker, he sensed that, in spite of Sanborn's perfunctory protestations about the need for independence,

22. Plan for the Defense of Kansas, Sanborn-Brown Collection, Houghton Library; Oates, *Brown,* pp. 184, 187; Sanborn to Higginson, January 5, 1857, Higginson-Brown Collection, Boston Public Library, Boston, Mass.; Villard, *Brown,* p. 271; Henry Steele Commager, ed., *Theodore Parker: An Anthology* (Boston, 1960), pp. 257–66.

the young man was ready to be led. And, as Sanborn himself had suggested, Brown was "used to leading."

John Brown looked forward to the meeting scheduled for Parker's home. While living in Springfield some years earlier, he had occasionally traveled to the Music Hall to hear the fiery abolitionist minister. Though Brown disagreed with Parker's Unitarian theology, he claimed to be "wonderfully taken up" with the minister's "discourse." And Brown's appreciation for Parker's violent rhetorical flourishes against slavery "constantly increased." The difference between Brown's Old Testament Calvinism and Parker's Unitarianism was partially reflected in the restrained but slightly heated debate which erupted between Garrison and Brown during the meeting. Garrison's New Testament pacifism and hopes of ending slavery by moral suasion were anathema to Brown, who based his religious convictions on the Old Testament. Brown interpreted its many injunctions literally and believed there was a wrathful God in Heaven who took an active part in human affairs through Divine Providence. Some men were even called to be God's instruments on earth and to mete out the severe and sometimes violent punishment of sinners.[23]

Parker listened attentively to this debate. Of course, he was doctrinally sympathetic with Garrison; yet, his brand of Unitarianism sought to incorporate the emotion Brown conveyed. Throughout his ministry, Parker hoped to demonstrate rational Unitarianism with intuitive and emotional proofs. Intellectually he agreed with Garrison, but his sentiment lay with Brown. Religion existed long before the Bible, Christ, or Christianity; natural laws had existed from creation. They were infinite and self-evident. Still, Parker knew that to believe in laws, one had to know them in more than a cold, intellectual way— they also had to be felt. The Emerson-Norton debate of the late 1830s had left this matter clear for him.[24]

But regardless of their religious differences or similarities, Parker liked Brown. The Kansas veteran believed slavery to be a crime against

23. John Brown, Jr., to Sanborn, March 27, 1885, Boyd B. Stutler Collection. For a complete examination of Brown's religious convictions, see Oates, *Brown*.

24. Commager, *Parker*, pp. 81–82, chaps. 4, 5.

humanity, and he understood the need to meet force with force. Though Brown was careful not to press his views on violence, Parker was glad he accepted its necessity.[25]

Parker noticed many of the same qualities in Brown that Sanborn had seen. Brown was a good family man, seemed to be very careful about his physical appearance, and spoke in measured tones. Undoubtedly, Brown's talk about the value of family inspired the minister, because he and his wife, Lydia, had never been able to have children and both revered those people who understood their worth. Like Sanborn, Parker recognized Brown's discipline and self-control as he presented his case for the formation of military cadres in Kansas.

Parker also felt a strong class kinship with Brown. Unlike Brown, Parker had had the advantage of a Harvard education, was financially secure at the moment, and had earned an outstanding reputation throughout New England; but the minister still felt an affinity with Brown. Like Brown, Parker was wellborn but poor; he was descended from distinguished ancestry, but had had no funds to pay his way during his youth. As the minister looked at Brown and sensed his bone-weary exhaustion, he knew it was a product of more than the man's sacrifices in Kansas. Parker was reminded of his own weariness after hours and hours of reading scholarly tracts and discourses. It was weariness acquired in the name of selfless learning, but Parker never forgot that his place in society depended on such exertions. Brown's exhaustion seemed to be born of the same struggle for survival in nineteenth-century America. Parker was flooded with memories of poor youths trampled by the exclusionary class system they encountered at Harvard. Like these young men, Brown had to sacrifice "pleasure, comfort . . . eye sight and health" to achieve his goals. Without the proper cultural background, these youths were forced to learn "all by . . . soul." They, like Brown, needed "iron" bodies as well as "iron" intellects in order to overcome their backgrounds. They required stamina, or they would "die in that experiment of the Cross." And like these wellborn poor boys at Harvard, Brown had "attained

25. Ibid., chaps. 10, 11.

a superior culture" at the expense of a crippled body. In a sense, Parker was familiar with Brown before the man entered his home. Both men had struggled with the handicaps of similar origins. One man had "succeeded"; the other had "failed"—until entering Kansas one year earlier.[26]

Three days after the meeting at Parker's, Brown met with Sanborn, Stearns, and Howe. He had just returned from a visit with wealthy industrialist Amos A. Lawrence, who was serving as director of the New England Emigrant Aid Society. When Howe heard this, he was prompted to share some remarks he had recently made to Lawrence with Brown. Howe wanted the Massachusetts Kansas Committee to suspend operations. In its place, the doctor suggested the Massachusetts legislature should "come out and take the high ground" by making an appropriation for Kansas. The legislature should "break through . . . the miserable trammels of statecraft" and do "what we would have a brave and generous man do in his own capacity." Such an appropriation would stimulate "fear" in slaveholders. Howe was still ambivalent about using force and did not specifically advocate direct attacks on slaveholders, but he did think that if the slaveholders' "fear" could be increased and they could be brought to "terror," Kansas would be kept free from the "curse of slavery." Slavery had always "beaten freedom," and it was time antislavery men acted as if "sons of our mothers and children of our wives were among the four million bondmen." Brown agreed and could scarcely contain his excitement. If Howe seriously believed what he said about "terror," Brown knew how to induce it. In a year he would ask Howe's assistance to implement a scheme for "practical abolition."[27]

For all Howe's talk of legislative action, by early 1857 he had become deeply disenchanted with politics. No doubt he lectured Brown about his concern that the Republican Party was "falling far short of its high mission." Men solely dedicated to the acquisition of political office ran the party. They were "disreputable" and used

26. Ibid., chaps. 1, 2; Story, "Class Development," pp. 137–38.

27. Oates, *Brown*, p. 187; Howe to Amos A. Lawrence, December 23, 1856, Amos A. Lawrence Collection, Massachusetts Historical Society, Boston, Mass.

"disgraceful" methods to get elected. Even Henry Wilson had acted as the supreme political opportunist, one who talked with his mouth and "not his eyes." He was "without . . . the heroic element." Howe wondered why men of character were constantly being displaced in party ranks.[28]

Brown concurred with Howe's observations. He could cite numerous examples of political ineptitude and opportunism hindering the free-state cause. Brown acknowledged the need for a state appropriation but was not optimistic that it would be approved. As Howe listened to Brown's response and watched him discuss Kansas affairs, he was inspired by the man's "capacity." Indeed, Brown "spoke with his eyes" and possessed "the heroic element." Howe saw Brown as the product of a frontier life that could bury talents, sacrifice taste, and throw away human accomplishment but, at the same time, could elicit by its "coarseness and hardness" all that was noble and righteous in the human spirit. Occasionally Brown's version of his role in the Kansas struggle seemed overstated and roused Howe's skepticism. But in the end, Howe considered such exaggerations insignificant. After all, as the doctor himself had suggested to George Luther Stearns some time before, "enthusiasts were prone to exaggerate what they had or could accomplish." The important thing to remember was that a great leader could be "used" and, therefore, should be "kept."[29]

Howe saw a number of other reasons why this potential leader of the Kansas free-state cause should be "kept." During the debate over the Kansas-Nebraska Bill, Howe had called upon Sumner to "send a blast through the land" because there was a need to "seize an opportunity" while public sentiment wasn't yet formed. In the wake of President James Buchanan's election and continued Kansas fighting, public sentiment was again ready for shaping. Howe felt there was a need for a "stern prophet to awaken mankind," and Brown seemed like such a prophet. With his penchant for quoting the Bible and his erect,

28. Schwartz, *Howe*, pp. 215, 247; Howe to Charles Sumner, n.d., September 21, 1856; Howe to Parker, n.d., 1854, Howe Collection, Houghton Library.
29. Howe to Charles Sumner, April 1852, May 19, 1852, ibid.; Oates, *Brown*, p. 187; Howe to Parker, February 27, 1860, Howe Collection, Houghton Library.

puritanical disposition, he might be the man to awaken a slumbering North. Then too, the prospects of Kansas being lost to slavery looked very real to Howe in the first weeks of January 1857, and he was "willing to aid anyone who would fight for freedom."[30]

Perhaps the most intimate, personal reason for the physician's support of Brown lay in the sad conclusion Howe had brought home from his Kansas trip. He realized he was no longer able to actively fight for freedom. The best he could hope for was to participate in the struggle by organizing and subsidizing someone else's actions. Soon after the meeting adjourned, Howe wrote to Lawrence, asking him to push hard for the state appropriation.[31]

During the entire meeting, George Luther Stearns remained silent, carefully watching and gauging the interaction among Sanborn, Howe, and Brown. He saw that Sanborn and Howe were moved by the man, but he knew that, as chairman of the Massachusetts Kansas Committee, he bore the ultimate responsibility for dispensing funds. It was crucial that he determine for himself the reliability of the men dealing with the committee. Stearns had to be sure his confidence was not misplaced. Having been raised by a staunch Calvinist who had rejected "optimistic theories" of religion, he was familiar with the tenor of Brown's religious convictions. What interested him more, however, was whether or not Brown understood the demands of careful organization. Could he make a businesslike analysis of his material needs? Did he understand that waste and inefficiency jeopardized the whole aid movement?

By the end of the meeting Stearns had his answer. He was convinced Brown was aware of the need for proper management, regularized payment schedules, and "full and fair" accounting of funds. Stearns sensed that Brown could be trusted and suggested the freedom fighter take possession of 200 Sharpe's rifles recently purchased with committee funds and turned over to the National Kansas Committee. On the following day (January 9), Stearns led the committee in voting Brown

30. Howe to Charles Sumner, January 18, 25, 1854, ibid.
31. Howe to Amos A. Lawrence, January 8, 1857, Amos A. Lawrence Collection, Massachusetts Historical Society.

$500 for "necessary expenses." At the same time, Brown was made a committee agent. Near the end of this second meeting, Stearns invited Brown to dinner at his Medford home. Two days later, on January 11, John Brown rode out to the Stearns mansion.[32]

Stearns hoped the informal dinner would allow him to test the validity of his favorable first impression, obtain more information about other "prominent Kansas men," and help assure Mary that, in his own way, he did look out for the interests of his family. Mary Stearns was pleased that her husband had invited the celebrated Kansas leader to their home and, by the end of the evening, she listened enthralled as Brown entertained her young sons with a description of the Battle of Black Jack. She was so taken with Brown's righteousness that she became one of his closest allies in Boston. For his part, Stearns maintained his favorable assessment of Brown's character. The Medford businessman was particularly impressed by Brown's "very clear ideas in regard to Lane, Robinson and others." Stearns felt much better about the men who would take possession of funds and supplies sent to Kansas by the committee. Though Brown probably did not discuss his numerous business ventures with the Stearnses, it is unquestionable that the committee chairman knew of his guest's experience in the business world. Only a man who understood the importance of dealing with trustworthy and competent associates could have constructed such an insightful analysis of the personalities directing free-state affairs. John Brown spoke like a true professional.[33]

Quite as important to Stearns as his analysis of Kansas was Brown's painful understanding of what dedicated antislavery work did to family life. Stearns was sensitive on this point. He had spent long hours away from home because of his Kansas aid work, and his absence had served as a further source of friction with Mary. But here was a man of heroic stature advocating the need for family

32. Oates, *Brown*, p. 189; Stearns, *Life of Stearns*, p. 129; U.S. Senate, Mason Committee, *Report on the Invasion of Harpers Ferry*, 36th Cong., 1st sess., 1860, I. Rept. 278, 2: 227–28 (hereafter cited as *Mason Report*).

33. Stearns, *Life of Stearns*, pp. 129–30, 134; Oates, *Brown*, p. 191.

sacrifices in the cause of freedom. Brown's theories made a deep impression. He persuaded Mary Stearns that she should be more tolerant of the demands on her husband's time, and he stimulated George Luther Stearns's feeling that his boys were being overindulged and spoiled. After listening to Brown's rather romantic assessment of how Kansas had strengthened his own sons' manhood, the Medford businessman was certain that his boys, Frank and Henry, "should be sent away from home for a year or two to prevent them from becoming soft and effeminate."[34]

The most touching moment of Brown's visit came just before he left. Young Henry Stearns boldly stepped up to Brown and offered his savings for Kansas. Brown took the contribution. Then, when Henry asked him to write and tell "what sort of a boy you were," he promised to send a brief autobiographical letter.[35]

Brown left the Stearns home confident the chairman would "hold up his hands" with committee funds. He believed the wealthy businessman might also be willing to personally subsidize his future abolitionist activity. The Stearns visit had been rewarding and a pleasant contrast to the meeting he had had with Thomas Wentworth Higginson two days earlier. Higginson had arrived in Boston on January 9, soon after the committee had voted funds to Brown. Sanborn had requested his appearance, thinking that if Higginson had confidence in Brown he might serve as a conduit to the substantial sums of money reputedly held by the Worcester County Kansas Committee. Sanborn had good reason to believe Higginson and Brown would appreciate each other. Only a few months earlier at a West Indian Emancipation Day speech, Higginson had hailed "the glory intrinsic to the white man fighting with arms to end slavery." Higginson went on to suggest that in a war against slavery, "the northern white man's present selfishness and money grubbing would be replaced by disinterestedness and self-devotion." Brown seemed the perfect exam-

---

34. Stearns, *Life of Stearns*, p. 155.
35. Oates, *Brown*, p. 192.

ple of those qualities. To Sanborn, Brown's disposition and personality reflected Higginson's contention that the "most favored race" found its "highest privilege" in aiding the "weakest" and "most ignorant race."[36]

Unfortunately for Sanborn, although Higginson did hold ideas similar to Brown's, a number of conditions unknown to the committee secretary prevented the minister from making any commitments. In November 1856, Higginson had recommended to Gerrit Smith that an "independent militia" be raised to fight in Kansas. What Sanborn did not know was that, while touring Kansas, Higginson had rejected a plan to organize such a militia group. Higginson had not been confident of the group's leadership. And as the minister would suggest in the near future, those who knew him best realized that under "apparent rashness, I have a great deal of caution."[37]

There were other reasons for Higginson's coolness toward Brown. It is possible that while he was in Kansas, Higginson and James Redpath had discussed Brown. If Redpath had hinted of Brown's role at Pottawatomie, Higginson might have been made wary of future "rash acts" by the Kansas veteran. Then too, Sanborn had exaggerated Higginson's access to Worcester County funds. In fact, Higginson was under pressure not to request any more funds until the accusations of Calvin Cutter had been cleared up. Cutter blamed the Worcester committee for loosely handling contributions. Seeking to account for funds the committee had dispersed, Higginson wrote Martin Stowell in Kansas asking him to itemize expenditures of some $2,000 sent from Worcester. When Higginson received an accounting in late fall of 1856, he found Stowell had lost $100 because he accepted a personal check from John Brown which was eventually returned "uncashed because of a closed account." Higginson was not about to make further

36. Thomas Wentworth Higginson, "West Indian Emancipation Day Speech" [given in August 1856], Higginson-Barney Collection, Houghton Library; Edelstein, *Strange Enthusiasm*, pp. 185–86; Higginson, *Journals*, p. 143; Higginson to Louisa Higginson, January 9, 1857, Higginson Collection, Houghton Library.

37. Harlow, *Smith*, p. 357; Edelstein, *Strange Enthusiasm*, p. 191; Higginson to G. W. Curtis, January 25, 1857, Higginson Collection, Houghton Library.

grants to an individual who regarded his financial obligations so casually.[38]

In addition, Higginson was held back from support of Brown by his deep involvement in the disunion movement. After he left Kansas in the fall of 1856, Higginson believed that if the cause of freedom were crushed there, the United States would separate into "two nations of North and South." The Constitution would not hold them together, and the drama of "Union and Disunion" would come closer every day. Higginson resumed his ministerial duties but was concerned about the "impending crisis." In fact, he wanted to do all in his power to promote it. By late December there was no doubt in his mind that freemen and slaveholders were living in "two nations."[39]

Early in January he sent out letters requesting attendance at the Worcester Disunion Convention. In the midst of the project, Sanborn called him to Boston. The timing was inopportune. Higginson had too much of himself invested in the convention. Disunion was the country's "destiny and duty," its "only hope," and he would not be distracted. As with the Burns rescue attempt and the Kansas trips, Higginson felt good to know he was in the forefront of a cause. From his early days in divinity school, he had always wanted to be a "leader of men." Symbolically, by his disunion efforts, he was again battering down Court House doors, and it made him feel "so much younger." Sanborn's request and Brown's presence were as much of an imposition as Parker and Howe's failure to send the Faneuil Hall crowd scurrying to his aid. He could not be bothered with Brown at the moment. Unlike his fellow Kansas committeemen, Sanborn, Stearns, and Howe, the minister reserved judgment on Brown. He was unsure of the man's character and was busy organiz-

38. James Redpath to Higginson, February 5, 1857, ibid.; Edelstein, *Strange Enthusiasm,* pp. 193–94; Martin Stowell to Higginson, November 12, 17, 1856, Higginson Collection, Houghton Library.

39. Harlow, *Smith,* p. 357; Thomas Wentworth Higginson, "A Ride through Kansas," pp. 10, 20–21; Edelstein, *Strange Enthusiasm,* pp. 186, 191; Thomas Wentworth Higginson, Untitled Speech [given August 8, 1856], Miscellaneous Pamphlets 1, Higginson-Barney Collection, Houghton Library.

ing the convention. The possibility of help from Worcester could be discussed later.[40]

Higginson's attitude stunned Sanborn and disappointed Brown. Still, the lack of commitment was not an outright refusal, and a brief examination of the views Higginson expressed during the convention indicate, at least partially, why it was inevitable that the minister eventually allied himself with Brown.

At the convention, held from January 15 to 17, Higginson openly clashed with Garrison. He rejected the theory of nonresistance, and he asserted that abolitionists must use "armed force" to thwart slavery— "two antagonistic nations could not live together any longer." Higginson was certain disunion must take place. The sooner it did, the better it would be for the North to "prepare for a peaceful and dignified policy." The Worcester abolitionist agreed with Wendell Phillips's contention that "peace between sin and servility" was not a benefit. Even if abolitionists gained control of the United States government, it would take "two or three generations" to rectify the abuses of the Slave Power. Thus, political abolition was too slow to "effect a cure." Violent, disruptive disunion was a "lesser evil" than the "gradual dying out of slavery."[41]

In his own speech to convention delegates, Higginson logically extended Phillips's position. He asked the audience why prior disunion attempts had failed, then answered his own question by pointing out that those movements had drawn a "glittering blade" only to tuck it back into a "neat little scabbard" after waving it for popular effect. This time things would be different. Higginson wanted a "convention of ten men who had drawn the sword for the right and thrown away the scabbard." All they needed was a "chance to come face to face with the United States government" and they could "revolutionize the world."[42]

40. *Liberator,* January 2, 16, 1857.

41. Edelstein, *Strange Enthusiasm,* p. 200; Higginson to Louisa Higginson, January 27, 1857, Higginson Collection, Houghton Library; *Proceedings of the Worcester Disunion Convention, January 15–17, 1857* (Boston, 1857), pp. 43–45, 51–52.

42. *Proceedings of the Worcester Disunion Convention,* pp. 25–30.

Incredibly, at the conclusion of his speech, Higginson dismissed the importance of the very convention he had helped organize, and he foreshadowed his commitment to Brown by suggesting that it was "vain" to speak of difficulty in promoting disunion. The time would be drawn soon enough by the "passions of men." At best, conventions could only partially prepare the way. By the spring of 1858, Higginson would come to believe that John Brown was the man to arouse such "passions," and it would be Higginson more than anyone else who would support Brown and embrace his plan to foment a slave insurrection.[43]

Except for Higginson's reticence, the first month of John Brown's presence in New England proved successful. He had acquired 200 Sharpe's rifles and $500 for "necessary expenses," and, above all, he had solidly established his personal character with those abolitionists in a position to help him in Kansas and in future antislavery efforts. He was viewed as a man of intense religious conviction, high moral character, and great physical self-control, a man who was unafraid of using forceful means to stop slavery. Brown had not attended Harvard but, as Parker indicated, he seemed to have "attained a superior culture." Most important, Brown's personal value system was not foreign to Sanborn, Parker, Stearns, Howe, or Higginson. These men initially interpreted Brown's beliefs as essentially the same as their own. He was neat, courteous, and disciplined. He preached industry, ambition, and calculation at the same time that he spoke of "character" as the ultimate prerequisite of leadership. He also felt a strong attachment to family. And like all of the men he met, Brown was concerned with conventional civic repute. Brown's "ideal person was comfortably within the nineteenth century mainstream." No doubt this gave great solace to the five urban, middle-class professionals who interviewed him.[44]

43. Ibid.
44. Story, "Injuries of Class," pp. 13–15.

CHAPTER 4

"Riding Free Horses": Kansas Funds and North Elba Land

THE ONE INDIVIDUAL most affected by Brown's personality after his initial foray in Boston was Franklin Benjamin Sanborn. When Brown asked the young man to accompany him to New York for a January 24 meeting with the National Kansas Committee, Sanborn eagerly accepted. At the meeting, Sanborn requested the committee to relinquish control of the 200 rifles turned over to them by the Massachusetts Kansas Committee. This request was honored, but the committee, led by Chairman Henry B. Hurd, balked at Brown's desire for "all the guns it had and over 1000 dollars worth of supplies." They also rejected Sanborn's plea for a pledge of $5,000 to $10,000. Hurd and the others thought Brown was too "violent and unpredictable" to be trusted because Brown refused to be pinned down by questions about what he intended to do with the arms and supplies. All he would say was that the committeemen knew him and his work in Kansas. If they wished to give him anything, he wanted them to "give it freely." Finally, at the urging of its eastern membership, the committee reversed itself and decided in Brown's favor by pledging $5,000 to help implement the "defensive measures" he felt were required to preserve a free Kansas. Brown was authorized to immediately draw $500 from the committee treasurer as a portion of that sum.[1]

Both Brown and Sanborn were pleased by the committee's action. Before leaving New York City, they discussed strategies which

1. Oates, *Brown*, pp. 192–93; Sanborn, *Recollections*, 1: 137; Resolutions of the National Kansas Committee, January 24, 1857, Brown Papers, Kansas State Historical Society, Topeka, Kans.

might force an appropriation out of the Massachusetts legislature. Such a grant coupled with the national committee's pledge would leave Kansas freestaters amply supplied to resist proslavery attacks. Upon returning to Boston, Sanborn wrote Brown and informed him of the schedule for legislative hearings on the appropriation. He advised the freedom fighter that his appearance at the hearings would improve the possibility of passage and would force a quicker consideration of the bill. Sanborn realized that Kansas had been relatively peaceful under the strong leadership of Governor John Geary but saw the proslavery legislature's recent attempt (January 12, 1857) to set up a rigged constitutional convention as an incident that could trigger renewed hostilities. Brown should make it a point to attend the hearings. His traveling expenses would be paid, and Sanborn hoped to "do something more."[2]

After leaving New York City, Brown journeyed to his North Elba home. On the way he stopped in Peterboro, New York, to see Gerrit Smith. During a previous visit he had been led to believe that Smith might make a contribution to his Kansas efforts. Brown also wondered if the wealthy landowner would help him purchase additional acreage near his North Elba farm. Brown thought the new acreage would relieve some of the financial strain on his family. Although he was elated by his acquisition of guns and money for free-state forces, his elation was tempered by anxiety about his family's poverty.

Gerrit Smith, born in Utica, New York, in March 1797, was the son of Peter and Elizabeth Livingston Smith. Peter Smith had been raised on a farm in Rockland County, New York, by parents who had only modest means. He moved to New York City at age sixteen in 1784 and found work as a clerk. Within a year, he was managing a bookshop, and by 1789 he had moved to Utica, where he opened a dry goods store, formed a three-year partnership with John Jacob Astor, and soon became a successful land speculator. Five years after arriving

2. Sanborn to Brown, January 28, February 11, 1857, Sanborn Letters, Atlanta University, Atlanta, Ga.; James A. Rawley, *Race and Politics: "Bleeding Kansas" and the Coming of the Civil War* (Philadelphia, 1969), pp. 178–79.

in Utica, Peter Smith married Elizabeth Livingston, a member of one of the state's most influential families. Gerrit Smith moved with his parents to Peterboro, New York, in 1806 and there received both an adequate education in local schools and the practical habits that are learned from long hours of toil on family lands. At age seventeen, Smith enrolled in Hamilton College at Clinton, New York, and after a period of adjustment, he became a very good student. However, he sometimes took himself too seriously and was occasionally haunted by visions of his impending death. A few years after leaving school, Smith began to display signs of hypochondria. He was to experience a variety of illnesses, both real and imagined, throughout his life but would live until 1874.

Smith graduated from Hamilton in 1818 and quickly followed in his father's footsteps by launching a career in real estate with the purchase of 18,000 acres of property near the town of Florence, New York—a purchase that stretched the limits of his available funds and nearly forced him into bankruptcy. In 1819 he married Wealtha Ann Backus, the daughter of Hamilton's president. Their union was short-lived; Wealtha Ann Smith died seven months later after a brief illness. About the time of her death, Peter Smith asked his son and Gerrit's uncle, Daniel Cady, to comanage the vast Smith holdings. The task proved to be an onerous one, and although it gave Smith access to great power and wealth, it put him on a financial roller coaster that peaked and bottomed with the erratic fluctuations of the national economy. Even though Smith's economic position was jeopardized only once— for a few years after the panic of 1837—that position never really stabilized until 1845.

In 1822 Smith married again, this time to Ann Carol Fitzhugh. The Smiths had four children, but two died before reaching the age of eighteen. In the early 1820s, Smith also began his lifelong study of religion. He was both fascinated and appalled by the labyrinths of Protestant theology and practice. During the same period, he made his first foray into politics by supporting the candidacy of De Witt Clinton for governor. But much of Smith's time in the years between 1822 and 1845 was spent managing and acquiring land and other assets—a process that alternately bored him with its routine and worried him with its possibilities for financial ruin. Smith did bring order to his financial affairs in the mid-1840s, but it took a recovering national economy, the help of some shrewd business associates, and a timely loan from John Jacob Astor to finally put his business worries to rest. During the years of economic stagnation following the panic, Smith had his wife and daughter help him with accounts when a cash shortage forced him to lay off clerks in his land office. Yet in spite of the financial pressure he sometimes felt, Smith did live well and had the time, motivation, and resources to indulge in a variety of reform efforts.

Throughout the 1830s and 1840s, he gave generously to the American Tract and Bible Society and the American Sunday School Union. He also fought what he termed the "soul shivering" nature of sectarianism; debated the pros and cons of baptism (finally allowing himself to be immersed in 1848); concluded that Saturday, and not Sunday, was the real Sabbath (1849); and founded his own church in Peterboro (1843). Smith strongly supported the temperance crusade. He also dabbled in the moral reform, prison reform, women's rights, and peace movements. Smith's initial answer to the problem of race prejudice experienced by free northern blacks (and one he continued to believe in throughout his life) was to sponsor a variety of educational projects aimed at promoting black self-help. In 1826 he toyed with the idea of organizing a seminary for "pious and promising" blacks and did establish a manual labor academy for black children at Peterboro in May 1834. The school remained open for almost two years. Smith contributed money to Oberlin College because it admitted blacks and gave to Beriah Green's integrated Oneida Institute. During the 1850s, he assisted Central College of McGrawville, New York, an abolitionist and American Free Will Baptist-sponsored school, which was integrated, coeducational, and founded on manual labor principles.

Smith's first response to the problem of slavery was to give funds to the American Colonization Society, and for almost two years after the formation of the American Antislavery Society in December 1831, he remained only mildly interested in the society's call for immediate emancipation. Between 1833 and 1835, however, the urging of various abolitionist leaders as well as his own reflections on the immorality of slavery and the way it infected all of American life prompted him to reconsider his colonization views. In October 1835, he attended the formation of the New York Antislavery Society at Utica. A month later, he enrolled in the American society and brought his considerable financial resources to the antislavery movement. In May 1836, Smith attended the annual meeting of the American society and sponsored a resolution calling for the use of free-labor products. That July he became an agent for the society.

When a debate arose within the organization about the advisability of using political action to further the antislavery cause, Smith let it be known that he favored some effort along those lines; but during the late 1830s and during the society's crisis and division in 1840, he did not directly oppose the Garrisonian contention that political affiliation would dilute the strength of the movement. When the society broke apart over this issue and others, Smith made great efforts to reconcile the differences between its members and the members of the newly formed Lewis Tappan-led American and Foreign Antislavery Society. Because reconciliation proved impossible, Smith gave up the effort (although he remained on good terms with both groups) and joined the political antislavery movement. He first backed the Liberty Party in the mid-1840s, then the Liberty League at the end of the decade. Finally, in 1852, after vacillating for a time over whether the political antislavery movement should broaden its base of support by embracing other reform issues and whether it should seek a coalition with anti-slavery Whigs and Democrats, he allied himself with the Free Soil Party.

During the 1840s, Smith allowed his name to be placed in nomination for a number of political offices on abolitionist tickets; but he also frequently lectured for the cause, used personal funds to buy the freedom of slaves, and provided assistance to fugitive slaves. He gave them shelter in his home, money for their journey, and, quite as often, a torrent of advice (at one time he noted, "I obtained strong promises from the slaves that they would totally abstain from intoxicating liquors, would be industrious, frugal and virtuous").

All in all, however, Smith gave as much money to the cause as he gave advice to the slaves. At one point during the mid-1840s, he estimated that he had contributed over $50,000 to the antislavery crusade.[3]

John Brown was confident that such a man would have money for the Kansas cause. Brown had known Smith since 1848, when he had come to New York to look in upon a number of black families who had settled 140,000 acres of land donated to them by Smith. The land was scrubbed and almost impossible to cultivate, but Smith had believed it would allow the blacks to improve their material condition and "give up notions of being servants and become independent mechanics and farmers." By cultivating their own land, they could avoid relationships with those who hated them. In the end, the land's poor quality had doomed the project. Still, Brown had been moved by Smith's desire to do something more than talk about aiding black people. Then, in 1849, Smith helped Brown purchase land in the North Elba area, and for the next few years the two men maintained a harmonious, if relatively superficial, friendship based primarily on their mutual antislavery sentiments. In 1855 Smith invited Brown to a convention of "radical political abolitionists" in Buffalo. Brown didn't attend but at the convention Smith read two letters from John Brown, Jr., which reportedly "drew tears" from many delegates.[4]

Besides hoping that their friendship and similar antislavery views would stimulate a Kansas contribution, Brown had specific information which led him to think Smith was ready to assist the cause of freedom in the territory. In his conversation with Higginson, Brown had learned that Smith had given full support to the minister's call for northern state governments to enlist "militia volunteers" for Kansas.

3. Harlow, *Smith*, pp. 1–363; Lawrence J. Friedman, "The Gerrit Smith Circle: Abolitionism in the Burned-Over District," *Civil War History* 26 (March 1980): 18–38. See also Friedman's *Gregarious Saints: Self and Community in American Abolitionism, 1830–1870* (New York, 1982).

4. O. B. Frothingham, *Gerrit Smith* (New York, 1877), p. 235; Harlow, *Smith*, pp. 245–46; Brown to Smith, February 14, 1850, Smith Collection, Syracuse University; Harlow, *Smith*, pp. 340–41.

Despite Smith's view that government was primarily established to protect property and overstepped its jurisdiction when going beyond that activity, Brown knew that Smith supported Vermont's state appropriation to Kansas. Then, too, in his brief meeting with Lawrence, Brown had discovered that Smith, in the early spring of 1856, had contributed $250 to the New England Emigrant Aid Society and had authorized Lawrence to use the money as he saw fit. Smith didn't mind if the contribution was used to purchase arms for free-state settlers, and he told Lawrence that there were "instances in which the shedding of blood" was "unavoidable." In March 1856, Smith had pledged $3,000 to Kansas, asserting that "we must stand by Kansas resistance." Although Brown did not know the extent of Smith's Kansas aid (it is estimated at $16,000), he was certain his information indicated a willingness on the philanthropist's part to fund the forceful defense of the territory.[5]

Brown's assumptions were justified. In fact, just before the Pottawatomie Massacre, in early May 1856, Smith had made very strong statements about his commitment to the defense of freedom. At that time he asked an abolitionist convention assembled at New York City to go with him in "voting slavery to death." If the assembled abolitionists were not ready to vote slavery to death, Smith announced he was personally ready to put "slavery to a violent death." He no longer opposed the "bloody abolition of slavery"; he was ready to have slavery "repulsed by violence" and "pursued even unto death by violence." Two months later, in the heat of Kansas fighting, Smith asserted that where government did not exist or when it failed, men had to obey the "necessity of the case," recognize themselves as government, stop "looking to ballots," and start "looking to bayonets." Those

5. Gerrit Smith, *The True Office of Civil Government* (New York, 1851). Most of Smith's theoretical assumptions about the nature and purpose of government are contained in this pamphlet. Harlow, *Smith*, p. 357; Smith to Higginson, November 26, 1856, Higginson-Kansas Collection, Kansas State Historical Society; Smith to Governor Ryland Fletcher, November 8, 1856, Smith Collection, Syracuse University; Gerrit Smith, printed letter to the *Syracuse Journal*, May 31, 1856; Frothingham, *Smith*, pp. 232–33.

who were truly antislavery men should be "mustering armed men and none but armed men." If "all manhood" had not left antislavery men, they would not allow Kansas settlers to be slaughtered. He was no "bloody-minded man" but he realized the South must be "dispossessed" of the idea that northern people were "cowards."[6]

Shortly after arriving at Peterboro, Brown described his successful fund-raising campaign in New England. Smith was pleased to hear that so many abolitionists had not lost "all manhood." When Brown discussed his family's difficult economic situation, Smith empathized and said he would see about additional acreage in the North Elba area. But when Brown finally asked Smith to give money for Kansas, he received a surprising and sharp rebuff. The philanthropist claimed his previous contributions to "save Kansas to Freedom" had "exhausted his current means"; he could not give more.[7]

The refusal jarred Brown, but he wisely refrained from pressuring Smith to reconsider his decision. Long years of negotiating various business schemes had taught Brown when a decision was final, and he knew further badgering would only antagonize Smith. It might even jeopardize Brown's plan to seek Smith's financial aid for a future assault on slavery. In a year Brown would return to Peterboro and unveil a scheme (already taking form in his mind) intended to demonstrate the power of black manhood. He would wait to press Smith.

If Brown had fully understood Smith's personality, he might have been more prepared for the abrupt refusal. Smith was an individual of "paradoxical intellect" whose fierce denunciation of the Slave Power and emotional outbursts in defense of violence were occasionally contradicted by his actions. From the beginning of his participation in the abolitionist movement, Smith never hesitated to advocate the use of

6. Harlow, *Smith,* pp. 350–53; Frothingham, *Smith,* pp. 232–33; Higginson to Smith, November 1, 1856; Smith to Higginson, November 8, 1856, Higginson-Kansas Collection, Kansas State Historical Society.

7. Harlow, *Smith,* pp. 358, 368, 369; Smith to Samuel J. May, December 22, 1856, Smith Collection, Syracuse University. On Smith's reputation for financial care even in his philanthropic efforts, see Frothingham, *Smith,* p. 225. Charles Sumner to Smith, October 16, 1855, Smith Collection, Syracuse University.

force against slavery. At Utica, New York, in 1835, during the first abolitionist convention he attended, Smith had responded to mob threats against the meeting by calling himself a "poor peace-man" and demanding the use of "deadly weapons" to protect the right of assembly. Four years later, when he was again disillusioned by the seeming fruitlessness of the abolitionist campaign and was feeling that it was "almost hopeless" to spread "correct views," Smith determined that slavery could only be abolished by "force" and never by "peaceable" means. He reasoned that if, as all antislavery men understood, violence was one of the products of slavery, the country would go on with "proslavery wickedness" until the institution had come "to a violent and bloody end." You fought fire with fire. When Higginson attacked the Court House during the Burns rendition, Smith applauded the attempt and was reminded of his own efforts to thwart the Fugitive Slave Law. He belonged to Syracuse's Vigilance Committee, helped establish a station on the underground railroad, and took an active part (along with black abolitionists Samuel R. Ward and Jermain W. Loguen) in the successful rescue of escaped slave William "Jerry" McHenry. When McHenry was arrested in early October 1951, Smith asserted that a judicial release was not good enough. Such an "acquittal" would be as "nothing" when compared to a "bold forcible rescue" that demonstrated the "strength of public opinion."[8]

Yet, in spite of forwarding these views, Smith stayed within the mainstream of abolitionist reform activity. Like Sanborn, Parker, and Howe, he was ambivalent about engaging in political violence. Rhetorical flourish was one thing, killing slaveholders was quite another. During the Jerry rescue, for instance, Smith advocated the use of force but was terribly afraid one of the policemen holding McHenry might get hurt. He cautioned those participating in the rescue not to do bodily harm to anyone guarding the fugitive. Always an office-seeker, Smith finally won election as an abolitionist candidate in 1852 on a platform that acknowledged "no law for slavery" and asserted that

8. Frothingham, *Smith,* p. 221; Harlow, *Smith,* pp. 122–23, 304–5; Earl E. Sperry, *The Jerry Rescue* (New York, 1924), pp. 24–25.

"national wars" and "the violence" of "misguided and frenzied individuals" were "unnecessary."[9]

Smith's term in the House of Representatives also suggests his paradoxical nature. The Peterboro squire voted against a homestead bill because he said it confined the "homestead privilege to white people." Then he turned around and refused to back Republican attempts to table the Kansas-Nebraska Bill by asserting that tabling was a political tactic that infringed on democratic principle. It was an odd position for one who had long claimed that the Slave Power controlled the political fortunes of the country.[10]

Smith had opposed the Kansas-Nebraska Bill from the moment of its introduction in December 1853, but he did not take part in "unofficial efforts" to defeat it or sign petitions circulated by Salmon Chase against it. He did make a speech condemning the measure in early April when he said that though he hoped slavery would "not end in blood," he "feared that it might." Smith considered the institution a "conspiracy of the strong against the weak," but he admitted having no plan to end it except "unconditional" and "immediate abolition." Finally, he argued that any institution that reduced a man to a "thing" had committed the "highest crime" against humanity.[11]

When Smith refused to join the maneuver to table the Kansas-Nebraska Bill, he rationalized his behavior by saying that in rescuing a fugitive slave, he took his stand "outside government"; however, in his role as a member of Congress, he was "bound to the will of the majority." If the will of the majority called for enactment of a measure perpetuating the "highest crime" against humanity, Smith felt obliged to obey it. Eventually the measure was put on the floor of the House, and Smith voted against it; but by that time it was too late.[12]

Smith's behavior was condemned by many abolitionists. The New York landowner was particularly upset by resolutions offered at the

9. Ibid.; Frothingham, *Smith*, p. 215.
10. Ibid., pp. 218–23; Harlow, *Smith*, p. 322.
11. Ibid., pp. 331–33, 323, 322, 327; Gerrit Smith, Speech on the Nebraska Bill, April 6, 1854, Smith Collection, Syracuse University.
12. Smith to *New York Tribune*, July 17, 1855, ibid.

National Convention of Colored People meeting in Cincinnati. The convention heartily regretted his refusal "to serve the cause of the oppressed." Such criticism stung Smith. When it was coupled with his hatred for "fixed routine," the feeling that his "talents were being wasted," continual subjection to charges of being "out of order" while on the floor of the House, and so little "admiration" or "applause" for his efforts, it prompted, in August 1854, his resignation from Congress. The resignation was the final contradictory gesture of his congressional career because, in one way or another, Gerrit Smith sought political office throughout his entire life.[13]

For over a year after leaving office, Smith retreated from antislavery activity. He remained aloof from initial efforts to organize and supply free-state settlers in Kansas. And, in the wake of his political rejection, Smith swung back to the position he had espoused intermittently for twenty years. He now entertained "slight hope" that American slavery would come to a peaceful conclusion. There wasn't enough "virtue" left in the American people. Law, education, politics, and religion conspired to blind men on the subject of slavery. Traditional institutions and traditional methods would no longer work. Slavery had to die a "bloody death."[14]

By early spring of 1856, Smith's wounded sensibilities had healed, and he cautiously returned to the conventional arenas of antislavery activity. Although he did not completely give up his belief that slavery must be violently overthrown, he reversed his assessment of the American people. He now felt they were "entirely ready" to destroy slavery and that all they needed were "leaders" to direct them in the work of destruction. It was a pity that "cowardly statesmen" could not forget their caution and "bid the masses to march—not with bayonets but with ballots."[15]

In Smith's refusal to give money for Kansas, Brown caught a

13. Smith to William Goodell, November 1, 1854, ibid.

14. Harlow, *Smith,* pp. 336–38; Smith to Wendell Phillips, February 20, 1855, Smith Collection, Syracuse University.

15. Smith to Charles Sumner, March 8, 1856; Gerrit Smith, Untitled Speech, March 13, 1856, ibid.

glimpse of his rapidly shifting and sometimes inconsistent behavior. Perhaps after their meeting Brown instinctively understood that personal slights and disturbing emotional experiences occasionally had a weighty impact on the wealthy landowner's ideological posture. In any case, Brown left Peterboro satisfied that Smith would try to find land for his family and optimistic that he could be counted on for a later contribution.

After spending a few days in North Elba, Brown again traveled to Boston for his February 18 appearance before the Massachusetts legislature's Committee on Federal Relations, which was charged with investigating the idea of a state appropriation for Kansas. Sanborn had suggested Brown's appearance before the group and worked hard prodding its members to quickly consider the appropriation proposal. His exertions were more than rewarded by the speech Brown gave. While poorly structured, haltingly delivered, and, at times, a simplistic assessment of the Kansas situation, the brief address revealed Brown's uncanny ability to make a calculated emotional appeal. He was a failed businessman who spoke in a monotonous cadence, but he had not forgotten the essentials of salesmanship. He knew what symbols elicited sympathy from his listeners. Brown stood before the committee and discussed the sacrifices of time and energy he and other free-state settlers had made in defense of Kansas. He spoke of farmers' lost crops, settlers terrified by continual violence, and the great loss of life and money in the territory. In a dramatic gesture, he held up the trace chains which proslavery men had used to imprison his sons, then lashed out at the "barbarous treatment" they had received and lamented his son Frederick's death. It was an impressive performance filled with uplifting maxims, biblical allusions, and the unstated but implied contention that, though John Brown had sacrificed much, he was willing to do more if supplied with the necessary funds.[16]

When Amos A. Lawrence heard about Brown's speech, he immedi-

16. Villard, *Brown*, pp. 277–78; John Brown, Speech to the Massachusetts Legislature, February 18, 1857, Boyd B. Stutler Collection.

ately contributed $70 for Brown's "personal use." Lawrence confided that although he had "no definite knowledge" on which to base his suspicions, he was sure Brown would be disappointed if he relied too heavily on the pledges of the National Kansas Committee. The committee had "not inspired confidence," and it would be difficult for them to raise funds. Lawrence's words were not unheeded by the canny Brown. Many times in the past his own business ventures had been ruined by poor management and lost confidence. He and his oldest son, John Jr., often discussed the best way to preserve trust among financial confederates. Brown wrote to Lawrence, thanking him for his "kind hints" and suggesting that they were an "exact expression" of his own "private conjectures."[17]

Brown had come to Boston with a lifetime of experience requesting funds for one enterprise or another. This letter to Lawrence, his performance before the Massachusetts legislature, and, in fact, the whole tenor of his behavior with Massachusetts Kansas Committee members indicate that he applied the lessons garnered from these experiences to the task of funding his Kansas work. He was adept at calculating the effect of his own actions and could evaluate, as well as manipulate, the personalities of the men and women around him.

After attending the legislative hearing and listening to Brown's speech, Frank Sanborn was even more committed to assisting the Kansas freedom fighter, and he claimed to be certain "we shall get a bill"—though a careful assessment of the legislature's attitudes would have indicated otherwise. Sanborn's use of the word *we* in his note to Brown is suggestive. It had been almost three months since he began work as a full-time committee member. At first, despite protestations to the contrary, he had been bothered by doubts about the wisdom of his decision. But since Brown had come to Boston, those doubts had disappeared. His belief in Brown and the correctness of his decision developed symbiotically—each nourishing the other until Brown himself had become a kind of living symbol of Sanborn's secure sense

17. Amos A. Lawrence to Brown, February 19, 1857, Brown Papers, Kansas State Historical Society; Brown to Amos A. Lawrence, February 21, 1857, Amos A. Lawrence Collection, Massachusetts Historical Society.

of place in the movement. Brown was also a prototype of all the personal qualities Sanborn imagined he required for success. Brown was someone to be studied as well as followed. The young man who spoke of independence yet "looked for authority" had finally found "something to do." Brown served Sanborn's need for cause, career, and identity.[18]

Because he was less certain about the state appropriation than Sanborn and because of the "hints" in Lawrence's letter, Brown looked elsewhere for funds. During the next three weeks, he rode rattling trains all over New England in his quest. These weeks were difficult ones. People were interested in his tales of Kansas life but had little cash to spare because the territory remained quiet (Geary seemed in full control) and financial panic swept the country. At the same time that funds for Brown's Kansas work dried up, the reality of his family's desperate financial condition pressed in upon him and affected his sons. They didn't want to "learn and practice war" anymore. Despite Brown's reminder that it was they, not he, who had engaged in fighting "in the first place" and that he had no "love for the business," they all seemed ready to leave Kansas and return home. Some pressure was lifted when, in early March, Samuel Thompson (one of the men who owned the North Elba land Brown was negotiating for) loaned a small sum of money to the family.[19]

In spite of a growing sense of desperation, Brown occasionally experienced moments of accomplishment. He sent newspaper clippings to his wife, Mary, showing the "different stories" being told about him but cautioned her that *"none of them tell things as I tell them."* Brown believed he could make people realize their "duty," though they stubbornly clung to the delusion that they had a "right to give or not

18. Sanborn to Brown, March 1, 1857, Sanborn Letters, Atlanta University; Sanborn to Amos A. Lawrence, February 19, 1857, Amos A. Lawrence Collection, Massachusetts Historical Society.

19. Oates, *Brown,* pp. 195; G. G. Hubbard to Brown, March 2, 1857, Brown, Papers, Kansas State Historical Society; Brown to Mary Brown, March 31, 1857, Boyd B. Stutler Collection; Brown to Mary Brown, March 6, 1857, Brown Papers, Kansas State Historical Society.

to give." Trying to promote his own conception of people's "duty," he published a broadside in early March which appealed to the "friends of Freedom." In it he asked people to "hold up his [Brown's] hands" with contributions and said that it was with "no little *personal sacrifice*" that he came before the public "in this manner." He thought that the appeal, when taken together with Buchanan's election, the Supreme Court Dred Scott decision, and Buchanan's seeming foreknowledge of it, would underline the price of freedom in Kansas.[20]

At this critical moment in his search for money, Brown welcomed an invitation from Sanborn to speak at Concord before an audience certain to be receptive and generous. Sanborn hoped it would prove how much "he regretted" that "so little" had been done for Brown and how much he understood what it was like to "suffer from the false confidence of the public." Besides, Sanborn was sure "the ladies would be glad" if Brown would speak.[21]

On the afternoon of March 11 Frank Sanborn paced nervously on Concord's train station platform awaiting Brown's arrival. When Brown did appear, the two men greeted each other warmly and went directly to Ellery Channing's (nephew of the famous Unitarian minister, William Ellery Channing) place. That evening Brown had dinner at Thoreau's home and afterward told of his role in the Battle of Black Jack, where he had relieved Henry Clay Pate of his magnificently mounted Bowie knife. The second night of his visit Brown was invited to Emerson's home. When the meal was finished, the party adjourned to the Town Hall, where Brown addressed an assemblage of about one hundred people. During his speech, the freedom fighter again exhibited the chains that had bound his sons in Kansas and spoke of Missouri proslavery "ruffians" as having the "perfect right to be hung." To those who listened carefully to Brown during the speech, and throughout his visit in Concord, some

20. Ibid.; E. Bingham to Brown, March 9, 1857; John Brown, "To the Friends of Freedom" [broadside], Brown Papers, Kansas State Historical Society.

21. Sanborn to Brown, March 1, 9, 1857, Sanborn Letters, Atlanta University.

foreshadowing of his wish to confront slavery in places other than Kansas should have revealed itself. Emerson, in particular, should have been forewarned. Earlier that evening Brown had remarked that "it was better that a whole generation of men, women and children pass away by violent death" than that a word of either the Bible or Declaration of Independence be violated.[22]

Concord residents missed Brown's hints, but they did not miss the personal qualities which persuaded certain abolitionists that he should be given a chance to confront slavery in a place other than Kansas. Those qualities would be eloquently described by Thoreau some years later when he composed his "Plea for Captain John Brown." What impressed Thoreau was Brown's rare gift of "common sense." He was a "man of action, ideas and principles," yet he did not yield to "whim or transient impulse." Brown's essence was reflected in his speech: He always spoke "within bounds." Thoreau remembered how Brown referred to his family's sufferings "without ever giving the least vent to his pent-up fire." Brown was a "volcano with an ordinary chimney flue." He was an "experienced soldier" who "kept a reserve of force and meaning." Listening to Brown was like listening to Cromwell. His puritan virtue and Old Testament enthusiasm moved Concord and Boston audiences alike. But it was his control, his unswerving discipline, which most inspired their confidence in his capabilities. Discipline and control, these were the virtues reverenced by reformers in mid-nineteenth-century America. Properly applied, they could help abate the social chaos stimulated by industrialization and immigration. Properly applied, they could help resolve economic uncertainty, dismantle the institution of slavery, and win freedom for settlers on the plains of Kansas. Properly applied, they could bring the return of traditional American values. Higginson had claimed his trip to Kansas was like revisiting the Battle of Bunker Hill. Those Concord men and women who listened to Brown speak that evening felt that and more.

22. Sanborn, *Recollections,* 2: 347, 353; Newbold, "Sanborn," pp. 10–11, 27; Sanborn, *Recollections,* 2: 104–8; Oates, *Brown,* pp. 196–97.

Brown was more than a religious prophet, more than a reincarnation of America's revolutionary spirit; he was a model for a developing urban middle class.[23]

In spite of the enthusiasm and sympathy which Concord residents expressed for Brown and the cause of freedom, they donated very little money. He left town dispirited and determined to change his fund-raising tactics. Until the Concord address, Brown had traveled widely throughout New England, speaking with large numbers of antislavery men and asking them to "help fill his hands" for freedom. He based the plea on the virtue of his own character, his willingness to fight for freedom, and his firsthand knowledge of the Kansas situation. These efforts earned him only a modicum of success. He was given guns and money by the Massachusetts Kansas Committee, a tentative commitment of funds from the National Kansas Committee, and a number of small donations from Connecticut citizens. But from mid-February to mid-March, Brown had not added substantially to these contributions. In fact, he heard rumors that Massachusetts would not make a state appropriation and that the National Kansas Committee was going to renege on its January agreement. When these fund-raising failures were added to his family's deteriorating economic situation and his sons' growing reluctance to fight unless something could be done for the family, Brown felt compelled to change his methods.

In the weeks following his Concord address, Brown pursued funds more aggressively. He showed less of the calm demeanor that made men wonder at his discipline and became more demanding. He more frequently pointed to his own and his family's sacrifice. He applauded the New England abolitionist community less and chastised them more for failing in their moral obligation to assist the Kansas free-state movement. Most important, Brown focused his appeal. He spent fewer hours traveling all over New England and more time applying pressure on the three people most receptive to him, Frank Sanborn and George and Mary Stearns.

---

23. Henry David Thoreau, "A Plea for John Brown," in *Thoreau: The Major Essays*, ed. Jeffrey L. Duncan (New York, 1972), pp. 149–50.

Immediately after his Concord appearance, Brown went to the Stearns mansion in Medford and outlined the poor response to his pleas. Stearns and Brown discussed the possibility that the National Kansas Committee would try to back out of its agreement. They both knew that chances for a state appropriation were slim. Brown mentioned that the only people who had shown any concern were the citizens of Collinsville, Connecticut, who contributed $80 and promised to ship his grandfather's gravestone to North Elba, where it could be "faced and inscribed" in the memory of *"Our Poor Fred"* who "sleeps" in Kansas. For the first time, Brown spoke at length about his family's desperate economic condition and the need to purchase more land around the North Elba farm site in order to relieve that condition. Although Brown admitted his needs more openly and discussed his activity in greater detail, it seems unlikely that he told the lead-pipe manufacturer everything. He certainly did not reveal his recent deal with blacksmith Charles Blair. While in Collinsville, Brown had met Blair and agreed to buy 1,000 steel pikes for a dollar a piece. As part of the bargain, Blair contracted to apprentice Brown's son Jason for one year, providing the young man with training, room, board, and $200 for his services.[24]

Stearns was sympathetic and understanding but not very helpful. He could make no personal commitment of funds because of his own pressing financial obligations. And he told Brown that the Massachusetts Kansas Committee did not have any more cash to spare. Stearns does seem to have advised Brown to write to Amos A. Lawrence about starting a subscription for the North Elba land purchase. After all, Lawrence had already contributed $70 for Brown's "personal use," and Stearns believed it was probable he would do more.[25]

24. Sanborn, *Recollections*, 1: 114–15; Oates, *Brown*, p. 199; Brown to Mary Brown, March 12, 1857, Brown Papers, Kansas State Historical Society; John Brown–Charles Blair Pike Agreement, March 30, 1857; Charles Blair to Brown, April 15, 1857; Oliver Brown to Family, May 16, 1857, Sanborn-Brown Collection, Houghton Library; Villard, *Brown*, p. 283.

25. Brown to Amos A. Lawrence, March 19, 1857, Amos A. Lawrence Collection, Massachusetts Historical Society.

Brown was encouraged by Stearns's suggestion. A few days later while soliciting funds at a March 19 meeting in New Haven, he took Stearns's advice and sent a short note to Lawrence. He asked the industrialist to assist some New Haven friends who had pledged to raise $1,000 to help purchase additional tracts of land around his North Elba farm. Lawrence balked at the request, claiming he had spent over $14,000 to aid the construction of public schools in Kansas and did not want to involve himself in yet another fund drive. He would think about "heading" such a subscription but could not do anything else. Lawrence assured Brown that if something happened to him while he was engaged in the "great and glad cause" of freedom, he could assume that his wife and children would be cared for "more liberally than you now propose." Such guarantees were good to hear but were not negotiable. Brown still needed funds. He refused to give up on the demand that a subscription be raised and in the next few weeks put pressure on Stearns and Lawrence to help him purchase the acreage. For the moment, he hoped to appease his family by sending them $150 from funds he had already received.[26]

By the last week in March, Brown was exhausted from traveling, discouraged by the continued fruitlessness of his efforts, and irritated by Sanborn's recent note hinting that the legislative appropriation would not pass. Summoning what little energy he had left, Brown asked the young committee secretary to accompany him to Easton, Pennsylvania, for discussions with Kansas ex-Governor Andrew Reeder. Brown hoped to persuade Reeder to return to Kansas as an agent for the National Kansas Committee and leader of free-state forces. Charles Robinson, who along with James Lane had initially organized the free-state militia, had lost the confidence of many antislavery men in the East because of timid and conservative policies. Brown was certain that this loss of faith had affected his own fundraising activity. With Reeder in a position of leadership, perhaps

26. Ibid.; Amos A. Lawrence to Brown, March 20, 1857, Brown Papers, Kansas State Historical Society; Brown to Family, March 25, 1857, Sanborn-Brown Collection, Houghton Library; Villard, *Brown*, pp. 279–80.

some of that faith could be restored and his own efforts enhanced.[27]

Sanborn was preparing for a trip to Washington, D.C., when he received Brown's invitation. He immediately wrote and told Brown that he would be happy to assist and would meet Brown at Easton upon his return from the nation's capital in early April.[28]

When he arrived in Easton, Sanborn received a summary of Brown's reasons for trying to persuade Reeder to go back to Kansas. Then both he and Brown entered into discussions with the ex-governor. They urged Reeder to take the committee agency, claiming that a man of his "great ability . . . foresight, boldness and prudence" would be an immeasurable aid to the cause of freedom. Reeder was flattered by their expressions of confidence, but he refused, saying simply that he did not want to return to the territory. Both Sanborn and Brown were disappointed by Reeder's reply and asked him to reconsider. When he stood firmly by his decision, the two men thanked him for the courtesy of hearing them and started back to Boston.[29]

There is little doubt that Brown was sincere in his request for Reeder's help, but he was just as interested in isolating Sanborn for a few days in order to thoroughly discuss his own financial difficulties. Brown used their trip back to Boston to gently prod Sanborn into exerting his influence to obtain more funds for the Kansas campaign. In very emotional terms, he discussed his family's sacrifices with the sympathetic young man. Brown admitted that his sons wanted to leave Kansas because of the privation their absence caused the rest of the family and said that he wanted to make the "best provision" he could for his wife and children. He spoke of his own disillusionment and uncertainty, his belief that Buchanan was a tool of the Slave Power, and his conviction that Robert Walker's recent appointment as gover-

27. Oates, *Brown,* p. 201; Brown to Mary Brown, March 31, 1857, Boyd B. Stutler Collection; Sanborn to Brown, March 21, 25, 1857, Sanborn Letters, Atlanta University.

28. Sanborn to Brown, March 25, 1857, ibid.

29. Sanborn to Parker, March 29, 1857, Sanborn Collection, Concord Free Public Library; Sanborn to Higginson, September 1, 1857, Higginson-Kansas Collection, Kansas State Historical Society; Oates, *Brown,* p. 201.

nor of the territory would jeopardize free-state exertions. Hoping to convince Sanborn of how much his trust and help were needed, it is possible that Brown hinted at his belief that even if freestaters gained control of Kansas, slavery would continue in the United States until the day black men and women rose up and violently destroyed it.[30]

Sanborn was moved by Brown's expressions of confidence. And though he was unsure about the necessity of slave insurrection, he agreed with the contention that there was no possible political solution for slavery in either Kansas or the United States. His recent experience in Washington, D.C., had persuaded him of that proposition. While in the nation's capital, he was dismayed by what seemed to be a cumbersome process of government and by "what sort of men rule us." The city was an incredibly "odd place," inhabited by a group of men whose characters were a "matter for tears." As far as Sanborn was concerned, of all the "creepy things" an "office seeker" was the "most loathesome." How could such men be expected to legislate slavery out of existence? They did not have enough character. Washington itself was an "absurd sanctuary" of that very institution; it was the home of the Slave Power and "full of abomination."[31]

Sanborn was confused and at a loss about what he could do to alleviate Brown's financial troubles. He had used all of his influence to get Brown Massachusetts Kansas Committee funds and weapons. He had pushed the Massachusetts legislature to act quickly on the Kansas appropriation bill, had set up Brown's meeting with the legislature's Committee on Federal Relations, had journeyed to New York with Brown to appeal for National Kansas Committee help, and had hurried to Easton for consultations with Reeder. Now Brown was pushing him to do more and was vaguely hinting about a plan to start an insurrection. It was disconcerting for the young secretary who, until the trip to Easton, had not fully realized the extent of the demands Brown would make on him and other committee members. Sanborn could only suggest they check on the progress of the Massachusetts appropriation.

30. Ibid.; Sanborn, *Recollections,* 1: 115–18.
31. Sanborn to Parker, March 29, 1857, Sanborn Collection, Concord Free Public Library.

When the two men finally arrived in Boston, they were confronted with more bad news. The National Kansas Committee had decided to cancel its pledge to Brown because of the state of "public opinion." Lawrence had guessed correctly; the committee lacked the confidence of the northern antislavery community and this, added to the relatively stable condition in Kansas that spring, made it impossible to collect the cash necessary to meet its commitments. Along with the notification of cancellation, Brown found a $50 contribution from Eli Thayer and $20 from Thomas Wentworth Higginson. The contribution from Higginson particularly irritated both men. They felt it was a mere pittance compared to what might have been sent if Higginson had made a serious attempt to inform the Worcester County Committee of Brown's real needs. Restraining his anger (as he had throughout the last week of February and all of March), Brown wrote a thank-you note to Higginson. He told the minister of his anxiety to secure a "mere outfit," and claimed he was being prevented from going to Kansas "at once" by lack of funds. But more upsetting than the National Kansas Committee's cancellation and Higginson's token contribution was a letter awaiting Brown from his son Jason which informed him that a federal deputy marshal had been making inquiries about him in Cleveland and was seeking his arrest for Kansas activities. In the midst of collecting funds, Brown was forced to postpone even these unsuccessful efforts by the threat of imprisonment. Luckily, Samuel Gridley Howe and other committee members were able to persuade the antislavery judge Thomas R. Russell to hide Brown in his home. For the next week, Brown took refuge in a third-floor bedroom at Russell's place, brooding about his failure to collect substantial sums and calculating ways to arouse the New England antislavery community from its lethargy.[32]

A few days after Brown began his seclusion, he started work on an essay called "Old Brown's Farewell . . . to Plymouth Rock," which he hoped Theodore Parker would read before his congregation. In it,

32. H. B. Hurd to Brown, April 1857, Brown Papers, Kansas State Historical Society; Brown to Higginson, April 1, 1857, Higginson-Brown Collection, Boston Public Library; Villard, *Brown,* p. 287.

Brown talked about his personal privations in seeking to assist Kansas free-state settlers and asserted that "every citizen" was under "equal obligation" to do all that he had done for freedom. Neglect of such duties would not be forgotten, and all men would be held "accountable to God." Brown complained that, although he had asked "no wages," he could not secure "the necessary supplies of a common soldier." As far as he was concerned, New Englanders had spurned their ancestors and their traditional support of liberty. "How were the mighty fallen!"[33]

The essay was similar to his broadside issued in early March, and Brown hoped for a positive reaction. But before asking Parker to read the piece, Brown used the essay (as he had the Easton trip) as a pretext. Claiming he was unsure of the essay's reception, he asked Mary Stearns to read it and offer her critical judgment. The request was not a random gesture but a carefully calculated move to convince Mary of the legitimacy of his financial needs. On at least one occasion (and probably many others), Brown and his son John Jr. had discussed the role of a woman in a business transaction. It was John Jr.'s opinion that when a woman "got an idea into her head," it was "very hard to get out." If properly inspired, a "talking woman" could "exert some influence in such a transaction." Brown could hardly have missed Mary Stearns's enraptured glances two months earlier as he sat telling her boys of his role at Black Jack. Nor could he have missed the influence she exerted upon George Luther. Now he used her evaluation of the "Farewell" as an excuse to pressure her for her husband's financial resources. Just a short time after Mary Stearns left the Russell home, George Luther arrived there, strode up three flights of stairs to Brown's room, and proceeded to authorize the Kansas veteran to draw on him for up to $7,000 should the need arise when he returned to Kansas. Brown's judgment about Mary Stearns had been correct.[34]

In addition to authorizing the $7,000, Stearns called a meeting of

33. Villard, *Brown,* pp. 287–88; John Brown, "Old Brown's Farewell," Brown Papers, Kansas State Historical Society; Oates, *Brown,* pp. 202–3.

34. John Brown, Jr., to Brown, March 1, 1850, Sanborn-Brown Collection, Houghton Library; Stearns, *Life of Stearns,* pp. 159–60.

the Massachusetts Kansas Committee to explore other sources of cash. On April 9 the committee met and decided to allow Brown to sell 100 of the 200 Sharpe's rifles he had been given in January at $15 a piece to "reliable" free-state settlers. The moving force behind this authorization seems to have been Stearns, who had originally purchased the rifles with his own funds. Six days later, on April 15, Stearns notified Brown that the committee had voted him a "further sum" of $500. The Kansas veteran was so exultant that he was hardly disturbed by Stearns's added stipulations to the April 9 grant requesting that the "proceeds" from the gun sales should be used for the "benefit of Free State men in Kansas" and that Brown keep an account of the sales "as far as practical." This somewhat vague injunction from the normally precise and business-minded Stearns only served to buoy Brown's enthusiasm and reaffirm his faith in Mary Stearns's influence over her husband.[35]

John Brown immediately notified his son John Jr. of the windfall. And it is fitting that the younger Brown shared in his father's joy. More than any other person, John Brown Jr. had helped his father prepare guidelines for successfully conducting business transactions. It was the younger Brown who stressed the importance of projecting a keen organizational sense, advised his father about the use of influential women in a transaction, and counseled his father to always keep his business partners apprised of his comings and goings. In his letter to John Jr., Brown spoke of acquiring his grandfather's gravestone and alluded to future plans which the younger Brown already knew about. Brown stated that the stone had "sufficient size" to contain more "brief inscriptions" and asserted that in one hundred years the stone would be a "great curiosity." Brown closed the letter by thanking his son for his past advice "about the value and importance of discipline." The counsel had been correct and was "fully" appreciated. Brown had managed to control his anger during the weeks when contributions had been poor, and he had been rewarded with substantial aid for Kansas.

35. Sanborn, *Recollections*, 1: 118–19; Oates, *Brown*, p. 204; Stearns to Brown, April 15, 1857, Amos A. Lawrence Collection, Massachusetts Historical Society.

He had also gained the confidence of the two men in the best position to assist his future insurrectionary plans.[36]

It is ironic and typical that after exerting such masterful control over his emotions during his weeks in the East, Brown's excitement about acquiring funds turned into an aggressiveness that nearly destroyed his relationship with Stearns and Sanborn, the two men who had done the most to insure his success. Because of an exaggerated belief in his ability to manipulate these two men, Brown tried to force them into filling a $1,000 subscription for purchase of North Elba property. And he did this in the face of their less-than-firm commitment to raise the sum. Brown tried to pressure both men into alleviating his family's financial difficulties as they had his Kansas needs.

Admittedly, there were some reasons for Brown's overly optimistic assumptions about his ability to move Sanborn and Stearns. Before he left Boston in mid-April, Brown received a letter from Sanborn which more than justified his conclusion that the young secretary would continue to be as easily managed in the future as he had been in the past. Sanborn thanked Brown for "remembering me as you have done" and said he would prize anything from Brown as a "memento of the bravest and most earnest man it has been my fortune to meet." The ex-schoolteacher did not want Brown to regard him as an "unprofitable servant" and indicated that Brown's Boston friends took great interest in his "future career." If anything happened to him in Kansas, Sanborn claimed he would see to it that Brown's family was made "more comfortable" and his "memory defended." Sanborn concluded his letter by suggesting that, if he could serve the Kansas veteran in any way, he would "reckon it an honor to do so." Brown had also spoken of his family's difficult situation with Mary Stearns when she came to evaluate the "Farewell," and he felt she could be counted upon to prod her husband on their behalf. Then, too, Brown had discussed the possibility of a subscription with Stearns throughout the spring. It was Stearns who suggested that Brown seek Lawrence's assistance in

36. Brown to John Brown, Jr., April 15, 1857, Boyd B. Stutler Collection.

raising the sum. Before Brown left Boston, he and Stearns had talked about the possibility of the Medford manufacturer's purchase of some two hundred revolvers for the Kansas effort. At the time, Stearns did not seem pressed for funds, and Brown assumed he was both willing and financially able to take on the burden of filling out the land subscription. Brown did not anticipate (perhaps refused to anticipate) the possibility that the primary task of collecting money for the land purchase would stretch Stearns's generosity to the limit.[37]

After remaining in North Elba for two weeks, Brown initiated his campaign to pry money for the land purchase from his Boston friends. On April 29 he wrote to Derrick Foster, a Boston State House clerk, asking him to inquire about the subscription. Foster talked to Stearns, then wrote back to Brown. In his letter Foster told Brown that Stearns said the aid for Brown's family (which had only been *partly* promised") would be made up with as "little delay as possible."[38]

Foster's inquiry, taken in conjunction with a letter Brown had sent a few days earlier, angered Stearns, who disliked the tone of both. Brown wanted to make a deal with T. W. Carter of the Massachusetts Arms Company for 200 revolvers and had written Stearns to tell him Carter was willing to sell the guns for $1,300 as long as the sale was "not made public." Near the end of the letter Brown tersely stated that "if Rev. T. Parker and other good people at Boston would make up that amount *I might at least be well armed."* The insinuation was obvious to Stearns: The subscription had been slow in coming and Brown was upset.[39]

Brown had been granted over $1,000 by the Massachusetts Kansas Committee, had been placed in charge of 200 Sharpe's rifles, 100 of which he could sell, and had been authorized to draw on Stearns for

37. Sanborn to Brown, April 16, 1857, Sanborn Letters, Atlanta University; Stearns, *Life of Stearns*, pp. 159–60; Brown to David Lee Child, April 27, 1857, Boyd B. Stutler Collection.

38. Derrick Foster to Brown, April 29, 1857, Brown Papers, Kansas State Historical Society.

39. T. W. Carter to Brown, April 25, 1857, ibid.; Brown to Stearns, April 28, 1857, Smith Collection, Syracuse University; Stearns to T. W. Carter, May 1, 5, 1857, Stearns Collection, Kansas State Historical Society, Topeka, Kans.

up to $7,000 once in Kansas. But he was pressuring Stearns for an additional $1,300 for revolvers and $1,000 for a land purchase. Stearns was enraged. He saw the demands as excessive and, indeed, had made no promise to Brown for either. He responded to Brown with two stinging letters. On May 4 Stearns told Brown that he and Lawrence had not been able to raise the full subscription and that, as a result, Lawrence had written to Gerrit Smith asking him to "accept the 600 dollars now raised." Smith was asked to take a mortgage from Brown for $400 and had agreed. Two days later Stearns told Brown to accept the proposition and advised him that the committee would try to raise the rest of the money at some other time.[40]

In these two letters and his response to Foster, Stearns had firmly presented his case. The subscription had only been "partly promised," and it had been difficult to fill. The committee was not reneging on its agreement, and Brown should understand the great difficulty in procuring funds by settling for partial payment. The Medford manufacturer believed his direct discussion of the matter would stop Brown from making any more unreasonable requests. In fact, Stearns was so sure he had resolved the problem that he made an appeal on Brown's behalf before the National Kansas Committee on May 10 in New York City.[41]

But if George Luther Stearns thought his frank statements about the subscription would placate Brown, he was wrong. The letters only relieved Stearns's anxieties; Brown was still irate. He was determined to have every penny of the land subscription and, on May 10, he met with Smith and the Thompsons at Peterboro, notified them of his intention to obtain the full subscription, and dismissed Smith's suggestion that he settle for what had been offered. Three days later, he wrote a long letter to Stearns explaining his position. Brown prefaced his remarks with a biting introduction in which he claimed that he "must have" the $1,000 "made up *at once.*" Brown said he had not started

40. Stearns to Brown, May 4, 6, 1857, Sanborn-Brown Collection, Houghton Library; Smith to Amos A. Lawrence, May 3, 1857, Amos A. Lawrence Collection, Massachusetts Historical Society.
41. Stearns, *Life of Stearns,* p. 139.

the measure though he was "sufficiently needy" and, in rather surly tones, apologized if his demands were "hindering" either Stearns or Lawrence. Brown then outlined the nature of his intended purchase in detail, believing this would give greater validity to his demand.[42]

Brown pushed Sanborn to see to it that the money was "promptly raised." Invoking the secretary's pledge to serve him or his family in any way possible, Brown wrote Sanborn on May 15 and said that a full subscription was "much the cheapest" and "most proper" way to provide for his family's welfare. It would be "far less humiliating" for his wife. Aside from highlighting the intensity of his campaign for funds, the letter to Sanborn indicates how well Brown had gauged the personality of the secretary during the first months of their relationship and how deftly he operated in terms of that assessment. He knew Sanborn would have a hard time backing down from his pledge to "take it on himself" to see that Brown's family needs were met. To the businessman Stearns, Brown had sent a detailed analysis of the purchase agreement, to Sanborn an emotional plea about family needs. Brown felt he knew his men well and acted accordingly. In addition, Brown knew how sensitive Sanborn was on the issue of organizing aid for Kansas but not participating in settlement, and he tried to exploit any lingering guilt in the secretary. Brown closed his letter to Sanborn by saying that he would never have uttered a syllable about the land purchase were he *not conscious* [of] performing that service which is equally the duty of millions who need not forego a single hearty dinner by efforts they are called to make." The lines stung the young committee secretary so badly that he was probably not consoled by Brown's concluding assertion that he really didn't want to burden Stearns and Lawrence nor "ride free horses" until they fell dead.[43]

Brown's letter caused Sanborn discomfort because he was being asked to force Stearns on the land subscription issue, and it was a task he did not relish. Sanborn realized how much Stearns had already done for Brown and what difficulty the Medford businessman was having

---

42. Brown to Stearns, May 13, 1857, Boyd B. Stutler Collection.
43. Brown to Sanborn, May 15, 1857, ibid.

in filling the subscription. Stearns was being unfairly pressured. After debating his course for a day, Sanborn went to Medford on May 16 still undecided about whether he should broach the issue with Stearns; he had not yet resolved where the bounds on his loyalty to Brown began and his friendship with Stearns left off.[44]

By the time he arrived at Stearns's Medford home, Sanborn had determined to at least show Brown's letter to the committee chairman. After reading it, Stearns reciprocated by showing Sanborn his own letter from Brown and denied that he and Lawrence had ever committed themselves to the subscription as fully as Brown implied. Stearns said he had originally refused to undertake the responsibility and had advised Brown to seek aid from Lawrence. When Lawrence refused, it had been Brown who kept the subject alive, not Stearns. But although the Medford businessman was upset by Brown's insinuations, Sanborn sensed that he was not angry enough to sever his connection with Brown. During the remainder of the meeting, Sanborn saw why this was so. Stearns showed the young secretary a letter he had recently received from Martin Conway, one of the committee's agents in Kansas. According to Conway, freestaters' efforts to organize their own legislature at Topeka were likely to be "suppressed by corruption." Free-state men were "increasingly . . . entering all around into business with proslavery men." James Lane and Charles Robinson were trying to counter the fraudulently elected proslavery legislature at Shawnee Mission with their own extralegal free-state legislative body but, if Conway's views were correct, the project was doomed. There would be no counterforce to proslavery political maneuvers. When Stearns tied this possibility to the realization that a rigged, proslavery constitutional convention was to meet at Lecompton in June and would surely vote a proslavery document, he was pessimistic about political attempts to win freedom in Kansas. Brown's words were biting, unfair, and partially untrue, but his valor and desire to fight for freedom in Kansas were beyond doubt. Stearns had resolved to continue his support. Sanborn was further convinced of Stearns's will-

44. Sanborn to Brown, May 20, 1857, Sanborn Letters, Atlanta University.

ingness to go on aiding Brown, despite the friction over the North Elba land subscription, when the committee chairman showed him a reply he had recently drafted to T. W. Carter of the Massachusetts Arms Company. In the reply, Stearns presumed Carter wished him to be "responsible" for the purchase price of the 200 revolvers "until . . . paid by Captain Brown." Stearns notified Carter that he "cheerfully" assented to the wish.

Before he left Stearns's home, Sanborn helped the chairman draft a letter to Brown explaining that he (Stearns) had agreed with Lawrence to make up the full subscription. Stearns told Brown that he would inform Lawrence that he "must fulfill the agreement." Four days later, Sanborn wrote his own letter to Brown, and in it he assured Brown that he need have "no fear" about the money, which would soon be gathered up and put in the "right hands." Sanborn agreed that it would be a "sad thing" if Brown's family was not cared for while he was exposing himself to danger in Kansas for "the good of others." The secretary did have some disappointing news: The "arts of politicians" had defeated the Massachusetts appropriation for Kansas.[45]

Sensing a distinct change in attitude about the subscription, Brown sent a temperate response to Stearns. His letter of May 23 was designed to ease the tensions which had arisen over the issue and to prevent any further misunderstandings. Once again he explained the North Elba deal to Stearns, assuring him that there had been no collusion between himself, the Thompsons, and Smith and that he had no "previous arrangement" with Smith about the land purchase other than the provision that Smith's contract with the Thompson's should be made over to himself on payment. Brown wished to demonstrate that he had pressed for the full subscription only because it was promised and not because he was bound to a prior contract. Brown swore that Smith had given him "no encouragement" about the purchase and had simply agreed to the "arrangement." Brown tried to prevent any mistaken

45. Ibid.; Martin Conway to Stearns, May 11, 1857, Sanborn Scrapbooks, 1, Boyd B. Stutler Collection; Stearns to T. W. Carter, May 11, 1857, Sanborn-Brown Collection, Houghton Library; Stearns to Brown, May 16, 1857, Boyd B. Stutler Collection.

assumptions about how much Smith had pledged in Kansas aid, prefer-
ring Stearns's annoyance at knowing Smith refused to give money
because the previous year's contribution had "embarrassed him" to
Stearns's anger at being deceived. Brown told Stearns that rumors
about Smith assisting his Kansas work were false. All Smith had
promised was that he would do "all he could" when the "struggle was
renewed."[46]

The letter does seem to have reassured the Medford businessman. He
forgave Brown's insinuations and considered Smith's behavior in the
affair to be proper. In fact, Stearns vigorously prodded Lawrence to
fill the subscription even though Lawrence continued to insist that he
had never intended to do any more than "write a 'heading'" for the
fund. Before leaving Medford that June for a vacation in New Hampshire with his family, Stearns exchanged letters with Martin Conway.
The letters further explain his willingness to continue Brown's support.
Conway was certain that the new territorial governor, Mississippi
ex-Senator Robert Walker, would attempt to disband the free-state
Topeka legislature. Although Conway claimed to have confidence in
the "instincts of the masses," he confessed that he agreed with Stearns's
evaluation of the situation. If free-state men were defeated in the
"Topeka business," they should, as Stearns had counseled, "marshal
armed forces for further action." Conway's agreement with Stearns's
fears about the destruction of free-state political efforts, Walker's
proslavery leanings, and the likely possibility of a proslavery constitution from the Lecompton convention, prompted Stearns's continued
assistance to Brown in spite of his irritation over the land subscription.
Political antislavery had been defeated too often by the Slave Power.
Only men who, like Brown, were willing to fight for freedom could
prevent a proslavery takeover in the territory. Brown must be supported.[47]

46. Brown to Stearns, May 23, 1857, ibid.
47. Amos A. Lawrence to Stearns, June 3, 1857; Martin Conway to Stearns,
May 29, 1857, ibid.

CHAPTER 5

Reevaluation and Revelation

NEAR THE END OF JUNE, Gerrit Smith resolved that "fighting for Liberty" was the only way to assure the survival of a free Kansas. He watched with mounting anger as free-state attempts to form a legislature were ruled illegal by Governor Walker and proslavery delegates debated the Lecompton constitution. Addressing a Milwaukee antislavery meeting, the Peterboro philanthropist also lashed out at the Supreme Court for the "naked despotism" it displayed in handing down the Dred Scott decision. A government that didn't "promise protection in return for allegiance" was "not a government at all." When asked if the decision would "arouse people to rebel against the Supreme Court," Smith labeled such a question "foolish." The Supreme Court was the "rebel."[1]

Smith met John Brown in Chicago late in June as Brown moved west to Kansas. It had been a month since the two men had spoken, and in the interim the unpredictable Smith had decided he would contribute to Brown's Kansas work. Despite his claims of a few weeks earlier that his means were "exhausted," he insisted Brown draw on him for $350 and left Chicago demanding that free-state men "not shrink" from fighting for freedom, even if federal troops were used against them.[2]

When Brown returned to Kansas in early June after an absence of almost eight months, he saw some promising signs for the triumph of

1. Harlow, *Smith*, p. 394; Smith to D. C. Littlejohn, May 18, 1857; Smith, Speech on Personal Liberty Bill, June 18, 1857, Smith Collection, Syracuse University.
2. Harlow, *Smith*, pp. 394–95.

the free-state cause. A large immigration that spring had swelled the ranks of free-state settlers in the territory to the point where they vastly outnumbered their proslavery counterparts. Lane, Robinson, and other leaders had accepted Walker's call to participate in legislative elections scheduled for the territory that October. They believed free-state men could gain political control of the territory and displace the fraudulent Shawnee Mission assemblage. While there were still isolated outbreaks of violence, most free-state men agreed with their leaders about deciding the issue of slavery in the territory with political methods.[3]

As he assessed the situation and recuperated from a debilitating attack of the ague, Brown realized that there was an excellent possibility for the peaceful resolution of problems in the territory. As a result, he spent more time thinking about and preparing for his insurrectionary strike. Some years before, at the time of his failure in the wool business, Brown and his son, John Jr., had discussed the reasons for that failure. John Jr. thought that one of the habits which had done "much injury" to them when they were engaged in "business connections" was their failure to maintain proper communication with business partners. They should have given a "narrative . . . detailed account of all transactions of interest as well as plans and bearings." This oversight led to "groundless suspicions" or, at least, "uneasiness" among their associates. Brown's son felt they must "mend" the habit so as to lessen occasions of faultfinding in the future. Thus, knowing that he might soon have to prevail on his Massachusetts "friends" for financing, Brown made it a point to keep them informed of his movements.[4]

Brown tried to prevent "groundless suspicions" from erupting with his conciliatory May 23 letter to Stearns. Shortly thereafter, he used the autobiographical sketch he had promised young Henry Stearns to quiet any doubts that might have developed over the North Elba matter and to lay the foundation for future proposals. Brown's letter to the Stearns boy is a revealing biographical and psychological document, but it is likewise a carefully constructed tactical device designed

3. Rawley, *Race and Politics,* pp. 204–17.
4. John Brown, Jr., to Brown, March 1, 1850, Sanborn-Brown Collection, Houghton Library; Oates, *Brown,* pp. 208–9.

(like Brown's March broadside and April "Farewell") to cultivate confidence in his character and, ultimately, support for insurrection. Although the letter tells us a great deal about Brown's beliefs, we should remember that Brown was conscious of who was reading the letter. Therefore, it is far from being a spontaneous, freely flowing expression of personality.

Brown began his brief autobiography by speaking of the "necessity" of a "severe but much needed course of discipline" in the early years of his development. He then moved to a consideration of the origins of his abolitionism by describing slavery's disruptive effect on family life. He spoke of his encounter with the brutal treatment of a "young negro boy" which brought him to reflect on the "wretched condition of Fatherless and motherless slave children" who had no one "to protect and provide" for them. Brown spoke of becoming "ambitious to excel in anything he undertook to perform" as a youth and indicated that "this kind of feeling" was one he would "recommend to all young persons." Vaguely suggesting his future plans and at the same time praising the virtue of having a well-thought-out direction in life, Brown wished young Henry Stearns to always have some *"definite plan."* Many men had none or, if they did, never stuck to it. This was "not the case" with John Brown. He followed up with "tenacity" whatever he set about doing as "long as it answered his general purpose" and, as a result, he "rarely failed" to effect the "things he undertook." In fact, he *"habitually expected to succeed,"* and he always united such expectations with the consciousness that his plans were "right in themselves." Near the end of the letter, Brown once again tried to mend any frayed sensibilities which might have been produced by the North Elba issue. Almost apologetically, he said that his "habit of being obeyed" occasionally prompted him to speak in an "imperious way."[5]

Brown appended a short note to his autobiographical account which informed his Boston associates of other sums that had been contributed to him. At Hartford and New Haven he had been promised $1,000 but

5. Brown to Henry Stearns, July 15, 1857, Boyd B. Stutler Collection.

had received only $285. He chose to forget Smith's Chicago draft for $350 and claimed the Peterboro squire had only supplied him with $50 for Kansas and $110 to pay the Thompsons while the subscription was being filled. Brown gently prodded his Massachusetts readers to continue to raise the land money, since the unpaid bill for the purchase had "exceedingly mortified" him.[6]

Although Brown was still careful to soft-pedal his belief that violence was the only way to destroy slavery, the autobiographical account was a brilliantly successful ploy to prepare his listeners for his future antislavery activity and a perfect reaffirmation of the value system which had ingratiated him with Boston antislavery men that spring. He was following John Jr.'s advice in trying to allay "groundless suspicions" and was again restating the beliefs that gave his Boston friends confidence in his character. He had a keen organizational sense, was disciplined, controlled, ambitious, confident of success and, like his Boston friends, loathed slavery for its attack on the fundamental institution of the family. The men in Boston who had contributed to his support admired his courage and his resolution to resist slavery forcibly, and this gave them confidence in Brown. But they were also looking for someone whose system of beliefs was similar to their own and who, by the logical extension of that system, despised the institution of slavery. Brown's mid-July letter to Henry Stearns reflects his own understanding of this situation as well as his understanding of their still uncertain attraction to violent means.

By early August, Lawrence and Stearns had filled the subscription and sent Sanborn to Peterboro with the $1,000 draft. The young committeeman was happy to make the trip. It gave him a chance to visit with Edwin Morton, his Harvard classmate who was tutoring Smith's children, and provided an opportunity to meet Smith himself. After delivering the draft, Sanborn wrote to Parker and said that he believed Smith to be a "greater man" than people in New England acknowledged. He was a superior individual who had "regular devo-

6. Ibid.

tion to his ideas" and "great personal influence." The real highlight of Sanborn's journey, however, was his visit with Brown's family. The young secretary gave Mary Brown a small sum of cash left over from the subscription after the payment to Smith and assured her that she could count on Brown's Boston associates if anything happened to her husband.[7]

No doubt the impressionable and somewhat romantic young man saw the Browns' poverty as a noble symbol of their heroic sacrifice for freedom. The deferential tone of his next letter to John Brown indicates how much the trip to North Elba reinforced Sanborn's desire to aid Brown. He told Brown that the autobiographical letter was "well appreciated" by all who read it and that the land purchase money had been turned over to Smith. The secretary "regretted" that the payments had been delayed so long and, momentarily forgetting Brown's pressure tactics, said that the entire delay was the committee's fault—the result of a "series of mistakes" on the part of Brown's Boston "friends."[8]

Nevertheless, for all of Sanborn and Stearn's concern about Brown, it is indicative of their ambivalence about nondefensive political violence and their post-North Elba reservations about the man who advocated it that they became somewhat more wary of Brown even while they were filling the land subscription. They thought there were good reasons to stop short of violent means—one being a belief that Governor Walker's promise to keep the October territorial election free from fraud was given in good faith. If freestaters could gain control of the territorial legislature, they could thwart any attempt to force slavery upon Kansas.

When Brown himself saw there was little chance of "major disturbances" erupting in Kansas that August and decided to "work back Eastward," he wrote Stearns on August 10 asking for "secret service" money with no questions asked. Stearns rebuffed his request by flatly

<hr>

7. Stearns, *Life of Stearns,* pp. 140–41; Sanborn to Parker, August 8, 1857, Sanborn Collection, Concord Free Public Library; Sanborn to Stearns, Report of the North Elba Land Purchase, Boyd B. Stutler Collection.

8. Sanborn to Brown, August 14, 1857, Sanborn Letters, Atlanta University.

refusing it. Stearns was caught up in the financial panic that struck the entire country that summer and fall. Peter Butler, the man who had rescued Stearns from financial ruin in 1853, was in desperate straits after losing large sums of money invested in the Michigan Central Railroad. It took Stearns and a number of others the summer and fall to gather enough money to cover Butler's debts. He could do nothing for Brown.[9]

There was, however, much more to Stearns's reluctance than Butler's fiscal headache. The Medford businessman was participating in the Massachusetts fund-raising campaign to assist free-state political chances in the October election. In the fall of 1857, when freestaters took control of the legislature, Stearns reversed his springtime assessment about using "force of arms" and decided that antislavery men would triumph by political methods. On November 17 he wrote Brown cautioning him not to attack proslavery forces unless he was attacked first. To make sure Brown heeded his advice, Stearns wrote to E. B. Whitman, an agent of the committee, and ordered Brown's access to committee funds and the $7,000 personal authorization closed. Stearns said Brown had been given authority to draw on him only "in a certain contingency" and that, since the contingency had not occurred, it would be "very unwise to attempt to establish *order* by force." Stearns believed the freestaters' "true policy" was to "meet the enemy at the polls and vote them down."[10]

Stearns's retreat from the advocacy of violent means mirrored a similar process in Samuel Gridley Howe. In late spring Howe journeyed to Kansas with small sums for the free-state cause. On the trip he encountered Senator Henry Wilson who was going to the territory. Wilson hoped to "persuade" freestaters to vote in the October

9. Rawley, *Race and Politics,* p. 204; Brown to Stearns, August 10, 1857, Boyd B. Stutler Collection; Brown to Family, August 17, 1857, Brown, Papers, Kansas State Historical Society; Stearns, *Life of Stearns,* p. 145; Oates, *Brown,* pp. 216–18. Stearns did send Brown $500 for "personal and family" needs.

10. Stearns, *Life of Stearns,* p. 144; E. B. Whitman to Stearns, October 25, 1857; Stearns to E. B. Whitman, November 14, 1857, Stearns Collection, Kansas State Historical Society; Oates, *Brown,* pp. 216–18.

election called by Walker. At the time Howe was "undecided" as to whether freestaters should participate because he was still confident in Brown and the logic of violent methods. This confidence is well documented in a letter Howe sent to the Kansas veteran in mid-June. Ostensibly the doctor was concerned with Brown's physical health, but his words reveal much about his allegiance to Brown and force. Howe, whose own physical condition had been ravaged by the tensions, cares, and the responsibilities of his personal and professional life, saw similar signs in Brown during the early spring. In Kansas, the Boston physician heard rumors that Brown was seriously ill. Howe wrote the veteran to give him the counsel of someone who could "understand and appreciate you." It was important for Brown "to live and be in health" in order to carry out his "noble purpose." Howe was convinced Brown could properly care for himself because Brown understood his own constitution and had the "self command" required to obey the "laws of God" when he knew them. Brown must not let excessive activity "burn him up." He had an "organization of rare power" and the doctor, who had dabbled in phrenology, believed Brown had an "uncommon development" of the "moral regions." It was a "great gift" to be "cherished" and used in the "cause of humanity."[11]

Despite his understanding about the demands of professional life and his regard for Brown's "self command," by the end of June, Howe looked for a political solution to Kansas's troubles. He backed away from his earlier, tentative commitment to the use of violence. At a private meeting called by Henry Wilson in late June, Howe joined Stearns, Lawrence, and others in raising $2,500 to help carry the October election. During mid-July the group appointed Thomas J. Marsh to bring almost $3,000 to free-state leaders to be "judiciously" used for election purposes. In less than three weeks Howe and the others had raised a sum it took Brown almost four months to acquire. By mid-November the Boston physician had fully followed Stearns's

11. Schwartz, *Howe*, pp. 214-15, 224; Howe, *Journals*, p. 431; Howe to Brown, June 13, 1857, Howe Collection, Houghton Library.

lead. In the wake of the free-state election success, he warned Brown not to attack Missouri border "ruffians."[12]

Like Stearns, Howe had also pulled back from Brown's support for financial reasons. That fall, when his good friend Horace Mann came east to collect money for a college building, Howe indicated the severity of the financial panic gripping New England and advised Mann that, though Moses got "water out of granite," he doubted Mann would be as successful among panic-stricken Bostonians. Howe himself was "cramped" and "pinched" by his falling income.[13]

Gerrit Smith joined Howe and Stearns in their retreat. Two months after he had given Brown $350 dollars to spur freestaters' "fight for Liberty," he was attending a compensated emancipation convention in Cleveland. In a speech before the group, Smith asserted that since slavery was a "national dilemma" and all men contributed to it, the North should help the South remove the institution. He was willing to make a "direct appeal" to the selfish slaveholder if it would prod him to dissolve his immoral relationship with the black man. Smith was careful to avoid accepting the Dred Scott decision. He was seeking to buy slaves, not because they were property, but because he believed northerners had a "moral right" to help "slave owner and slave." Smith, like most abolitionists, was as worried about slavery's effect on white slaveholders as on black slaves. Although his position on compensated emancipation did not cause him to completely break away from past ideas about force, his support for the movement does indicate a growing willingness to try to buy off slavery before fighting it off.[14]

When William Lloyd Garrison labeled Smith's address as "another

12. Howe, *Journals*, p. 431; Howe to Brown, November 7, 1857, Howe Collection, Massachusetts Historical Society.

13. Howe, *Journals*, pp. 452–53; Howe to Horace Mann, November 18, 1857; Howe to Charles Sumner, November 22, 1857; Howe to Horace Mann, December 16, 1857, Howe Collection, Houghton Library. Samuel Gridley Howe constantly worried about excessive "family and personal" expenses. He claimed that before he was married, he had "nearly twenty thousand dollars well invested and owed not a dollar," but since his marriage "joint expenses" had exceeded "joint income."

14. Gerrit Smith, Speech on Compensated Emancipation, August 26, 1857, Smith Collection, Syracuse University.

gyration," the Peterboro squire said he was "pained" at so "palpable an injustice." However, he soon dropped his backing for the scheme. Perhaps in an attempt to reestablish his abolitionist credentials with Garrison and other antislavery proponents, Smith used his annual Jerry rescue speech on October 1, 1857, to reassert his belief in moral suasion and political abolition and to play down his advocacy of violent methods. In the speech, Smith asked if "we would have the slaves rescued by violence" and answered with a resounding "No!" Smith claimed it would be "wicked" to make such a request because there was a better way to proceed. All people had to do was "vote the Federal Government into the hands of abolitionists and every chain would fall peacefully from every slave."[15]

Unlike his colleagues who backed away from belief in the necessity of forcible means as soon as the possibility of a favorable political solution presented itself in Kansas, young Frank Sanborn left that conviction more reluctantly. For him, retreat from force was tantamount to a retreat from Brown himself. This was difficult for the young committeeman because he felt his whole role in the free-state movement, abolitionism, and reformist Boston society depended on his relationship with Brown. To withdraw his support from Brown was, in many ways, to deny the symbol of his own significance. Nor would the crafty Brown allow such a withdrawal to take place. After Sanborn sent his deferential confirmation of the North Elba purchase, for instance, Brown was quick to document his gratitude and imply his great need for Sanborn's continued assistance. Brown was thankful his wife and daughters would not be "drawn to beg" or become a "burden" to his "Poor Boys," who had "nothing but their hands to begin with." Brown was grateful to have found friends to "look after his family," friends who were acquainted with their "real condition."[16]

15. *Liberator,* September 18, 1857; Gerrit Smith, Speech at Jerry Rescue Commemoration, October 1, 1857, Smith Collection, Syracuse University.

16. Brown to Sanborn, August 27, 1857, Boyd B. Stutler Collection; Sanborn to Brown, August 28, 1857, Sanborn Letters, Atlanta University. In the letter to Sanborn, Brown also continued efforts to smooth relations with Stearns. Brown

Prompted by the confidence Brown seemed to be placing in him and his own desire to preserve their relationship, Sanborn, in early September, made a bold attempt to tap the seemingly untouchable reserves of the Worcester County Committee. Claiming he had been informed that there was "a large sum" of money (some $3,000) being held by the committee, Sanborn told Higginson there was no reason why it should be "kept idle." He wanted it donated to Brown. Higginson was furious at Sanborn for making such a demand. He immediately wrote and explained to the secretary that he had no control over the money of the Worcester committee and that if he did, he would not have given it for Brown's "useless" efforts. The sharp response flustered Sanborn, and he toned down his condemnation of the Worcester group, admitting his "own two or three" committees had not excelled in giving Brown aid and that all free-state committees were "culpably negligent." Worcester's committee was "no worse than the rest." Sanborn was disconcerted by Higginson's assertions and defended Brown's inactivity during the summer by saying that Governor Walker had knowledge of his purposes and was "watching for him." John Brown was as "ready for Revolution" as any man. All he needed was money and he would be the "best Disunion champion" found. Perhaps hinting at Brown's plans for insurrection or at least restating his own resolute commitment to Brown and forceful means, Sanborn concluded his letter to Higginson by suggesting that, with one hundred men raised and drilled, Brown would "do more to split the Union than any man alive."[17]

Sanborn's letters to Brown during the late summer and early fall further indicate his refusal to desert the veteran's side. When it seemed that the bogus Lecompton constitution would not be submitted to the people of the territory, Sanborn declared to Brown that it would be best if the officers of the proslavery government were *"hung."* Sanborn

claimed that if he was able to, he would avoid *"such a speculation* as shall swallow up all property I have been provided with." He would "hasten to keep it *all safe,* so that he [Stearns] may be remunerated."

17. Sanborn to Higginson, September 11, 28, 1857, Higginson-Kansas Collection, Kansas State Historical Society; Edelstein, *Strange Enthusiasm,* p. 207.

apologized for Stearns's failure to send "secret service" money, explaining that money was "very scarce" and the committee's treasury was depleted. When Brown continued his correspondence with Sanborn in spite of the other committee members' waning interest, the young secretary became even more respectful. He was glad to be getting these regular reports because they convinced him that Lane and Brown were the only "real generals" to be found in the territory.[18]

In December, two months after free-state settlers had captured the territorial legislature and seemed in a good position to prevent the Lecompton constitution from being imposed on Kansas, Sanborn finally conceded that the situation could be settled politically but said he would "not be surprised" if Brown's "courage and arms" were needed there again.[19]

Sanborn's absorption with Brown is reflected not only in his seemingly die-hard support for force but also in the Brown-like tones of his speech and thought. By late fall of 1857, Sanborn was worn out by his committee work. The constant trips to Boston, never-ending committee correspondence, and his occasional schoolteaching activity tired him. His response to this state of mental and physical fatigue is reminiscent of Brown's. In order to regain his strength, Sanborn decided to forego the "pleasures of visiting Boston." It was time to "deny" himself the company of "social flatterers" and retire to "regions where everything passes for what it is." Like Howe and Higginson who had looked for simplicity and privacy in Kansas, Sanborn wanted a place where he could "avoid the distractions of life," where he could order his existence, and, like Brown, he wanted a place where he could devote himself more closely "to study and meditation," not only of books, "but of life itself." Sanborn hoped to rid himself of the pressures and tensions which arose when one made abolitionism a "business and study." He needed to "eradicate" certain "evil tendencies" from his "present way of life." He was looking for the benefits of "severe discipline" and was willing to

18. Sanborn to Brown, August 28, September 14, 19, October 19, 1857, Sanborn Letters, Atlanta University.

19. Sanborn to Brown, December 11, 1857, ibid.; Rawley, *Race and Politics,* pp. 228–36.

"live like a monk" for a while. It was time to retire to his "cell." Husbanding precious energy was imperative for the young, nineteenth-century professional; a career could be exhausting.[20]

During mid-March 1857, in the midst of his quest for Kansas funds, John Brown journeyed to New York City for an interview with an ex-soldier of fortune named Hugh Forbes, whose lecture-circuit appearances in the East had earned him a modest reputation as a military expert. Forbes, an Englishman, had come to New York a few years earlier after spending two years as a field commander in Garibaldi's army of Italian volunteers. His particular expertise lay in the use of guerrilla tactics, and Brown wanted to recruit him for Kansas and future attacks upon slavery. After lengthy discussions, Brown hired Forbes for six months. As soon as the Englishman could put his personal affairs in order, he was to go to Kansas and begin training Brown's recruits. Forbes was to receive $100 a month for his services, and Brown hinted that he might count on a longer term of employment if certain "New England humanitarians" agreed to finance other plans. Hugh Forbes was quick to enter the arrangement. His lecture-circuit appearances and part-time newspaper work had not provided sufficient funds to take care of his wife and children, who still lived in Paris, and he needed money desperately.[21]

From the start of their relationship, problems developed between Brown and Forbes. The ex-soldier demanded to be paid the $600 in advance and then was slow in joining Brown. When Forbes did reach Mt. Tabor, Iowa, and began drilling Brown's recruits in early July, he asked Brown to reimburse him for money he had spent preparing a military tactics manual. In addition to the friction caused by his tardiness

20. Sanborn to Parker, November 1, 1857, Sanborn Collection, Concord Free Public Library.
21. Oates, *Brown*, pp. 200–201; W. D. H. Callender to Brown, July 2, 1857, Brown Papers, Kansas State Historical Society; G. M. Trevelyan, *Garibaldi and the Making of Italy* (London, 1914), pp. 98–99; G. M. Trevelyan, *Garibaldi's Defense of the Roman Republic* (London, 1907), pp. 349–51. See Forbes's statement in the *New York Herald*, October 27, 1859. Villard, *Brown*, pp. 285–86.

and financial demands, Forbes argued with Brown about how the recruits should be trained. Both men were proud of their "unchallengeable expertise" in guerrilla warfare and had a difficult time accepting criticism. Then, in August, when Brown partially revealed his scheme for a slave insurrection, their arguments grew more heated. Forbes had his own ideas about which type of foray would be most successful. He wanted to "muster along the northern slave frontier" with a highly trained group of "carefully selected colored and white persons." The former field commander wanted to "instigate a series of slave stampedes, running Negroes into Canada." In the process he hoped to render "slave property untenable." Brown firmly rejected Forbes's approach, claiming he had his own plan, one which he had been working on for "many years." Brown said he had prepared himself by reading numerous works on guerrilla tactics and carefully examining topographical maps of the southern states. He would recruit twenty-five well-trained, well-armed men, "colored and white mixed," and supply them with pikes, then use this cadre to "beat up a Slave Quarter in Virginia." Though both plans seemed similar, major disagreement arose over the predictability of a slave response to such a venture. Forbes was uncertain the slaves could respond and strongly believed that they should be warned of the impending attack. Brown was sure a warning wasn't necessary. He felt that, once the attack had begun, between 200 and 500 slaves would join him. He would then take 80 to 100 men and "make a dash" against the federal arsenal at Harpers Ferry. After the assault, Brown would lead the entire group into the Virginia mountains and hold on there until his "New England partisans" called a convention to "overthrow the proslavery administration."[22]

Because of constant disputes with Brown about training techniques, tactics, and finances, Forbes left Mt. Tabor in mid-November. Brown was disappointed to lose Forbes's obvious military skills. At the same time, however, he was relieved to be rid of the only man in the small group who seriously questioned his authority. But this was not the last Brown would hear from the ex-soldier of fortune. Two months later,

22. Oates, *Brown*, pp. 211–13.

in mid-January 1858, the disconsolate Forbes threatened to destroy Brown's plan before it could be implemented. In letters to Sanborn, Forbes alleged that the "New England humanitarians" and, in particular, Sanborn, had violated their financial obligations. According to the soldier, Brown had promised to pay him $100 a month for a year and had reneged on his commitment. Forbes suggested that Brown had not been able to pay him because the New Englanders had failed to supply sufficient funds.[23]

Sanborn was angered by these allegations and said he had never heard of "such an arrangement." The secretary assured Forbes that if he or other committeemen had known about such a contractual obligation, they would have made it their business to see that it was kept. Sanborn angrily asserted that he would never have let Forbes's family suffer for want of money and further stated that he was "not guilty" of cheating on or lying about the agreement. Although he rebuked Forbes for his "abusive language," it was more than Forbes's accusations which upset Sanborn. For the first time, the young secretary doubted Brown's competence. He realized, as Stearns had during the land subscription episode, that Brown could be something less than selflessly heroic. Indeed, Brown could be "imperious," insensitive, and mistaken in his judgment of character. Sanborn immediately wrote to Brown and asked what misinformation Forbes had been given. He wondered why Brown had not written the soldier to defend his Boston "friends."[24]

Sanborn's letter jarred Brown, who could not afford to lose the confidence of his most dedicated and efficient Boston agent at a time when he was about to request money for his Harpers Ferry raid. And Brown could not allow Forbes to threaten his plans with any further disclosures. Such revelations not only destroyed confidence but also neutralized the plan's element of surprise. Once again, in a moment of desperation, Brown turned to his son, John Jr., and asked him to deal

23. Ibid., p. 218; Sanborn to Brown, January 12, 1858, Sanborn Letters, Atlanta University.
24. Sanborn to Brown, January 12, 1858, ibid.; Sanborn to Parker, January 17, 1858, Sanborn Collection, Concord Free Public Library.

with the situation by sending Forbes a "sharpe" and "well-merited rebuke." John Jr. should notify the disgruntled soldier that he had not been engaged for a year as he claimed and that Brown did not "accept it well" to be asked to state an "untruth." John Jr. followed his father's advice. He wrote Forbes and berated him for his "spiteful letters," stating that they had done "great injury" because they had "weakened" his father's "hands" with Massachusetts supporters. The letter John Jr. sent was temporarily effective. Hugh Forbes was silenced—but only for a few weeks.[25]

Forbes's defection and his resulting attempt to seek funds from the Boston committeemen worried Brown. Yet it was only one of a number of aggravating problems he faced in the fall and early winter. During that period he was plagued by recurring attacks of the ague, his funds dwindled, and he had to watch as free-state settlers voted themselves into power and eliminated the need for his Kansas activity. The October elections of 1857 put a free-state representative in Congress and captured thirty-three of fifty-two seats in the territorial legislature. By early January 1858, the legislature had also blocked submission to Congress of the fraudulent, proslavery Lecompton constitution before it could be voted on by the territory's settlers. It troubled Brown to see this political solution, for he realized it would hasten the retreat of his Boston allies from their radical professions of the previous spring. He had to move quickly if he wanted to capitalize on whatever sentiment remained for the use of violent means against slavery. By mid-January, he had gathered his recruits, arms, and supplies at Mt. Tabor, traveled eastward through Ohio, and settled in upper New York State. During the journey Brown continued to discuss his scheme, slowly revealing additional segments, and preparing his men for their "ultimate destination" in Virginia.[26]

On January 28, 1858, Brown sequestered himself in the Rochester

25. Oates, *Brown*, p. 225; Brown to John Brown, Jr., February 9, 1858, Brown Notebook, 2, Brown Collection, Boston Public Library, Boston, Mass.; Franklin Benjamin Sanborn, *The Life and Letters of John Brown* (Boston, 1885), pp. 432–33; John Brown, Jr., to Hugh Forbes, January 15, 1858, Boyd B. Stutler Collection.

26. Oates, *Brown*, pp. 224–26; Rawley, *Race and Politics*, pp. 213–14, 228–36.

home of Fredrick Douglass and set about perfecting his "Virginia Plan" by drawing up a "Provisional Constitution" which he hoped would eliminate "anarchy and confusion" once he was established in his mountain fortress. He also thought it would demonstrate the care with which he had developed his "definite plan" to end slavery. After completing work on the document, he initiated his quest for support from Gerrit Smith and his Boston allies: Sanborn, Stearns, Parker, Howe, and Higginson. The letters Brown sent to these men testify to his understanding of the people with whom he was dealing. Each request was carefully worded and neatly tailored to the personality of the recipient.

Brown appealed to Higginson (who was perpetually concerned with his manliness) as both a "true man and true abolitionist" and sought "secret service" money for the most important undertaking of his whole life. Brown said he needed $500 to $800 in sixty days. Indicating that he had already written to Parker, Stearns, and Sanborn about the project, Brown continued his appeal to Higginson's ego by noting that he was depending on the Worcester activist because he did not know whether "Mr. Stearns or Mr. Sanborn are abolitionists." In view of Brown's past assistance from both Sanborn and Stearns, his comments to Higginson were a rather cynical assessment of their abolitionism, but Brown was determined to have Higginson's participation in the venture even if he had to flatter the minister at the expense of those who had already done so much for him. Besides, Brown was as determined that this would be his "last effort in the begging line." He would do whatever was required to insure a successful effort.[27]

Higginson's response was equal to Brown's plea. Higginson claimed he was "always ready to invest money in treason" but at present had "none to invest." His friends were either unwilling or "bankrupt." The minister also spoke of prior obligations that demanded his attention— he was gathering funds for underground railroad activity in Kansas.

27. Oates, *Brown*, p. 224; Villard, *Brown*, p. 319; Brown to Higginson, February 2, 1858, Higginson-Brown Collection, Boston Public Library; Sanborn, *Life and Letters of John Brown*, pp. 435–36.

However, Higginson did not want to dissuade Brown entirely and therefore slyly alluded to the very funds Brown was trying to obtain by hinting that he might be able to interest his county committee in supporting Brown with the "trifling balance" they had left. That "trifling balance" was exactly what Brown was pursuing, and he immediately replied to the minister. Indeed, "railroad business on a somewhat extended scale" was the "identical object" for which he was "trying to get means." Brown had been connected with the underground railroad since boyhood and had "never let an opportunity slip." Would Higginson meet him at Gerrit Smith's during the last week of February? He had a "measure on foot" that he was sure would awaken something more than a "common interest" if Higginson could hear it.[28]

Higginson did not go to Smith's and wasn't sure what "railroad business on an extended scale" meant, though his discussions with Sanborn led him to believe there was a possibility that Brown was contemplating a slave uprising. The thought excited him. Recently he had read about the problems caused by the "defiant and hostile attitudes of the Negro population in Louisiana, Tennessee and Arkansas." One insurrection had been fomented by a white abolitionist named Hancock, who was eventually caught, tried, found innocent, and shot. If Brown was contemplating the same sort of escapade, Higginson was sure he was worth supporting. After the Burns episode, the minister had few scruples about using political violence to end slavery, and he had repeatedly said so. It was quite likely that Brown could free substantial numbers of slaves by such an insurrection. Higginson was intrigued by the possibility, as well as by the effect a raid would have on public opinion. He had grown disturbed by the declining influence of radical antislavery and thought that backing Brown's scheme might be a good way to reestablish that influence. Hadn't his Burns rescue

28. Higginson to Brown, February 8, 1858, Higginson-Brown Collection, Boston Public Library; Higginson, *Journals,* p. 191; Brown to Higginson, February 12, 1858, Brown Collection, Massachusetts Historical Society, Boston, Mass.; Sanborn, *Life and Letters of John Brown,* p. 436.

attempt, Sumner's beating, and the bloody struggle for a free Kansas done much to rekindle antislavery fervor?[29]

John Brown also wrote to Theodore Parker during the first week in February. He told Parker that he was "perfecting arrangements" for an "important measure" and was counting on Parker's assistance because their "mutual friends" were not as "deeply-dyed" in abolition as the minister. None of them understood his views as well as Parker. Brown's determined attempt to secure Parker's assistance is revealing. Of all the Boston friends, Parker had been the least supportive. The minister had done little to obtain funds for Brown in 1857 and had refused Brown's request to read the "Farewell" before his congregation. But Brown sensed Parker's ability to inspire activity on his behalf and believed that Parker was the one whose counsel Howe, Stearns, and Sanborn would seek in attempting to defend their support of the plan. The importance of the meeting at Parker's home one year earlier had not been lost on Brown. Boston abolitionists had not gathered there simply as a matter of convenience. The meeting was symbolic. Parker was the undeclared leader of all Massachusetts antislavery men who entertained thoughts of using violent means against slavery. His theoretical justification could be vital.[30]

Brown wrote to George Luther Stearns requesting that the Medford businessman come to Smith's home in late February and listen to the plan. Stearns, however, had recently returned from a business trip to New York City, was too tired to make another journey so soon, and wasn't sure he wanted to do anything for Brown. In fact, the pressures of economic panic prompted Stearns to ask Brown to return money provided for his Kansas work. The financially harried lead-pipe manufacturer was no longer ready to "invest in treason." Brown had received funds previously, but they had not been given "under obligation." Kansas settlers no longer needed aid in "defending themselves

29. Thomas Wentworth Higginson, Collection of Clippings on Slave Insurrections, 1856; Higginson to Louisa Higginson, March 16, 1858, Higginson-Barney Collection, Houghton Library.

30. Brown to Parker, February 2, 1858, in Parker, *Correspondence,* 1: 163.

from marauders." Their "true course" was to vote the enemy down. Because the contingency for which Stearns had given his pledge had ceased to exist, he wanted the remaining cash returned without conditions. Stearns said he was not "indifferent" to Brown's needs but would only give aid when it was "proper" to do so. At present, with friends being dragged under by economic panic and Kansas ready to resolve its problems politically, Stearns doubted the "propriety" of a contribution. Stearns was also disturbed by Forbes's accusations and wanted to know why the soldier wrote such "abusive letters" to Brown's Boston associates. Unquestionably, Stearns's reluctance to contribute was partially due to a growing skepticism about Brown's competence.[31]

Frank Sanborn received two letters from Brown in the first week of February, but this time the young secretary was more cautious in his response to Brown's pleas. Writing to Higginson on February 11, ostensibly to seek funds for Brown, the secretary spoke uncertainly, claiming only to have enough "confidence" in Brown to trust him with a "moderate sum" for his new venture. Sanborn was still upset by the "slanderous and insulting tone" of Forbes's letters, and there is little doubt that he placed most of the blame on Brown. In addition, Sanborn was bothered by Brown's manipulation of Edwin Morton. Sanborn had received a note from his Harvard classmate saying that Brown needed $500 to $800 to "overthrow slavery in a large part of the country." Morton's phrasing was so reminiscent of Brown's that Sanborn could hardly fail to recognize who had inspired the letter, and the young secretary disliked the pressure. Sanborn's reticence, however, was precipitated by more than Forbes's letters, Morton's seeming manipulation, and his own scanty financial resources. The young secretary clearly understood that Brown contemplated an "uprising of slaves" and that worried him more than anything else. His attempt to dispel his fears about such a scheme are obvious in the conclusion of his letter to Higginson. Sanborn half-heartedly suggested that "the Union" was "evidently on its last legs" and, because Buchanan and others were

31. Stearns, *Life of Stearns,* pp. 161–62.

"trying to tear it to pieces," he believed "treason would not be treason that much longer but patriotism." The statement was more of a question than an assertion.[32]

During the next week Sanborn was finally able to persuade himself of his own definition of patriotism. When Brown refused the secretary's plea to come to Boston (Brown's reasons for "keeping still" were strong enough to prevent him from seeing his family), Sanborn unenthusiastically prepared for a visit to Smith's home at Peterboro. It is obvious that the trip stretched the limits of his trust in and deference to Brown. Indeed, from now on Sanborn would continue to function efficiently for Brown but never with the kind of unflagging confidence and unfailing enthusiasm which had characterized the first year of their relationship.[33]

John Brown did have an important reason for keeping still at Gerrit Smith's home. He wanted to unveil his plan among those who would receive it most favorably, and Smith seemed to accept the basic assumption on which the venture was premised. After a week of discussions with Brown, the Peterboro philanthropist said he no longer doubted the need for slave violence. It was the only way white America would acknowledge black manhood. This position was not solely the result of his intense conversations with Brown. Smith had debated the issue with himself for over sixteen years; Brown's urging merely culminated the next stage of that debate.

As early as 1842, Smith had addressed slaves on how best to change the image white men had of them. They were to cultivate dispositions which were becoming to "poor and afflicted men." They should always display patience, trust, and hope. A few years later, the wealthy landowner advised free blacks to cultivate "self-respect" in order to "peacefully regain" their rights. Although he gave such advice, Smith doubted whether they would ever "exert an influence for the redemp-

32. Sanborn to Higginson, February 11, 1858, Higginson-Brown Collection, Boston Public Library.

33. Brown to Sanborn, February 17, 1858, ibid.; Sanborn, *Life and Letters of John Brown,* p. 436; Sanborn to Higginson, February 11, 1858, Higginson-Brown Collection, Boston Public Library.

tion of their enslaved brethren." By January 1851, some three years after Smith had attempted to found an independent black agricultural community where men could "avoid" those who hated them, the landowner's perspective on the issue of black manhood had shifted. While speaking at a state convention on the Fugitive Slave Law, Smith contended that the days of American slavery would be numbered only "when white America was inspired with respect for the black man." Smith entreated all blacks to be less deferential, to "rise up" and "quit themselves like men" in their political, ecclesiastical, and social relations. Smith said that he no longer accepted a black man's degradation on the grounds that it was "forced." He had "comparatively no concern" for the "degradation" that came from others; rather it was the black man's "self-degradation" that filled him with sorrow. It grieved Smith to know that white men had murdered blacks, but his deepest grief was that black men were "suicides." As is indicated by the tone of these words, Smith had gradually moved to a position that required all black men to actively resist white control. The world was in sad condition until "man as man . . . for his mere manhood shall be held in honor." Then, in January 1856, Smith wrote a letter to Salmon Chase saying that nothing but prejudice sustained slavery. "Not for a moment" could slavery "co-exist with a full sense of his [the black man's] manhood." In the third week of February 1858, as Brown awaited Sanborn's arrival (none of the others were coming), Brown confirmed Smith's idea that only slave violence could truly demonstrate that manhood.[34]

Huddled next to a small desk in Edwin Morton's third-story bedroom at Smith's mansion, John Brown roughly outlined his proposal for Sanborn. The specifics of this February 23 meeting are not fully recorded, although it is certain Brown told the young secretary that he had gathered a small cadre of recruits for a raid on slavery in the South. He planned to "beat up a slave quarter," arm those slaves who

34. Frothingham, *Smith*, pp. 94, 228–30; Harlow, *Smith*, pp. 345–47; Smith to Salmon Chase, January 30, 1856, Smith Collection, Syracuse University Library.

rallied to his banner, attack a federal arsenal in order to get additional weapons (Brown listed a number of federal installations), and then retreat to a mountain fortress in Virginia. The fortress would serve as a station on the underground railroad and as a base from which to launch further strikes at slavery. Brown said his many discussions with free black men had made him confident he could count on a slave response. To demonstrate that his plan had not been hastily conceived, Brown unveiled the provisional constitution he had drawn up at Douglass's home in late January. Throughout the discussion, Brown repeatedly stressed his belief that it was necessary for slaves to fight for their freedom. In so doing, they would break through the debilitating effects of slavery and show their manhood in the only way white men could appreciate.

Sanborn had anticipated a plan of this sort, but he was incredulous as Brown revealed it. The committeeman was amazed that Brown neither expected nor desired a large force to make his strike, and he was again unsettled by the thought of slave insurrection. From Brown's hints in 1857 and the recent "intimations" of Hugh Forbes, it had become obvious that Brown contemplated an "uprising of slaves." Sanborn had known this before he came to Peterboro. He had said as much to Higginson two weeks earlier. But when Brown laid the plan before him, the young secretary's response was confused and uncertain. Brown's careful methods of organization and fortification and his elaborate theory of the way in which the invasion would be received in the country at large failed to stem the committee secretary's fears. Sanborn wasn't sure whether slaves would fight for their freedom and complained of the "manifest hopelessness" of the scheme. Brown met such expressions of doubt with quotations from the Bible and references to his numerous discussions with free black leaders. In the end the young man felt cornered, left only with the alternatives of "betrayal, desertion or support."[35]

After hastily scribbling a note to Higginson in which he said that

---

35. Sanborn to Higginson, February 23, 1858, Boyd B. Stutler Collection; Sanborn, *Recollections*, 1: 143–47.

the minister ought to be in Peterboro because their "friend" was "about
. . . entering into the wool business in which he has been engaged all
his life" and that he had a "plan" which was the "result of many years
of careful study," Sanborn asked to speak privately with Gerrit Smith.
For over an hour, as the sun set on the snow-covered hills surrounding
the Peterboro estate, the two men walked and discussed Brown's plan.
Smith said he understood Sanborn's reservations. He, too, had some
doubts about slave participation and the "slender means" with which
Brown sought to spark the attack. He, too, feared the possibility that
Hugh Forbes would break his silence at any moment and reveal the
scheme. But black manhood could only be shown by the slaves' own
efforts for freedom. Besides, Brown was a noble individual and a truly
religious man. If slaves must rise up and kill their masters, what better
person to lead them? Slowly Smith's words diffused the young secretary's anxiety—but not entirely.[36]

The next day, February 24, Sanborn prepared to leave Peterboro
only "half convinced" that he should support Brown. He would
convey the plan to his Boston associates but could only unveil the
general outlines of the scheme. If Brown wanted to be sure of assistance, he must come to Boston and fill in the details. Brown agreed and
promised to be there during the first week of March. He apologized
for not being able to come sooner but said he had to travel to New
York City for important meetings with black abolitionist James N.
Gloucester and Jermain W. Loguen (the minister with whom Smith
had worked during the Jerry rescue) who had "whole heartedly"
approved his plan.

Although Sanborn had left Peterboro only "half convinced,"
Brown was confident about his aid and that of the other Boston
committeemen. While in the city he wrote a short note to his family

36. Ibid., 1: 155, 138, 143–46; Frothingham, *Smith,* pp. 229–30; Ralph V. Harlow,
"Gerrit Smith and the John Brown Raid," *American Historical Review* 38 (October
1932): 32–37. Sanborn first wrote the note on the back of a piece of paper Brown
had used to sketch in the "rude outlines of Virginia forts." But the secretary scrapped
this when Brown cautioned him about the necessity of developing the plan in
absolute secrecy. Sanborn rewrote his note on a second piece of paper.

which indicates his optimism. Brown stated that in the last few weeks he had had "a constant series of secret discouragement and encouragement" but knew his discussions with Sanborn would bear fruit and that it would be "a very strange thing" if Sanborn "did not join me."[37]

When Frank Sanborn returned to Boston he immediately contacted Howe, Parker, Stearns, and Higginson and informed them of the plan Brown contemplated. He advised them of his own reservations and prepared them for Brown's arrival in the first week of March. As promised, Brown appeared in Boston on March 4 and registered at the American House hotel. That same day all five of his Massachusetts confederates met with him in his room. Before Brown could explain his plan, he was vigorously cross-examined about Hugh Forbes. Why had Forbes made threatening accusations? What had Brown done about the soldier of fortune? What was the nature of their contractual arrangement? Brown calmly addressed their questions. He spoke of John Jr.'s letter to Forbes, told the group why Forbes had been contracted, and gave his interpretation of their agreement. Brown said Forbes had lied when he said he had been promised $100 a month for a year; he had only been promised $600 for six months' service. Forbes had been advanced the whole sum in order to take care of family problems but had vainly squandered the sum publishing his manual of tactics and then demanded to be reimbursed. Brown probably admitted that Forbes knew about the cash Brown was receiving from New England "humanitarians," but he certainly denied that he had ever led the soldier of fortune to believe his salary was contingent on those funds. Brown denied that Forbes knew enough about his plan to jeopardize it, even if he took it upon himself to disclose what he knew. In the end he approached the five men as he had the National Kansas Committee one year earlier. They "knew him" and "knew he could be trusted."[38]

37. Sanborn, *Recollections*, 1: 154–55, 77; Oates, *Brown*, p. 231; Brown to Mary Brown, March 2, 1858, Brown Papers, Kansas State Historical Society.
38. Brown to Higginson, March 4, 1858, Higginson-Brown Collection, Boston Public Library; Sanborn, *Life and Letters of John Brown*, p. 447; Oates, *Brown*, p. 234.

In spite of some uneasiness, his Boston allies agreed to renew their commitment to him. Indeed, they should have; Brown had spent over a year carefully demonstrating that he possessed the character and values each one of them believed essential to produce a stable, ordered, and virtuous society. By now they could hardly reject the image he had so self-consciously displayed and they had so self-consciously demanded. To reject Brown on the basis of his character would have been to reject themselves.

After allaying the anxiety caused by Forbes's letters, Brown discussed his insurrectionary scheme. Again, as at Peterboro, he stressed his belief in the importance of black efforts for freedom. No one could give freedom to anyone. Each man had to take his own. Again, Brown explained his conviction that slaves would fight; black leaders throughout New York, New England, and Canada had assured him of this. Only slave insurrection would prove to southern slaveholders and their northern sympathizers that slaves were not content to remain incarcerated.

Brown certainly revealed significant details of his plan and it seems likely that he spoke of alternative geographical areas into which his select force might strike. He shrugged off assertions that his cadre was too small by saying that the scheme depended on surprise and not numbers. Brown praised the "highly moral" men he had recruited and hinted that he would obtain the services of Canadian blacks. He boasted of the rigorous training his men had undergone in preparation for their "dash" south and displayed the constitution he had drawn up to govern his mountain-fortress community. He concluded his remarks by suggesting that if the proposed insurrection lasted only one day, the whole country from the Potomac to Savannah would be "ablaze."[39]

As Sanborn had so aptly commented, the Boston confederates all felt they were faced with the question of "betrayal, desertion or support." Although they had doubts, Brown had to be assisted. And, no doubt, they realized they would have a noble martyr to abolition if the escapade failed. Brown would be a positive human symbol of the

39. Ibid.

antislavery movement in the same way Commissioner Edward Loring had served as a negative symbol after the Burns episode.

By the time Brown had finished presenting the plan on March 8, four days after his arrival, the five Massachusetts abolitionists hesitantly decided to join with Gerrit Smith to raise funds for him. They formed the Secret Committee of Six, made Stearns chairman, Sanborn secretary, and began collecting $1,000 for Brown's "business operations." The five from Massachusetts were to raise at least $100 apiece and more if they could. Brown would be sure of at least $500 and $1,000 "in all probability." While Dr. George Cabot and Thomas R. Russell were given hints of the "speculation," the committeemen resolved that no other member of the abolitionist community should be "admitted to a share of the business." Brown himself continually cautioned them about secrecy and, during the meetings, vetoed Sanborn's suggestion that Wendell Phillips be brought into the "operation." According to Brown, Phillips was not a "man of action" and, therefore, should not have knowledge of the venture.[40]

Between March 8 and March 17, Sanborn pressed his colleagues to raise the money they had pledged. On March 18 he called a meeting of the group at Howe's home to coordinate their labors. At this meeting Stearns was made treasurer and took control of approximately $150 which had already been raised. It was decided that since Sanborn and Higginson were less able to raise money than the others, they should be limited to a $100 contribution. Stearns, Howe, and Parker should raise that sum and more if possible. Stearns promised to raise an additional $200. Parker also claimed he "would do more," and Howe hoped to raise at least $50 beyond the required sum. Sanborn was pleased with his fellow committeemen. Sometime after the meeting, he wrote to Brown and advised him that the enterprise still looked "hopeful" to "speculative people." By April 1, $375 of the minimum pledge had been raised.[41]

40. Ibid.; Villard, *Brown*, pp. 324–25; Sanborn to Higginson, March 8, 1858, Higginson-Brown Collection, Boston Public Library.

41. Sanborn to Higginson, March 14, 1858, Sanborn Collection, Concord Free Public Library; Sanborn to Higginson, March 21, 1858, Higginson-Brown Collec-

Despite their formation of a secret committee to assist Brown and their collection of funds to finance the raid, the Boston members of the group felt much like Sanborn had when he first heard the plan at Peterboro. They remained only "half convinced" that they should support the scheme. Only gradually, in the weeks following Brown's revelations, were their doubts abated by Higginson's and Parker's theorizations. At the moment, there were good reasons for their apprehension. All of them wondered about the venture's chances of success, given the slender means Brown sought. The plan seemed well conceived and organized, but a number of unanswered questions still remained. Brown never did say how many men could be counted on to join him in the initial foray. At Smith's, Brown had "casually" asked Sanborn what he thought of a strike on the federal arsenal in Harpers Ferry, but at Peterboro, and again in Boston, Harpers Ferry was only mentioned as one of a number of places where the raid could be started. When Brown left Boston, the group still had no idea which place he favored. Brown said he expected Canadian and free, northern blacks to join him in his Virginia mountain fortress; yet he never said whether leaders of the black community were recruiting volunteers or whether he was depending on a spontaneous reaction like the one he expected from southern slaves. Sanborn's euphemistic communication with Brown and other members of the secret committee (the secretary always referred to the raid as a "business operation," "speculation," or the "wool business") was at first prompted as much by the demands of secrecy as by a lack of precise information and specific detail.[42]

Then, too, despite the fact that each of these man trusted Brown,

tion, Boston Public Library; Villard, *Brown,* p. 326; Stearns to Higginson, April 1, 1858, Higginson-Brown Collection, Boston Public Library.

42. Sanborn, *Recollections,* 1: 151. Sanborn's assertion that after Brown revealed his plan in March 1858, he gave "no impression" that he meant to begin at Harpers Ferry is probably true. So, too, is the secretary's contention that throughout 1858 the "place" of the attack was never made known to Boston members of the Secret Six. But his suggestion that Brown "never" revealed the location to anyone but Smith and Douglass is certainly not true. Well before the attack in October 1859, Sanborn, Stearns, Higginson, and, most likely, Howe knew of its location.

all of them were forced to confront personal convictions which struck at the heart of Brown's plan and raised strong doubts about its chance for success. All of the committee members (excluding Higginson) had ambivalent feelings about financing a violent, offensive thrust at slavery. Their Kansas aid had always been for defense against the Missouri "ruffians." Now Brown wanted to incite an insurrection. Everyone except Higginson had been relieved by the successful political solution to the Kansas struggle; now they were being asked to finally and firmly reject a political settlement on the question of slavery. In effect, each member of the committee was being asked to incite a Faneuil Hall crowd and send it storming into Court Square. And each of the members faced that request with the same doubts that Parker and Howe had encountered four years earlier.

In addition to Brown's unanswered questions and their own ambivalence about using violence as an offensive weapon against slavery, all of the committee members (including Higginson) had uncertainties about the central premise on which Brown's insurrectionary thrust rested: the willingness of slaves to fight for their freedom. All of the conspirators held a romantic racialist image of the slave's nature and did not believe he was capable of fighting his white oppressors. As recently as January, in a speech called the "Present Aspect of Slavery," Theodore Parker had perfectly explicated their racial sentiment. Indeed, Parker fully accepted the racial stereotype adhered to by the defenders of slavery, though he claimed that far from marking the black race for slavery, such traits indicated that the black man had achieved an advanced form of Christian piety and should, therefore, be a free member of society. Parker spoke almost reverently of the African as the "most docile and pliant" of all races of man. He applauded the fact that the black man had "little ferocity" and that vengeance, which was "instantial" with the Anglo-Saxon (as well as being the ultimate source of his freedom), was "exceptional" in African history. In their "barbarous state" Africans had never been "addicted" to revenge and were "always prone to mercy." The black man was strong in the "affectional instinct," was "easy" and "indolent." Unlike his Anglo-Saxon brothers who owed their freedom to their ability to fight for it, the African was "little warlike."[43]

Brown was asking far more than money from members of the committee. He sought their trust without fully revealing his plan; he asked them to overcome their apprehension about using violence, and, just as important, he asked them to accept views of black capabilities that did not square with their own conceptions of the African's nature. It is no wonder that in the first days after Brown left Boston, the committee members remained only "half convinced" about supporting the "dash." As Parker noted sometime later, they simply weren't sure that Brown's scheme was the "right way" of getting at slavery.[44]

Clearly, Parker's personal debate about the rectitude of Brown's plan was the most profound. This is revealed by the minister's reaction to a request Brown made of him before leaving Boston. Brown asked Parker to write two addresses for his use during the invasion. One was to be sent to the "officers and Soldiers of the United States army on the Duty of a Soldier." In it, Brown wanted Parker to "powerfully assert" the conviction that a soldier's duty (if he understood what was morally right) "was to desert the army and join up with Ossawatomie Brown." The second address was to be used by Brown to inspire his insurrectionary forces. But his stipulations for it also show the method Brown used in trying to cultivate the confidence of his Boston allies. The second speech must be short so as to be read easily and must be written in the "simplest and plainest language." The address must not have the "least affection of a scholar" about it and should be constructed with "great clearness and power." The whole tone of the speech (like Brown's tone with his conspiratorial associates) must demonstrate that he was " 'after other' and not 'after himself, at all, at all.' " Furthermore, Parker should bear in mind that "women were susceptible of being carried away by the kindness of an intrepid and

43. Theodore Parker, "The Present Aspect of Slavery and the Immediate Duty of the North" [a speech given on January 29, 1858], in *Works* (Cobbe edition), 6: 289. Refer to Chapters 5 and 6 in Fredrickson's *Black Image* which deal with romantic racialism.

44. Parker to Francis Jackson, March 15, 1860, Parker, *Letterbooks,* Massachusetts Historical Society.

magnanimous soldier even when his brave name was but a terror the day before."[45]

Parker refused Brown's request. Instead, he sent Brown a copy of General McClellan's "Report on the Armies of Europe." The refusal indicates Parker's initial skepticism about Brown's plan. The minister, like the rest of his colleagues (except Higginson), had begun to collect funds for Brown but had not resolved his qualms about bankrolling slave violence. His trust in Brown's character and values carried him a long way, but his doubt about the use of force and the potential for a slave response prevented his unreserved commitment to the project. Yes, he would raise funds for an attack he wasn't sure would take place, but he would not write speeches that were premised on the fact that such an insurrectionary thrust had been made. Subsidizing theory was one thing, writing speeches for reality quite another.[46]

Although Parker's tentative early attachment to Brown rested on a faith in the man's character, as weeks passed he gave his most serious attention to Brown's thoughts about the slaves' willingness to fight. Slowly Parker's theoretical commitment quickened, and slowly he dispelled his anxiety about the slaves' capacity to exhibit "vengeful emotions." Perhaps Brown was correct. Perhaps it was necessary (and possible) that slaves fight for their freedom. Brown's assertions forced Parker to reflect upon numerous instances of black valor in the Boston area and prompted him to make inquiries of William C. Nell and William Wells Brown, two moderate black abolitionists from Boston who had recently been engaged in research on the question of both free black and slave military exploits.[47]

45. Commager, *Parker*, p. 253; Parker, *Correspondence*, 1: 164–65.
46. Commager, *Parker*, p. 253.
47. Parker, *Correspondence*, 1: 152–53, 234–35 (hereafter to be cited as Parker, *Works* [Weiss edition]). In early February 1856, Parker had been considerably impressed by the courage and iniative of Anthony Burns. After spending two years in slavery following rendition, Burns's freedom had been purchased by leading abolitionists in Massachusetts. When Burns returned to Boston to express his gratitude, he spoke of his future plans. The ex-slave claimed that he eventually wanted to work in the South as a minister to help his people out of bondage and he speculated that it might take a "general uprising" of slaves to overthrow the institution (*National Anti-Slavery*

Parker had known William C. Nell for a number of years and respected his abolitionist activities and opinions. Indeed, Nell's work in the movement predated Parker's own involvement by ten years. Nell had been born in Boston, the son of a tailor who fled Charleston, South Carolina, during the War of 1812 and who provided an activist model for his son by helping found a black protective association. Nell graduated with honors from the all-black Smith Grammar School, and his experience there, particularly his exclusion from citywide ceremonies honoring outstanding scholars, caused him to lead the successful struggle by Boston blacks in the 1840s to overturn public school segregation. Nell's staunch integrationist sentiments, his friendship with William Lloyd Garrison and Frederick Douglass (Nell served as Douglass's assistant editor on the *North Star* during the early 1850s), and his extensive literary and historical studies attracted Parker, forever a writer and researcher himself. Undoubtedly Nell and Parker's early conversations had covered an array of topics both abolitionist and nonabolitionist, but after the passage of the Fugitive Slave Law, Parker must have noticed an increasing urgency in Nell's abolitionist speculations as well as a shifting in his antislavery posture.[48]

Originally a Garrisonian in the sense that he believed strongly in the tactics of moral suasion and nonresistance, Nell's outlook turned partially political after 1850. He joined the Boston Vigilance Commit-

---

Standard, March 10, 1856). If Burns's words stimulated even the briefest memories of past fugitive slave rescues in Boston, Parker would have realized that for all the Boston Vigilance Committee efforts, only the Lewis Hayden-led attempt by black Bostonians to free the fugitive Shadrach in 1852 had been successful. Howard Bell, "Expressions of Negro Militancy," *Journal of Negro History* 45 (January 1960): 11–20; Herbert Aptheker, "Militant Abolitionism," *Journal of Negro History* 26 (October 1941): 438–84; George August Levesque, "Black Boston: Negro Life in Garrison's Boston, 1800–1860," (Ph.D. diss., State University of New York at Binghamton, 1976). Levesque's work on Boston is outstanding. In it he carefully chronicles Nell's career in abolitionism and his growing commitment to black solidarity in the 1850s. Levesque also discusses black Boston's increasing willingness to see a violent solution to slavery during the late 1850s. This work is soon to be published.

48. Robert P. Smith, "William Cooper Nell: Crusading Black Abolitionist," *Journal of Negro History* 55 (July 1970): 185–99.

tee and ran for a place in the Massachusetts legislature on the Free Soil Party ticket. In the mid-1850s Nell's position as an integrationist also shifted slightly. Throughout his early years in the movement, Nell had stood firmly by the ideal of integration. Though he had attended all-black conventions, he often reminded his fellow black abolitionists of the need for cooperative black and white efforts. On occasion his strict adherence to this principle caused friction with some of his black friends. Then, in the wake of the Dred Scott decision, as he bitterly watched black citizenship wiped away by the Supreme Court, Nell became increasingly persuaded about the need for black solidarity. By the time Parker sought his counsel in 1858, Nell was engaged in the planning stage of a black citizens' convention to be held in Boston during August 1859.[49]

In the course of redirecting his abolitionist position, Nell researched the contributions of black soldiers during the wars of 1776 and 1812. It was this research that Parker specifically wanted to talk about. Nell had published *Services of Colored Americans in the Wars of 1776 and 1812* in 1852 and *Colored Patriots of the American Revolution* in 1855. Both works sought to "stem the tide of prejudice against the Colored race" by showing that "in days of our country's weakness [when black men had] . . . power to help or harm," they had served. Claiming his predilections were *"least and last* for what constitutes War," Nell went on to chronicle the courage and physical valor of blacks during wartime, citing incidents in each state which showed that blacks had proved "loyal and ready to worship *or die,* if need be at Freedom's shrine." He concluded, however, that the white man's banquet had been held and "the colored American's share had been to stand outside and wait for crumbs to fall from Freedom's festive board." After his conversation with Nell, Parker clearly understood the implications of Nell's thought and writing: Slaves and free blacks might not wait much longer for "crumbs." Nell may have advised Parker to continue their discussion with William Wells Brown, whose work on the slave revolts in Santo Domingo had been published in 1854 and who had

49. Ibid.

begun an extensive investigation into black American history.[50]

Whether at Nell's suggestion or on his own, Parker did contact Brown. William Wells Brown was born a slave in Lexington, Kentucky, but in 1834 at the age of twenty he escaped slavery and fled to Cleveland, Ohio. By the early 1840s he had moved to Buffalo, had refined his ability to read and write, and had begun to work in the antislavery movement. In 1843 when Buffalo hosted the National Convention of Colored Citizens, Brown joined Charles Lenox Remond and Frederick Douglass in condemning Henry Highland Garnet's call for slave insurrection. When Douglass went to England, Brown replaced him as a lecture agent for the American Antislavery Society and then traveled to England himself late in 1849. Passage of the Fugitive Slave Law forced Brown to remain in England for the next four years, where he lectured, wrote *Clotel,* the first novel by a black American, and moved away from the belief in nonresistance he held at the time of Garnet's appeal in 1843.[51]

Brown touched on the topic of insurrection in an indecisive way at a lecture during his first year in England when he talked about the plight of fugitive slaves and indicated that he had heard reports of a meeting where fugitives vowed to die rather than go back into slavery. He went on to say that slaves were already arming themselves and "if they were strong enough, he wasn't adverse to them protecting themselves, [although] he would not . . . encourage them to rise." On the other hand, "if he were to hear of a successful insurrection he would thank God for it."[52]

50. William C. Nell, *Services of Colored Americans in the Wars of 1776 and 1812* (Boston, 1852), pp. 4, 6, 37; William C. Nell, *Colored Patriots of the American Revolution* (Boston, 1855).

51. William Edward Farrison, "A Flight Across Ohio: The Escape of William Wells Brown from Slavery," *Ohio State Historical Quarterly* 11 (July 1952): 273–83; William Edward Farrison, "William Wells Brown in Buffalo," *Journal of Negro History* 50 (October 1954): 299–314; William Edward Farrison, "William Wells Brown, Social Reformer," *Journal of Negro Education* 5 (December–March 1949): 29–39; William Wells Brown, *Narrative of William Wells Brown, A Fugitive Slave* (Boston, 1848).

52. *Liberator,* October 19, 1849.

As time went on and his stay in England lengthened, Brown concluded that slave violence was essential to dismantle slavery. He talked about the need to use "new instrumentalities" in the fight for the slaves' freedom. By 1853, after spending two years writing and researching, he reflected on the historical lessons which could be learned from men's willingness to fight for freedom. He was fascinated with Toussaint L'Ouverture and the slaves' struggle for freedom in Santo Domingo. Shortly before leaving England, during May 1854, he gave a lecture about Toussaint at the Metropolitan Athanaeum in Manchester. On his return to Boston he published it as *St. Domingo: Its Revolution and Its Patriots*. With this publication, his thinking about insurrection came full circle, and he used the work to outline his position. Brown warned southern slaveholders that the time was short in which blacks would continue to bear the burden of slavery and that "slaveholders in our Southern States [should] tremble when they shall call to mind these events [the willingness of St. Domingo slaves to shed blood for their freedom]." In Brown's view, "American slaves were only waiting the opportunity of wiping out their wrongs with the blood of their oppressors." Like Nell, it was Brown's opinion that "the spirit that caused the blacks to take up arms, and to shed their blood in the American revolutionary war is still amongst the slaves of the South; and if we are not mistaken, the day is not far distant when the revolution of St. Domingo will be reenacted in South Carolina and Louisiana."[53]

Nell's and Brown's words had a powerful effect on Parker. Unlike the claims of Henry Highland Garnet, Jermain W. Loguen, Martin R. Delany, and other black abolitionists who had advocated the use of political violence, Parker considered the opinions of Nell and Brown to be reflective ones. They had evolved over a period of time and were based on careful investigation and analysis. They were radical opinions offered by two men who ordinarily held

53. Ibid., January 24, 1851; *Bristol Gazette,* April 18, 1850; William Wells Brown, *Santo Domingo: Its Revolution and Its Patriots* (Boston, 1855), pp. 25, 32.

moderate views. Parker could not dismiss them. When he coupled these views to what John Brown said about the slave's willingness to fight for his own freedom, they helped stimulate some new thoughts about antislavery reform. In early April 1858, Parker asserted that it was time for a reassessment of white "outdoor charity." Parker was convinced that seventy percent of these charitable activities had only a "reflex good action." That is, only thirty percent of white charitable activity actually helped the intended "receiver." Most of the time it was the "giver" who benefited by gaining a sense of his own "righteousness." Parker believed it was important to reverse these percentages and that the best way to do this (as John Brown intended) was to enable people to help themselves. Parker's reflections about "outdoor charity" and conversations with William C. Nell and William Wells Brown say much about his growing desire to support Brown's "dash." Brown's claims had forced Parker to reevaluate the effects of white reform. He now conceded that such efforts were "mainly bad" and did "more harm than good." The Unitarian minister also formulated a new law. He hypothesized that "charitable demand" was often "equivalent to the organization to meet that demand." When organized "dependence" became "institutionalized," both giving and receiving were simultaneously bureaucratized. In the name of perfecting society, reformers might be inadvertently thwarting the one thing that could bring about such perfection: the individual's own effort for it.

If Parker dared carry his new theories to their logical extreme (and the minister seems to have done just that), he must have looked with suspicion on abolition's highly organized and institutionalized structure. Maybe abolitionists weren't helping slaves. Perhaps their actions only provided antislavery advocates with a sense of their own "righteousness." Perhaps Brown was correct when he said that only slave self-help could be effective. Parker's slowly developing enthusiasm for a plan he once listened to with reservation is linked to this reasoning. Parker's thinking counterbalanced Brown's lack of specific detail about the venture, his own ambivalent attitude about political violence, and his own romantic racialist prejudice.[54]

There was another reason why Parker gradually embraced Brown's plan. A "revival of religion" was taking place in Massachusetts and throughout the country that spring, but the radical Unitarian minister was not at all pleased. He believed it was a "false revival," especially when ministers in the Boston area attributed it to prayer. To Parker it wasn't prayer that brought religious reawakening but "effectual fervent work" for the right, the "head-work" and "hand-work" of "a righteous man." Simply gossiping before bedtime, "tattling mere words" and then asking God to do one's own duty, was not true religious revival. Uncertain as Parker may have been about Brown's plan, the minister could not overlook the fact that in "Ossawatomie Brown" religion had an "effectual" and "fervent" worker. Brown wanted action not mere words. He not only spoke for the right, but demanded that slaves cease praying for salvation and start striking for it with their own hands. In addition, Parker viewed Brown as more than a righteous man. In his own way, the man from North Elba was an intensely dedicated and emotional minister of the Gospel, and Parker had always contended that it was a minister's duty "to awaken, strengthen and quicken the religious power" of men. It was the minister's duty to "diffuse ideas" which "molded society" so that it could develop well under the direction of men of great "natural powers." Wasn't this precisely what Brown sought to accomplish by insurrection? Brown wanted to change white views of the slave and thereby remold white attitudes toward the institution of slavery. At the same time, he was asking slaves to assert their manhood. Could there be a more competent "minister" to "diffuse" the proper ideas and values to both black and white society? Weren't Brown's values precisely those which Parker and his colleagues hoped to impart to their fellow Americans?

54. Parker to Frank E. Parker, April 15, 1858, Parker Letters, Harvard-Andover Theological Library.

Hadn't Howe and Higginson felt there was something much more "real" about Kansas settlers in their warlike surroundings than about the rest of the "diseased" American society? Wasn't Brown a real American who embodied the ideals of Bunker Hill? Couldn't Brown bring the proper values to black men—maybe even impart the "vengeful" emotions so essential for freedom?[55]

Parker's thoughts calmed the fears of the "half convinced" Sanborn and his Kansas committee sponsor, George Luther Stearns. Each of these men shared Parker's concern about political violence and his doubts about slave capabilities. In addition, they still wondered if they had heard the last from Hugh Forbes, worried if the convulsion Brown sought to induce could be controlled, and pondered their responsibility if Brown was caught. In the face of these doubts, Parker's speculations were reassuring.

Samuel Gridley Howe was particularly influenced by his good friend Parker. Parker's views echoed his own theory of diffusion. When he thought about it, Howe realized that he and Stearns had made a similar case for self-help in their discussions about the handicapped. If it was important for the handicapped to be exposed to "normal" people, wasn't it just as important for slaves handicapped by a debilitating institution to have that opportunity? Could slaves be exposed to a better man than Brown? Howe may also have remembered a four-year-old image as he debated about his commitment; he may have heard again the shouts of a young, black woman as she watched Anthony Burns being taken back to slavery. He should "kill himself," she cried as Burns walked by, "kill himself" rather than be taken back into slavery. At that time Howe had realized that this ultimate gesture of self-sacrifice was really the only thing which would disabuse white America of the idea that blacks were suited for slavery. Perhaps Brown was correct; perhaps a fight to the death for freedom was the only way to demonstrate black

55. Parker, *Works* (Weiss edition), 6: 252; *Boston Daily Bee*, March 17, 1858; Parker to Sarah Hart, March 23, 1858, Parker Letters, Harvard-Andover Theological Library.

manhood. Wasn't the willingness to fight to the death for freedom the central racial trait of the Anglo-Saxon? Didn't the black man have to adopt the trait in order to earn his right to freedom and show his ability to live in it?

It is possible that Parker's thoughts may also have caused Howe some guilt. His own trip to Kansas had been an attempt to do more for the "giver" than the "receiver." The excursion had been as much a way of resolving personal questions about his character as it had been a journey to assist Kansas settlers. It had been a "last chance" to test the purity of his motives, to overcome his fear of danger, and to recapture a romanticized past. In the end, the trip had only served to compound the uncertainty he felt about his character, and he realized that if slavery was to be actively resisted, it would have to be done by someone other than himself. At the moment, he had the chance not only to subsidize someone else's effort but, in a somewhat less extravagant way, to recapture a sense of his own self-worth. All Brown asked was a chance to act. Howe and his committee associates were growing more confident each day.

While the Boston allies collected money to pay for Brown's "dash" at slavery, gradually dispelled their apprehensions about the advisability of the scheme, and built a fragile rationale for their support, Brown went to Philadelphia with John Jr. for discussions with free blacks. His conversations with Rev. Stephen Smith, William Still, and the militant minister Henry Highland Garnet reaffirmed his convictions about the desire of northern blacks to assist their slave brethren. Brown left Philadelphia full of confidence, traveled to North Elba where he recruited the services of his sons Henry, Watson, and Oliver, then quickly moved on to Syracuse. There, he again visited Jermain W. Loguen, who suggested that he seek the assistance of famed underground railroader Harriet Tubman. Brown sought the black woman out in St. Catherines, Canada West, but she made no commitments to his venture, although she said he might obtain aid from Martin R. Delany, the black nationalist who was living in Chatham, Canada West. Indeed, Delany was helpful. He agreed to set up a convention in early May where Brown could outline his plan to radical abolitionists residing in Ontario and recruit interested parties. After a trip to Springdale, Iowa, to advise his Kansas volunteers about the state of his plans, Brown returned to Chatham on May 8 and prepared for the convention. Everything seemed to be proceeding smoothly. Brown had the financial backing of the Secret Six, the approval and support of militant black leaders, and an opportunity to recruit more men for his raid at Chatham.[56]

56. Schwartz, *Howe,* pp. 221–23; Howe, *Journals,* p. 241; Oates, *Brown,* pp. 241–43; Villard, *Brown,* pp. 315–16, 328–30; Brown to John Brown, Jr., April 8, 1858, Boyd B. Stutler Collection.

CHAPTER 6

The Hugh Forbes Postponement

As JOHN BROWN PREPARED for the Chatham meeting, further letters from Hugh Forbes shattered the confidence of the Secret Six and forced postponement of the raid. Once again Forbes lashed out at the New England "humanitarians" ("especially" Sanborn) for their negligent treatment of him, and this time he made it clear that he would not allow Brown's "speculation" to continue. The letters Forbes wrote to Howe and Sanborn did not indicate that the soldier knew of the secret committee, but did imply that he had greater knowledge of the scheme than Brown had led the group to believe during the March meetings. Sanborn had wanted to attend the Chatham convention and bring Brown $600 dollars, but in the wake of the Forbes ultimatum, there was no chance of his traveling to Canada. The committee had to act swiftly to prevent Forbes from "giving statistics" and "quoting prices" to newspapers while they were trying to "start a march on buyers and sellers."[1]

And act they did. On May 5, Sanborn, Stearns, Parker, and Howe met to consider their proper course. A careful reexamination of the contents of Forbes's letters indicated that the soldier knew some details of the plan and knew that Stearns, Howe, and Sanborn had been informed about it. Parker and Stearns were quick to react: They decided the plan had to be "deferred." Sanborn claimed to be "in doubt" though "inclining to their opinion." Only Howe balked. He

1. Sanborn to Higginson, April 20, May 1, 1858, Higginson-Brown Collection, Boston Public Library.

wasn't sure a postponement was called for but could not persuade his fellow conspirators to change their view and, ultimately, accepted their decision. It was decided that Stearns should go to Chatham and speak to Brown. In the meantime, Sanborn would write to Gerrit Smith telling him of the situation and ask his assistance in explaining the secret committee's action to Brown. The Boston members also wanted Smith to go to Chatham to discuss Forbes's threats and to reevaluate the project.[2]

Two days after the meeting, Sanborn received another letter from Forbes in which the soldier of fortune said that he would stop at nothing to destroy Brown's plan. After reading the letter, Sanborn no longer "inclined" to postponement, but clung to it in panic-stricken desperation. The committee secretary immediately wrote to Higginson saying that Forbes had "exact knowledge" of the secret project, that there was "a leak" somewhere in the secret committee's boat, and that, since everything was so "uncertain," the plan was best terminated for the present. Before they did anything, the secret committee must "get rid" of Forbes because he had a "grudge" against all of them. In addition, Sanborn openly questioned Brown's competence. After asking Higginson to make discreet inquiries about Forbes and requesting the minister to go to Canada and discuss matters with Brown (Stearns now claimed he was unable to do it), Sanborn flared angrily at his erstwhile warrior-patron. The secretary told Higginson that he realized news of postponement would be "hard" for his "old friend" but suggested that the delay was entirely Brown's fault. Brown's "too great confidence in Forbes" had forced this decision "upon the speculators." Sanborn had been a bit upset by Brown's imperiousness during the North Elba subscription effort, had occasionally been disappointed when he did not receive news of Brown's whereabouts, and had been annoyed by the abusive letters Forbes wrote in January, but he had never been tempted to quit Brown's side. Now, just as Parker's speculations had nourished his own and the others' belief in the advisability of the scheme, Forbes's behavior created serious concern in the young

2. Sanborn to Higginson, May 5, 1858, ibid.; Sanborn, *Recollections,* 1: 156.

committeeman about the wisdom of ever having supported "Ossawatomie Brown."[3]

Thomas Wentworth Higginson agreed with Howe's initial assessment and would not be stampeded into postponement. Higginson was irate when Sanborn notified him about deferral. He was determined not to go to Canada to appease Brown. He rejected the committee's decision and he wrote to Brown saying that he was absolutely against postponement. If the plan was postponed, it was "postponed forever." After all, couldn't Hugh Forbes "do as much harm this year as next?" Higginson believed everything had gone "too far"; hesitating at this moment meant "certain failure." When Theodore Parker tried to placate his protégé by suggesting that if Higginson knew the extent of "Forbes' knowledge," he would "not counsel" continuation, the Worchester activist refused to listen.[4]

Parker also had to persuade Howe that the May 5 decision was correct. Howe certainly knew the extent of Forbes's threats, since he had received one of the soldier's letters. Initially the physician had flown into a "tempestuous rage" over the matter. He had been particularly angered by Forbes's oblique effort to inform Henry Wilson, Charles Sumner, and William Seward of the conspirators' plans "to overthrow slavery." But Howe had not panicked like his colleagues and still desired to continue the project after Stearns, Parker, and Sanborn settled on deferral. Instead of abandoning Brown, Howe thought it would be possible to confuse and divert Forbes. He fired off a "blistering" note to the soldier of fortune labeling his accusations "utter fallacy." Howe said it was "absurd" for Forbes to infer that the committee's (Massachusetts Kansas) relationship with Brown invested them with "any responsibility for his acts." As far as the doctor knew, there was no legal or moral contractual arrangement between the two soldiers. And if Brown had entered into an agreement, the committee had "never delegated power to anyone to bind it by legal and moral

3. Sanborn to Higginson, May 7, 1858, Higginson–Brown Collection, Boston Public Library.

4. Higginson to Brown, May 7, 1858, ibid.; Higginson, *Journals,* p. 191; Parker to Higginson, May 7, 1858, Higginson–Brown Collection, Boston Public Library.

obligation." Howe sought to "dissolve" Forbes of any "lingering notion" that he or any members of the "late committee" had "any responsibility for Captain Brown's actions." Howe falsely suggested that in the "last communication" sent to Brown, the committee had urged him to go "at once" to Kansas and assist in the coming elections. In his letter Howe also tried to keep Forbes from any further meetings with Charles Sumner, who was still suffering from his beating on the Senate floor two years earlier. Howe told Forbes that he had personally notified Sumner of Brown's "integrity" and "ability" and indicated that any future attempt by Forbes to convince Sumner that his Boston friends were negligent would be wasted.[5]

A few days after Howe wrote Forbes, he also tried to "dissolve" the suspicions of Henry Wilson. Forbes had approached the junior senator from Massachusetts with vague references to Brown's plan and unclear accusations about possible misuse of Massachusetts Kansas Committee funds. Wilson was shocked and immediately contacted Howe seeking to determine the truth about the soldier's statements. Wilson was afraid that if Forbes's revelations were accurate and were made public, they would jeopardize the Republican Party's election chances in the fall. Wilson demanded to know what was going on in Massachusetts. Howe was quick to reply. He assured Wilson that the Massachusetts Kansas Committee had given "no countenance" to Brown for "any operations outside of Kansas." Measures had been taken "to prevent any such monstrous perversion of a kind as would be the application of means raised for the defense of Kansas to a purpose which the subscribers to this fund would disapprove and vehemently condemn." Technically, Howe was being "truthful" with Wilson. Forbes did not realize that Brown's support had been taken over from the Kansas Committee by

5. Schwartz, *Howe,* pp. 228–29; Howe to Hugh Forbes, May 10, 1858, Howe Collection, Massachusetts Historical Society. Forbes had first contacted Sumner in December 1857 in order to obtain the names of Massachusetts Kansas committeemen who were supporting Brown. Apparently Forbes didn't tell Sumner why he actually wanted the information. It was on the basis of the information he received from Sumner, however, that the soldier eventually wrote his "abusive letters" to Howe and Sanborn in January 1858.

the Secret Committee of Six. Also, in the days immediately following the May 5 conference, possession of the guns originally donated to Brown by the Massachusetts Kansas Committee and later reconfirmed in his possession by the Secret Six had been transferred back to George Luther Stearns who had paid for them in the first place. Bureaucratic subterfuge allowed Howe to tell Wilson "truthfully" that the Massachusetts Kansas Committee had not "countenanced" the plans Forbes alluded to in his statements.[6]

While Howe diverted Forbes and Wilson, Sanborn again tried to bring Higginson into line with the view of the other secret committee members. He notified Higginson that Gerrit Smith agreed that postponement was the wisest policy. The secretary said that he could not "quite yield" to Higginson's arguments because Forbes had it "in his power" to remove "the terror" of Brown's proposed insurrectionary thrust. Wasn't the element of surprise the most essential feature in the plan Brown outlined during March? There was no question in Sanborn's mind about deferral and the need to put Forbes "off the track." Near the end of his letter to Higginson, Sanborn further rationalized his attitude by explaining that, even if he agreed with Higginson, nothing could be done to change the May 5 decision because the largest "stockholders" in the venture (Stearns, Smith, and Parker) were adamantly opposed to any movement by Brown and would not raise money to support him. Because there was "little the rest of us can do . . . in that way," Sanborn claimed he must abide by the decision.[7]

Higginson was cynically amused by the timorousness of his fellow conspirators and particularly angered by Sanborn's new found obsequiousness. As secretary of the Massachusetts Kansas Committee, Sanborn had never hesitated to wield the authority of his office in Brown's

6. Howe to Henry Wilson, May 12, 1856, in *Mason Report,* p. 216; Howe to Henry Wilson, May 15, 1856, Howe Collection, Massachusetts Historical Society; Sanborn to Higginson, Letter No. 674, Higginson Collection, Houghton Library; Schwartz, *Howe,* p. 230.

7. Sanborn to Higginson, May 11, 1858, Higginson-Brown Collection, Boston Public Library.

behalf. Whether he was badgering Higginson for Worcester funds or soliciting Stearns's generosity during the North Elba subscription drive, Sanborn had frequently been aggressive and calculating, not often cowed by his own lack of financial resources. But in the face of possible exposure by Forbes, he had become uncharacteristically sub-missive to the major "stockholders." As Higginson reread Sanborn's letter, he was struck by the secretary's use of the word *terror*. For an individual who, along with the other secret committee members, had steadfastly avoided personal contact with it, terror was an unknown commodity, a mere abstraction justified by another abstraction known as Higher Law. Higginson believed that, for Sanborn and the others, political violence was a topic to be discussed in lecture rooms, the gracious confines of the Bird Club, or in front of an abolitionist gathering. They only threatened slaveholders with insurrection or used the promise of forcible means as a rhetorical device to arouse public opinion. As far as Higginson was concerned, Sanborn, Parker, Stearns, Smith, and Howe would never confront the reality of force and never take responsibility for subsidizing it. Higginson suspected that some-thing more than Forbes's disclosures held his colleagues back; a greater fear gripped these men than concern about exposure. Although they had committed themselves to Brown early that spring, they all were ambivalent about the use of violent means and continued to look for a reason not to follow through with their support. Forbes's revelations provided them with the perfect opportunity to swap abstractions. They traded the principle of justifiable violence for that of self-interest, thereby relieving their own doubts and fears. Higginson was furious.

George Luther Stearns also worked to order the chaos unleashed by Forbes. He warned Brown to hold on to the rifles and sidearms he had been given, pending further directions from the committee. In a few days a member of the secret group would arrive at Chatham to discuss the "best mode" of "disposing" of the weapons.[8]

The letters Brown received from the Boston conspirators telling of

---

8. Stearns to Brown, May 14, 1858, *Mason Report*, p. 227.

Forbes's behavior and postponing the raid capped an already disappointing convention. Harriet Tubman had failed to appear, fewer men
than Brown expected had showed up to discuss the plan, and some who
had come expressed the opinion that he would be "disappointed in the
slaves because they did not know sufficient to rally to his support." By
the end of the Chatham meeting, he had not recruited anyone to join
him, was stranded in Canada without money to pay his hotel bill, and
seemed to have lost all credibility with a majority of the secret committee's membership. Like so many other times when his ventures were
on the brink of failure, Brown turned to his eldest son, John Jr., and
asked if he could shed "light on the subject." Brown knew he had to
act quickly. He must regain control of the situation or face the possibility of complete loss of support by the Secret Committee of Six.[9]

Calming himself, Brown took the first step toward reclaiming the
confidence of his "stockholders" by writing to the one man who stood
most firmly against postponement, Thomas Wentworth Higginson.
The letter Brown wrote at this critical juncture in the conspiracy is
an important one. It tells as much about the image he sought to
promote as does his letter to young Henry Stearns. Brown made no
appeals to the justice of his cause, no allusions to his providential
instrumentality, no use of biblical quotation or inflated antislavery
rhetoric. Rather, he labored to reestablish himself as a pragmatic,
self-controlled, and calculating "leader of men." He told Higginson
that it was "invariable" with him to be "governed by circumstances."
He would "not do anything" while he did "not know what to do."
None of his Boston friends "need have any fears" about "hasty or rash
steps being taken." Only "knowledge" was "power." Brown assured
Higginson that arrangements had been made to quiet Forbes, asked for
funds to pay his Chatham bills, and concluded his letter with the pledge
that he would "not . . . act other than to secure perfect knowledge of
the facts in regard to what Forbes had already done." The course to

9. James Monroe Jones to *Cleveland Leader,* August 10, 1860, Boyd B. Stutler
Collection; Jermain W. Loguen to Brown, May 6, 1858, Sanborn-Brown Collection,
Houghton Library; Brown to Family, May 12, 1858, Boyd B. Stutler Collection;
Oates, *Brown,* pp. 243–47; Villard, *Brown,* pp. 330–38.

be taken in both Chatham and Boston should not be decided "under excitement."[10]

Brown also wrote to George Luther Stearns. Covering much of the same ground with the Medford businessman, Brown closed his note with the injunction he would live by: "In all ways acknowledge Him, and He shall direct thy paths." Stearns, however, was not as deeply affected by such biblical flourishes as he had once been. Despite Brown's calm assurances, the businessman was too upset to be moved by religious incantations. He wanted to know why Forbes was acting so irrationally, how much Forbes knew about the plan, why Brown had been so indiscriminate in trusting such an erratic character, and what the true nature of Brown's arrangement with the disgruntled soldier had been. Most important, Stearns, like Sanborn, Parker, and Smith, had lost confidence in Brown. In March Stearns had believed Brown's version of the Forbes arrangement; at the moment he was unsure what to think. The businessman's slowly developing willingness to commit himself to slave insurrection had been shattered by Brown's indiscretion. Could Brown really lead a successful raid on slavery when he couldn't govern the behavior of a former military associate? Shortly after receiving Brown's letter, Stearns wrote to Higginson, notified him that Brown had been relieved of the arms in his custody, invited the minister to Boston in order to discuss postponement, and coldly advised the recalcitrant committee member that if he would only listen, "we can convince you it [postponement] is for the best." Brown's religious injunction hadn't made a dent in the lead-pipe manufacturer's decision to temporarily withhold support from the scheme.[11]

In the week between receiving Brown's letter of May 15 and Stearns's request that he come to Boston to be "convinced" on May 21, Higginson continued his vigorous attempt to salvage the raid. On

10. Brown to Higginson, May 14, 1858, Higginson-Brown Collection, Boston Public Library; Sanborn, *Life and Letters of Brown*, p. 457; Brown to Friends, May 21, 1858, Boyd B. Stutler Collection.

11. Stearns, *Life of Stearns*, p. 185; Stearns to Higginson, May 21, 1858, Higginson-Brown Collection, Boston Public Library.

May 18 he wrote Parker and again warned that "postponement was abandonment." Forbes could do "as much harm next year." He firmly believed threats of exposure could only be countered by swift action. There was still time to capitalize on the element of surprise, still time to "steal a march." He had "little doubt" that a successful raid could be executed. Any "betrayal *afterwards*" would "only *increase* the panic" caused by the raid. To Sanborn's contention that Forbes could "injure the operation" by exposing the "smallness of its resources," Higginson made a telling rebuttal, one that indicates much about the nature of the plan unfolded by Brown in early March. Higginson told Parker that Sanborn had forgotten that by Brown's *"original program"* the raid "was to be regarded [at first] as a mere local flurry with no resources at all." From the beginning Brown had argued that the small size of his group would act as a perfect camouflage to the ultimate design of general insurrection, and Higginson was "amazed" his fellow conspirators hadn't considered this before making their decision.[12]

Higginson fought hard for Brown's plan on other grounds as well. In a May 12 speech before the New York State Antislavery Society, he prodded his associates by echoing Parker's ideas about some reformers' shortcomings. Higginson stated that "white Anglo-Saxon abolitionists" were "too apt to assume the whole work" of ending slavery and tended to "ignore the great force of the victims of tyranny." If slaves were "ever to free themselves," they "must strike the first blow." For many years he had been "disposed to think" that the "salvation of the slave" had to be worked out "not by him but for him." Presently, he had begun to "see otherwise." Higginson admitted to wondering at the "patience of the Negro" but was sure that the time would come when, witnessing the "aroused strength" of the African, whites would "at last give him credit for the prudence which has waited until these preliminary agitations [Fugitive Slave Law, Kansas] . . . created the sympathy . . . needed for his support." Abolitionists often spoke of the African as "weak, down-trodden, degraded," and

12. Higginson to Parker, May 18, 1858, Higginson-Brown Collection, Boston Public Library; Higginson, *Journals,* p. 191.

"cowardly because exposed to the institution of slavery." In so doing, Higginson felt that abolitionists may have been inadvertently perpetuating the institution by failing to see that "behind all those years of cheerful submission . . . there may be a dagger and power to use it when the time comes." The African had been degraded by the institution of slavery, but it was time all Americans saw what he had once been and what he "may be again." Ironically, Higginson made his claims for the slave partially on the basis of his own romantic racialist notions about the origins of race traits. In the end, he based his confidence in black capabilities on the fact that they had received blood from "heroic races," the Maroons of Surinam and Jamaica, and these races had "mingled blood" with "a race [Anglo-Saxon] which was the strongest in the world." Higginson spoke of previous indications of the willingness of blacks to fight for freedom. Fugitive slaves demonstrated the black man's desire for freedom, and the Shadrach rescue executed by Boston blacks was a prime example of northern freeman's regard for his chained brethren. Then, too, as Brown had noted in early March, the underground railroad had "lodged tens of thousands in Canada" and these black men and women "proved the possibility of African civilization and African agriculture." Echoing Howe, Higginson remarked that blacks had "learned their strength" in Canada by being exposed to "normal people"; now they were ready to use that strength in the cause of liberty.[13]

On May 18, the same day that Higginson sent his letter of protest to Parker, Sanborn wrote and told the Worcester committeeman of Howe's attempt to "baffle" Forbes, Wilson, and "God knows how many more" who had heard about the plan. At the same time, the secretary informed Higginson that a committee meeting had been called for May 24 in order to formally reevaluate their support of Brown. Gerrit Smith promised to attend, since he had to be in town for an American Peace Society meeting.[14]

13. Thomas Wentworth Higginson, Speech to the New York Antislavery Society [May 12, 1858], in *Liberator,* May 28, 1858.

14. Sanborn to Higginson, May 18, 1858, Higginson-Brown Collection, Boston Public Library; Villard, *Brown,* p. 339.

Reeling from his brother's recent death as well as the Forbes disclosures, Gerrit Smith came to Boston in late May to speak before the American Peace Society. It is possible that when Smith wrote his speech he was laboring under the emotional burden of these two events. In any case, his words to the society on the morning of May 24 are another example of his "paradoxical intellect" at work. The address contained two separate arguments about the use of force. In one Smith spoke against a nation's involvement in external war, and in the other he spoke in favor of armed force to maintain internal order. Smith believed war in the international sphere "could be avoided always" and that "no nation known to refuse to engage in it need fear it." A country's refusal to fight would "unequivocally express" the "confidence" that war would not be made on it. In addition, a nation must give "ample proof" of its "professed principles" by dismantling forts and disbanding its army. Smith's advocacy of this position on external warfare did not make him a nonresistant (even Christ had practiced nonresistance only from "expediency"), for he firmly believed that "armed force" was essential to the domestic life of a nation. There was a definite need to "suppress frontier violence" and to support the "irregular but righteous governments" set up in Kansas. Above all, domestic violence was necessary to deliver the slave from bondage "at whatever harm to the slaveholder and to restrain slaveholders by whatever terrors it is necessary to hold over them."[15]

By two o'clock in the afternoon, Smith had left the peace meeting to join with other members of the secret committee in his Revere House hotel room. But faced with possible exposure by Forbes, Smith backed away from his call for the use of domestic force. He agreed with Sanborn, Stearns, Parker, and Howe that support should be temporarily withdrawn from Brown. The secret group decided that the best way to diffuse Forbes's threats was to send Brown back to Kansas. Howe had already said as much to Forbes, and Brown's return to Kansas might be enough to persuade Forbes that the doctor was

15. Harlow, *Smith*, pp. 400–401; Peter Brock, *Radical Pacifists in Antebellum America* (Princeton, 1968), pp. 229–31.

telling the truth. In order to induce Brown to go back to the territory and to assure him that he had not been abandoned, the committee promised to raise $2,000 for resumption of the project at a later date. The committee also decided to send Brown $500 to pay his Chatham bills, to return control of the rifles to him, and to request his presence in Boston for further discussion of the entire matter.[16]

All of the secret committee members, with the obvious exception of Higginson, were relieved by the actions they decided upon in their afternoon meeting. Surprisingly, the man who seemed to relax most was Samuel Gridley Howe. He had not capitulated to postponement until a few days before the meeting, but when he did, he was happily unburdened of the great pressure it took to stand by Brown. Writing to George Woods, Howe revealed part of the reason for his relief. The doctor explained that he could now "powerfully" and "truthfully" assert that Forbes was "all wrong" in his description of Brown's "intended movements."[17]

Indeed, it was more than just being able to speak "truthfully" which eased his mental and physical strain. Again, as in the summer of 1856, the clash between Howe's abolitionist activity and his genuine friendship for Charles Sumner had become a source of paralyzing guilt. Earlier in the month Howe had been forced to lie to Sumner when the ailing friend asked about the statements Forbes was making in Washington that spring. The doctor claimed he was amazed Sumner didn't "see through" a man whose "hot temper" had blinded him to the wrongfulness of his course. Howe assured Sumner that the Massachusetts Kansas Committee had never "directly or indirectly employed" Forbes and that Brown's contact with the soldier had been made on his "own responsibility." What bothered Howe was a growing fear that Sumner would be drawn into the Forbes situation and be subjected to undue emotional stress. Such stress might further retard the already slow recovery Sumner was making from his attack. Howe wasn't certain that the senator hadn't already been affected. Writing

16. Sanborn, *Recollections,* 1: 155–60.
17. Howe to George Wood, May 26, 1858; Howe to Charles Sumner, April 6, 1858, Howe Collection, Houghton Library.

to Sumner on May 17 in the midst of the crisis, he cautioned his friend to get plenty of rest, exercise, and fresh air and advised him to "avoid taxing his brain by keeping away from people and events" which "demand too much." Howe frankly admitted that his own "doubt" had been "painfully incurred" by Sumner's failure to improve his health and by his recent relapse. In a comment that goes a long way toward explaining why Howe finally agreed to postpone Brown's effort, the doctor stated that his doubts would have "disappeared in a sad certainty" if he could have been sure that the relapse "was not occasioned by any sufficient *external cause* but was a natural consequence of the *internal condition* of the injured organs." Howe was concerned that the Forbes accusations had contributed to Sumner's failing health. In fact, on the next day, May 18, Howe advised his old friend to resign his office and "stay away in Europe" for "a year or two."[18]

By the time Brown received the secret committee's request for a meeting in Boston at the end of the month, he had steadied himself and had started working to hold his cadre of recruits in line during the period of postponement. Writing to John Kagi and other members of the group who had left Chatham earlier, Brown informed them that "such has been the effect of the course taken by Forbes on our Eastern friends that I have some fears . . . we shall be compelled to delay further action *for the present.*" Brown told Kagi that he had been urged to postpone but had been promised "liberal assistance after a while." If they did have to "defer" efforts, no problem should arise in "great and noble minds," and they should not indulge in "useless complaints." It was in a "time of difficulty" that men showed what they were made of, and it was at such times that "men *mark* themselves."[19]

John Brown marked himself with his eastern friends on May 31 in Boston when he held the first of a series of meetings in his room at the American House hotel. Once again Brown was asked to explain

18. Howe to Charles Sumner, May 17, 18, 1858, ibid.
19. Brown to Friends in Cleveland, May 21, 1858, Boyd B. Stutler Collection.

his relationship with Forbes. Once again Brown accused the soldier of being vain and irresponsible. This time though, Brown did admit that he had not fully perceived the man's character when he first recruited him for the scheme and that Forbes knew more about the plan than Brown had previously suggested. Nevertheless, Brown still argued that Forbes did not know enough to jeopardize the project. Howe, Stearns, Parker, and Sanborn listened attentively as Brown presented his case for continuation, but, of course, his words did nothing to change their determination to postpone the operation. After Brown finished, the committee members spelled out the way they thought it was best to handle the situation. Brown was formally notified of the committee's desire to defer his "dash" at slavery, was asked to decoy Forbes by returning to Kansas, and was told that the secret committee intended to back his venture next spring. As a way of demonstrating their continued commitment, they gave Brown another $500 for expenses.[20]

Thomas Wentworth Higginson was noticeably absent during all four days of the meetings held between Brown and the other four Massachusetts members of the committee. He continued to fume about the attitudes and actions of his fellow conspirators and believed that by disregarding their invitations to attend the meetings and thereby boycotting those meetings, he could most effectively register his protest. However, Higginson was in Boston while the June 1 session was being held and afterward met privately with Brown to explain his behavior. Higginson's memorandum of his conversation with Brown adds substantially to our understanding of the meetings and of the relationship Brown had with the other committee members. Higginson noted that Brown had been "pushed to postpone until next winter or spring," had been "promised 2000 dollars to 3000 dollars" if he did so, and had been asked to blind Forbes by returning to Kansas. Though Brown kept control of the weapons committed to him in 1857, he was

20. Sanborn to Higginson, May 31, 1858, Higginson-Brown Collection, Boston Public Library; Oates, *Brown*, pp. 250–51; Sanborn to Higginson, June 4, 1858, Higginson-Brown Collection, Boston Public Library; Villard, *Brown*, p. 396; Higginson, *Cheerful Yesterdays*, p. 222; Sanborn, *Recollections*, 1: 167; Edelstein, *Strange Enthusiasm*, pp. 212–13.

to legally "transfer property" so as to relieve the committee of responsibility, and in the future, the conspirators were "not to know of his plans." Higginson reported that Brown was very disappointed by the committee's decision to postpone and considered those in favor of it not to be "men of action." He was angry that they had been "intimidated" by Wilson, believed Gerrit Smith to be a "timid man," and thought Stearns and Parker "did not . . . abound in courage." Brown did admire Howe for initially standing fast against postponement. He made no comment about Sanborn.[21]

Brown's harsh words did not offend Higginson, for his own evaluation coincided with the Kansas veteran's assessment. More than at any time in their relationship, Higginson was impressed with the man and regarded him as a "sly old veteran" who carefully calculated his actions. Brown admitted to Higginson that in the meetings he had "appeared to acquiesce far more than he really did" because *it was essential they did not think him reckless.* Brown's behavior in the wake of Forbes's disclosures truly "marked" him.[22]

The five members of the secret committee who had voted to defer aid to his project were not the only people he tried to manipulate with the image of a self-controlled fighter for the right. Higginson earned his share of Brown's attention by his steadfast refusal to postpone the venture. After their exchange on June 1, Brown was determined to pay closer attention to the Worcester activist. In ensuing weeks he corresponded with Higginson more frequently, spoke of his plans more freely, and regularly requested Higginson's views of them, hoping all

21. Ibid., pp. 212–13; Higginson-Brown Memo, June 1, 1858, Higginson-Brown Collection, Boston Public Library. It is interesting to speculate why Brown remained silent about Sanborn. Certainly Brown realized that Sanborn had panicked like the others; yet Brown said nothing derogatory about him to Higginson. It is possible Brown sensed the personal tension that existed between the young committee secretary and the minister from Worcester. Brown realized how much he needed Sanborn's assistance and understood that if he censured Sanborn, the assistance might be jeopardized. If, in a moment of anger, Higginson used Brown's remarks against the secretary, there was no telling what effect they might have on Sanborn's future disposition to work in Brown's behalf.

22. Ibid.

the while to deepen the minister's interest in the scheme and receive funds from the Worcester County Committee.[23]

After seeming to "acquiesce far more than he really did," Brown left Boston on June 3 and headed back to Kansas as the "decoy" that "T. P. and the S's envisioned." He refused, however, to let the committee forget their obligation to him simply because he was out of sight. Within three weeks he wrote from Kansas prodding his Boston friends to be "in earnest . . . to carry out as soon as possible" the measures he had put forward to Boston "during the early spring." Brown pushed them to collect money by saying he wanted "no delay" in the matter. Brown also tried to reestablish his image as a disciplined leader of men who had the ability to smoothly carry out his proposed "dash" against slavery. While in Kansas he "concealed his presence," surfacing only long enough to let people know he was in the territory, but not long enough "to create any excitement." He was not in Kansas to "open a quarrel or be the first to seek revenge." Although the Kansas situation was gradually resolving itself politically, Brown could not help exaggerating the possibility of new turmoil in order to sustain the interest of his readers and further highlight his own discretion. According to Brown, freestaters lived in "constant fear" of "new troubles," and some thought the whole Kansas problem would start "afresh."[24]

In addition to these attempts to pressure the Secret Six and refurbish his image with them, Brown seems to have enlisted the aid of James Redpath, the frenetic young journalist who had journeyed into Kansas with Higginson. No specific documentation exists to prove that the two men entered into an agreement, but a number of facts point to that conclusion. For one thing, Redpath enjoyed the confidence of Thomas Wentworth Higginson, the only man on the committee who

23. Brown to Higginson, September 13, 1858, Brown Collection, Massachusetts Historical Society; Edelstein, *Strange Enthusiasm,* p. 213; Villard, *Brown,* p. 340; Higginson to Brown, October 29, 1858, Higginson-Brown Collection, Boston Public Library. Hugh Forbes also communicated with Higginson for the first time in early June: Hugh Forbes to Higginson, June 6, 1858, ibid.

24. Brown to the Six, June 28, July 20, 1858, ibid.; Villard, *Brown,* p. 353; Sanborn, *Life and Letters of John Brown,* pp. 474–77.

stood by Brown during the Forbes affair. Certainly Higginson could use help in pressing Brown's cause. For another, Redpath had more impressive credentials than Brown when it came to assessing the slaves' willingness to fight for their freedom. The young journalist had traveled extensively in the South with the expressed purpose of finding out whether or not slaves were primed for insurrection. Indeed, before Redpath went south, he noted that if blacks were not ready for violence, he would "disseminate discontentment" and prepare the way for "revolution." Here was a man with firsthand knowledge of the South, and it is hardly possible that the "sly old veteran" would have missed the opportunity to put a primary source in the hands of Harvard scholars. There is a further reason to believe Brown recruited Redpath to promote his scheme among the reluctant conspirators in Boston: Redpath was as certain as Brown that the only way slavery could be ended was by insurrection. Soon after a meeting with Brown on June 27 in Kansas, Redpath started east. During the next year he would press for the implementation of Brown's scheme while residing in Medford, Massachusetts, and preparing a manuscript for publication entitled *The Roving Editor: or Talks with Slaves in the Southern States.* An examination of this work, which was eventually published in November 1859 and dedicated to Brown, undoubtedly reveals much of what Redpath told Brown's Massachusetts supporters.[25]

In this work Redpath agreed with Brown's disrespect for the "efficacy of political antislavery action." Political action was founded on "expediency" and "the morals of the counting room"; therefore, it could do nothing to solve the slaves' problems. Like Brown, Redpath urged friends of the slaves to "incite insurrection and encourage in the North a spirit which shall culminate in civil and servile wars." If, after all, the founding fathers had been justified in "their rebellion, how much more will the slaves be justified in their insurrection?" Redpath, asserted that he was ready to "slay every man who attempted to resist the liberation of the slave" and was willing "to recognize the negro

25. Oates, *Brown*, p. 253; James Redpath, *The Roving Editor: or Talks with Slaves in the Southern States* (New York, 1859), Intro.

as brother however inferior in intelligence and actual endowments, as having rights which to take away or withhold is a crime that should be punished without mercy."[26]

Redpath's book contained his own reflections on the slaves' condition as well as those of other informed observers. Samuel Gridley Howe contributed a piece on a slave prison in New Orleans. Another part of the book, which the journalist obviously felt went a long way toward documenting his contentions about slaves' desires to fight for liberation, was a section called "The Insurrection Hero." Here Redpath quoted long passages of a story written by John Vaughn which studied the motivations of a slave leader named Issac who, Vaughn claimed, led an abortive insurrection in the South. According to Vaughn, Issac was "kind, affectionate, and simple as a woman" and "never tired of doing for others"; yet he had determined that insurrection was the only hope for freeing his people. Issac's own rationale for this position was included in Vaughn's account. The slave said he "knew there was and could be no help for me, for my wife or my children, for my race, except we were free, and as whites would not let this be so and as God told me he could only help those who helped themselves, I preached freedom to the slaves and bid them strike for it like men." Whether Vaughn's piece was fact or fiction is really not significant. It is Issac's thinking that is important. It confirmed what both Brown and Redpath had been saying all along: Slaves knew they must fight for their own freedom.[27]

Redpath's belief in the possibility of a spontaneous general uprising to be ignited by an attack like the one Brown contemplated is contained in a section he wrote for the book entitled "The Underground Telegraph." According to Redpath, slaves would rally to the banner of those leading an insurrection because there existed a rapid and efficient system of communication among them, which could effectively disperse the first news of a raid over a wide area of the South long before slaveholders could hear of the attack and organize forces

26. Redpath, *Roving Editor*, pp. iii–iv, 507.
27. Ibid., pp. 271–83.

to subdue it. Redpath said that this elaborate "underground" telegraph had originated as a "system of secret travel" among slaves and had then grown into a communication network initially because of the slaves' "love of gossip" and, later, because of their "yearning for freedom." The journalist asserted that this system linked hundreds of plantations and that there was no question in his mind that its existence gave "power" to stir a "formidable insurrection . . . directed by white men."[28]

It is certain that all the Massachusetts secret committee members who heard Redpath's descriptions were at least a bit skeptical. All of them had studied slaves and slavery and had not discovered such a system. Yet it seems likely that they continued to listen to him throughout the year, for none of these men had the journalist's experience. And, it was becoming more difficult to refute evidence which seemed to indicate the slave's burgeoning desire for freedom.

In the first few weeks after Brown left Boston, neither his pressure tactics, Redpath's appearance, nor the justice of slave liberation concerned Stearns, Sanborn, and Smith because they were all too relieved at having narrowly escaped exposure by Forbes. George Luther Stearns rekindled his belief in a political solution to slavery and was cheered by the continually improving condition of Kansas. He agreed with E. B. Whitman that if freestaters were "moderately diligent," they would thwart the Slave Power and send the institution to "political perdition." While Brown was in Kansas acting as a decoy, struggling to recapture the confidence of supporters, and suffering with the ague, Stearns did little for Brown's "wool business." Instead, he began remodeling his Medford mansion, followed the Lincoln-Douglas debates, plotted the course of Donati's comet, and argued against those who believed the superstition that "all great comets have been closely followed by devastating wars."[29]

Brown's "recklessness" in the Forbes affair had petrified Sanborn.

28. Ibid., pp. 284–87.
29. E. B. Whitman to Stearns, May 26, 1858, Stearns Collection, Kansas State Historical Society; Stearns, *Life of Stearns,* pp. 178–79.

All along his commitment to the forceful dissolution of slavery had been based on his attachment to Brown. In spite of Parker's thoughts about the importance of black self-help, the secretary found that once his confidence in Brown was shaken, he had great difficulty in defending the proposed raid to himself or others. Throughout the summer and fall of 1858, he drew back from his support for a slave uprising. After all, if Brown bungled the raid as badly as he had his relationship with Forbes, it was possible the entire secret committee would be faced with more than abusive letters or the wrist-slapping criticism of people like Henry Wilson. "Treason" had not yet become "patriotism" as Sanborn had advised Higginson weeks earlier, and a jail term still awaited anyone convicted as an accessory to Brown's scheme. Sanborn's reflections on Kansas partially indicate his increasing desire to see slavery removed by other than forcible means. He even lectured Brown on the subject, saying he was glad Kansas was at peace and he now believed her "true course" lay in formulating an effective free-state constitution to guide territorial fortunes. It was best for Kansas to use traditional "political means" to end slavery.[30]

In May, at the time of the Forbes blowup, Gerrit Smith had only wanted Brown's plan "deferred." By July, he was telling Sanborn he didn't want to know anything about Brown's future efforts. Although Smith still claimed Kansas had been saved by her "own brave spirits" and applauded Brown's efforts in beating back "border ruffianism," he returned to political antislavery activities during the late summer and early fall. The Peterboro landowner reentered the political arena and ran for governor of New York. Beginning in August, he attended some fifty-three campaign meetings, traveled some four or five thousand miles, and spent about $5,000 seeking office. Throughout the effort, he said he had accepted the nomination "in faith that frank, bold, persuasive speech backed by moral truth would be more than a match for the [proslavery] press." Smith knew his chances for election were not great, but he believed in the aims of the campaign, vigorously

30. Sanborn to Brown, August 25, 1858, Sanborn Letters, Atlanta University.

justified his "spontaneous" nomination, and forcefully promoted his antislavery views.[31]

Though Smith had known from the start that his chances for election were slight, defeat in November still left him feeling indignant and self-righteous. It seemed to him that people simply were not ready to receive the "democratic theories" he had spent his life inculcating. Smith supposed that he must "live and die an unpopular politician." What was worse than his loss (one is never sure Smith wasn't intrigued by the cultivation of his own political unpopularity) was his feeling that throughout New York State antislavery sentiment was dead. By late fall, he had again changed the direction of his thinking and his pessimism about the prospects of a political solution to slavery returned. The "public mind" had been drawn away from abolition into the nonextension of slavery. Again, in the face of his own political failure and the death of antislavery sentiment, he resurrected his ideas about political violence. Kansas owed her salvation not to politics, but to "ample preparations to repel by physical force the aggressions of slavery." It was "men money and munitions" brought to Kansas by "eastern enterprise and liberality" which had really saved the territory. The Republican Party had become the "protector of slavery." Perhaps Brown's raid would fail. Perhaps Brown's mishandling of Forbes was portentous. But in the wake of political defeat Smith overlooked such possibilities and renewed his commitment to "men money and munitions." At the minimum, an insurrectionary thrust would rekindle a "demoralized" public sentiment.[32]

In the first weeks after Brown's departure, Theodore Parker retreated from his theories, but unlike his friends, Stearns, Sanborn, and Smith, he never entirely turned his back on them. Before beginning

31. Sanborn, *Recollections,* 1: 176; Harlow, *Smith,* pp. 361, 363, 380–82. Smith's nomination on the People's State Ticket was also promoted by Democrats who were hoping to siphon off votes from Republicans.

32. Frothingham, *Smith,* pp. 194–95; Gerrit Smith, Letter of Acceptance, August 4, 1858; Letter to Abolitionists and Prohibitionists, August 19, 1858; Letter to the Men who put me in Nomination, November 5, 1858; Smith to J. Giddings, November 12, 1858, Smith Collection, Syracuse University Library.

a restful journey to the Green Mountains that June, Parker outlined his position to an audience at the annual meeting of the New England Antislavery Society. Parker stated that it was such meetings that were the "best manner" in which to agitate the slavery question. However, he did admit to this group that, in the various struggles between freedom and slavery, the battle had always been "settled by war," and it seemed to him that the "great and final" abolition of slavery in America would have to be accomplished in that way as well.[33]

During midsummer, with Brown safely in Kansas and the Forbes episode seemingly settled, the minister intensified his pleas for slave violence. Examining the effects of slavery in a July speech, he suggested that "compulsory toil" was "not necessarily degrading." Slaves learned "certain special things" which they could not have learned in Africa. Indeed, it was a sign of the slave's "excellency" that he was "pliant before his master's will" while he learned these special things. But, ultimately, the institution of slavery was "essentially degrading" because it denied Africans "history . . . science . . . arts . . . literature" and "a great war to look back on." The minister did not wonder at the slaves' "despair" and went on to point out that the wrongs slaves suffered had awakened "very little sympathy in the mass of men, who in their rudeness reverence strength and not justice." Parker also warned of the potential for slave violence and wondered aloud what blacks would do if the United States became engaged in a war with England (a speculation William C. Nell had engaged in), then answered his own question by asserting that "at least three million [slaves] would take sides with the enemy." Free black men would "spontaneously" do the same thing. It is obvious from both of these speeches that, although the Forbes affair had initially jarred Parker's confidence in Brown, the ideas Brown had helped summon about insurrection continued to intrigue him.[34]

33. Theodore Parker, Speech to New England Antislavery Society [May 26, 1858], in *Worcester Daily Spy,* May 28, 1858.

34. Theodore Parker, "The Effect of Slavery" [a speech given on July 4, 1858], in Parker, *Works* (Cobbe edition), 8: 146.

CHAPTER 7

A Theory of Violence
and Assimilation

THOMAS WENTWORTH HIGGINSON'S certainty about Brown's ideas increased in the months following the veteran's departure from Boston. During the early fall Higginson advised William Lloyd Garrison to read an article he had prepared on "African Proverbial Philosophy," explaining that it would present "quite a new view of the character and capabilities of the [black] race." In fact, Higginson's most revealing expression of these "new" views are found in an article he prepared for the September 1858 issue of the *Atlantic Monthly*. Here, in an elaborate theoretical framework, Higginson fused his own romantic racialist attitudes; the assertions of Brown, Redpath, and free black leaders about the slaves; Parker's speculations on "outdoor charity"; and Howe's "theory of diffusion" into a comprehensive justification of insurrection. Higginson achieved his fragile synthesis by reexamining the typology of courage and suggesting that political violence could help slaves assimilate a new system of values.[1]

In Higginson's view, there were three forms of courage. The greatest form was possessed by all "heroic races" and was called the "courage of blood." According to Higginson, men who possessed this type of courage dared perils not merely for the sake of principle, but for "their own sake," and there was no special merit in such courage—one either had it hereditarily or one did not. Indeed, the courage of blood often concealed itself under the finer names of self-devotion and high princi-

---

1. Higginson to William Lloyd Garrison, September 28, 1858, Garrison Collection, Boston Public Library, Boston, Mass.; Thomas Wentworth Higginson, "Physical Courage," *Atlantic Monthly* 2 (September 1858): 728–30.

ple. As an example of this kind of courage, Higginson spoke of the activities of evangelist George Barrow, "who convinced himself that he was activated by evangelical zeal to spread the Bible to Spain." In Higginson's opinion, it was "chiefly adventure" which had lured Barrow to Spain.[2]

In Higginson's typology there was an environmental complement to the "courage of blood" which was called "transmitted courage." This second type was produced by constant training and practice and could "give steadiness" to less powerful, inherited forms. This "transmitted" variety was the type shared by a captain with his men. John Brown spoke of this kind of courage (though not using the same terminology as Higginson) in 1857 when he spoke of organizing free-state settlers into militia groups. In these groups "strong" men would bolster the courage of "weak" ones.[3]

It was, however, in the examination of a third variety of courage that Higginson revealed his "new view" of black capabilities. The third type of courage was the "courage of self-devotion" or "courage of emulation." Women and Africans possessed this kind of courage. It was evoked by "special exigencies" and was powerful enough to alter the character of slaves who had been "suppled" by long years of slavery and "softened" by mixed blood. This courage allowed them to pass from "cowering pusillanimity" to daring. Under its influence a slave's "giddy laugh" vanished, his "idle chatter" hushed, and "Buffoon" became hero. Self-devotion was the most noble form of courage because it entered the "domain of conscience" and was engendered by outstanding moral leadership. If slaves were exposed to the right leader, they would be sure to fight violently for their freedom and produce "results which seemed miraculous." Higginson himself had a hard time determining where this courage came from or what it was. In the end, he could only claim that it was an "element of inspiration" or a "superadded something" which was "incalculable" in effect. Though he never said so directly in the article, one is left with the impression

2. Ibid., pp. 730–32.
3. Ibid.

that Higginson was certain that John Brown was the man to induce this "superadded something," the man to kindle slave desires for freedom.[4]

It is unimportant whether Higginson fully believed in his own theoretical analysis or merely forwarded it as yet another prod to his reluctant colleagues. The attempted synthesis suggests that Higginson was trying to resolve for himself and his fellow conspirators a basic contradiction between their romantic racialist thinking and the contentions of Brown, Redpath, and black leaders. Each of the conspirators, to one degree or another, maintained a racial stereotype which was at odds with the underlying reason for Brown's willingness to incite a slave uprising. Although each of the six men believed in the free black man's "spontaneous" desire to assist enslaved brethren, none of them believed the slave was by nature capable of anything more than "docile" and "pliant," though virtuous, behavior. Brown, Redpath, and black abolitionists asked them to think differently. Parker began the attempt to resolve the contradiction with his preliminary reevaluation of the usefulness of white reform activity. Higginson brought this thinking to fruition in his article by providing the mechanism (the courage of self-devotion) which, though it did not erase the contradiction, allowed romantic racialism and the possibility of slave violence to coexist. By the fall of 1858 other members of the committee had major doubts about Brown's competency, but Higginson, at least, had gone a long way toward putting aside their racial skepticism and their ambivalence about using political violence. Higginson had traveled beyond Higher Law to a new and further justification for insurrection.[5]

4. Ibid., pp. 732–33.
5. Ibid., pp. 728–33, 736, 737. In his article, Higginson did more than provide a theoretical rationale for Brown's contentions. He also criticized his fellow conspirators for their behavior toward Brown during the Forbes episode. In so doing, he adds further insight about the motivation of the other members for supporting the Kansas warrior. Higginson began his criticism of the others in the introduction to his piece. Here he claimed that it was a "foolish delusion" to believe that the combined power of gunpowder and peace had "banished" the necessity for physi-

Higginson had advocated execution of Brown's plan in the face of the Forbes disclosures. He had displayed his disdain for the secret committee's faintheartedness by boycotting their May postponement meetings and censuring them for their moral bankruptcy in the last section of his *Atlantic Monthly* article. But he understood the limits to which his colleagues could be pushed, and he realized that any additional public furor would most certainly destroy their little remaining inclination to support the project. As a result, he was alarmed by a short letter he received from Lysander Spooner near the end of November. Spooner was an abolitionist who had been active in Boston reform society for years and had recently pressed for the use of forceful means to end slavery. In his note to Higginson, Spooner asked for an opinion of a "scheme" he had devised to foment slave uprisings. He enclosed two documents which he proposed to have printed and circulated exten-

---

cal courage. The demand would never pass away. Physical courage was neither "easily set aside" nor "a mere corollary from moral courage" as "our reformers" seemed to assume. In fact, it often occurred that the leaders of an age who had ample "moral courage" were "physically timid." Certainly these introductory remarks were aimed at the men Brown had ridiculed a few months earlier for being "intimidated" by Wilson and "not abounding in courage." But these introductory remarks were mild when compared to those words Higginson saved for the conclusion of his piece. Here Higginson claimed that men who were committed to the "right side" of an issue too often got credit for "moral courage." In his view the credit was unjust, for their supposed moral courage wasn't really courage at all but merely an "intense egotism." This "intense egotism" helped these supposedly courageous men to isolate themselves from "all demand for human sympathy." In the "best cause," men of this type actually preferred to belong to a party which was "conveniently small" and upon the "slightest indications" of "popular approbation," began to "suspect themselves of compromise." The "abstract martyrdom" of "unpopularity" was "clear gain" to them. But when it came to the "rack . . . revolver and the Bowie Knife," their "habitual egotism" made them "cowards." Such men were annoying "in themselves" and annoying because they threw discredit on "noble and unselfish reformers." Clearly, Higginson addressed these angry words to the men who had postponed Brown's raid. Clearly, he was suggesting that their actions made both their radical abolitionism and allegiance to Brown suspect in his eyes. He implied that both were a product of egotistical and self-serving principles and that, in the end, these same principles had been the reason Brown's plan was postponed.

sively through the South; both called for the violent overthrow of slavery.[6]

In the longer broadside entitled "A Plan for the Abolition of Slavery," Spooner demanded that slaves be rescued from the "hands of their oppressors" by the "formation of associations" dedicated to that purpose. He wanted private war waged against slavery by private individuals. He called for compensated emancipation, separation of government from the interests of slaveholders, and the destruction of the "security and value" of slave property. The second, shorter document was addressed to "non-Slaveholders" and went farther than the first one. In it, Spooner stated that slaves had a "right to be free" and had a "right to take that freedom by force." It was the duty of all able men—particularly nonslaveholding whites—to assist this effort. While slaves were flogging and kidnapping their oppressors, forming military cadres, and building forts from which to "carry on warfare," it was up to nonslaveholders to be supportive and let the black men "know they have your sympathy." Such support would give slaves courage and self-respect as well as "making men of them."[7]

From the moment Higginson saw the Spooner plan he realized what disaster would befall Brown's project if the documents were circulated. He knew the other committee members would abandon Brown and disband their secret group. Somehow he had to dissuade Spooner. In his reply to the Boston abolitionist, Higginson claimed to have read the broadsides with "great approbation" and suggested that increased interest in the subjects Spooner alluded to was "one of the most important signs of the times." He agreed that the freedom of slaves had to be accomplished "by action of slaves themselves in certain localities with the aid of *secret* cooperation from whites." Insurrection would

6. John A. Alexander, "The Ideas of Lysander Spooner," *New England Quarterly* 23 (June 1950): 204, 207; Lysander Spooner to Higginson, November 28, 1858, Higginson-Brown Collection, Boston Public Library; Edelstein, *Strange Ethusiasm*, pp. 214–15.

7. Lysander Spooner, "A Plan for the Abolition of Slavery," Higginson-Brown Collection, Boston Public Library.

undercut slaveholders' confidence in the institution and would force northerners "back on the fundamental question of Liberty." Obviously remembering Brown's words as he responded, Higginson went on to say that a "single insurrection with decent *temporary* success would do more than anything else to explode our present political platform." What nineteenth-century America needed was a sharp slap in the face to clear its head.[8]

But near the end of his note Higginson cautiously moved to prevent Spooner from circulating the two pamphlets. He agreed that blacks needed help from whites but said that the cooperation should be kept "secret." Admitting to Spooner that the proposed circulation might serve to prepare the "public mind," Higginson went on to suggest that this had already been accomplished by the "fugitive slave cases" and "Kansas excitement." He then asked Spooner not to distribute anything until they could speak further. This plea was repeated by Wendell Phillips and Theodore Parker, who had also received notes from Spooner. Phillips said the plan was impractical. Parker, like Higginson, requested Spooner not to do anything until the two of them could "talk about it."[9]

Spooner did postpone distribution of the leaflets. Then, throughout December, he met with Parker, Higginson, and the other Massachusetts members of the Secret Committee of Six. In order to derail Spooner's scheme, the committee gave him a vague description of what Brown intended, told him how Brown was counting on the element of surprise, and warned him that if his documents were connected to Forbes's revelations, they might ruin any chance for successful insurrection. At first Spooner strenuously objected to these arguments by saying that the slaves needed "previous preparation," but by early January 1859 he relented and decided to drop all plans for distribution of his documents. Later in the spring when Brown had returned to

8. Higginson to Lysander Spooner, November 30, 1858, Spooner Collection, Boston Public Library, Boston, Mass.

9. Ibid.; Parker to Lysander Spooner, November 30, 1858, Spooner Collection, Boston Public Library; Wendell Phillips to Lysander Spooner, July 10, 1858, ibid.

Boston, Spooner met with him and came away from their discussion "wholly" convinced his decision was correct.[10]

Just how much Lysander Spooner had to be told about Brown's plan in order to be "wholly" convinced is difficult to ascertain. Spooner made some telling remarks years later, however, which suggest the limits of his knowledge. He claimed then that "very few knew much about the *details* of Brown's plan until it was actually developed at Harper's Ferry." Brown had broadly hinted where his assault was to begin, specified theoretical considerations upon which he based his plan, and continually asserted his own ability to execute the project, but he had not outlined the specific tactics he hoped to use in the raid. Spooner came away from his meeting with Brown feeling that the aid furnished by the secret committee was given primarily because of a "general confidence" in and sympathy with Brown rather "than from any intimate knowledge of the plan." Spooner's observation is only partially correct. The committee did base some of its support on confidence in Brown's character, but by late spring of 1859 four members of the committee—Sanborn, Stearns, Smith, and Higginson —did know many details of the plan.[11]

In December 1858 Brown, though still in the West, played a major role in influencing Spooner's final decision. In the midst of the secret committee's negotiations with Spooner, newspaper reports revealed that Brown had run off eleven Missouri slaves during the third week of the month. The raid was proof of what Boston committee members had been telling Spooner for some time: Brown had returned to Kansas to divert attention and to discredit Hugh Forbes. He would soon come east to prepare his insurrectionary strike. If Spooner sent his pamphlets south, the entire effort to "decoy" Wilson, Seward, and all those to whom Forbes had spoken would be ruined.[12]

10. Lysander Spooner to Higginson, December 2, 1858, Higginson–Brown Collection, Boston Public Library; Lysander Spooner to Governor Henry Wise, November 2, 1859, Spooner Collection, Boston Public Library.

11. Lysander Spooner to O. B. Frothingham, February 26, 1878, ibid.

12. Oates, *Brown*, pp. 261–64; Villard, *Brown*, p. 370; [Floyd C. Shoemaker], "John Brown's Missouri Raid: A Tale of the Kansas-Missouri Border Retold with Some New Facts," *Missouri Historical Review* 26 (October 1931): 80–83.

Brown's Missouri raid did more than help turn Spooner from his circulation scheme. It also informed the secret committee that Brown was "in earnest" and would soon be in Boston to make good on their pledge of the previous spring. Higginson was particularly excited by Brown's feat. The Missouri venture stimulated his confidence and made him optimistic that Brown would be able to "make a dash" into the South. Higginson was desperate for an insurrection. Writing in the *Atlantic Monthly* that winter on the need to educate women (who shared the "courage of emulation" with Africans), the minister stated that if "contempt did not originally cause failure," it certainly "perpetuates it." Any systematic effort to discourage a class or individual would "in nine cases out of ten" cause that class or individual to "acquiesce in their degradation," if not claim it as a "crown of glory." Brown's successful Missouri raid meant that in spite of the Forbes disclosures, he might yet regain the secret committee's full support for his proposed venture. And in so doing, Brown would be given the opportunity to destroy black "acquiescence" and white "contempt." To Higginson the Missouri raid was not merely a diversionary gesture, but a tactical masterstroke. Still, Higginson was very careful to hide his rekindled enthusiasm. When Sanborn wrote excitedly about the possibility of Brown getting "great results from this spark of fire" (the Missouri raid), Higginson responded by claiming to have "serious doubts" that Brown would execute his plan. The minister obviously sought to prod his youthful committee colleague with pessimism and to remind him of the committee's previous faintheartedness.[13]

Like Sanborn and Higginson, Theodore Parker was enthused by Brown's raid. When it was suggested to the Boston minister that Brown's conduct was motivated by a desire to avenge the murder of his son Frederick, Parker sprang to Brown's defense and labeled the accusation as unjust. If Brown had been motivated by vengeance, he would have sought "cheap and easy revenge on actual transgressors in

13. Thomas Wentworth Higginson, "Ought Women to Learn the Alphabet?" *Atlantic Monthly* 3 (February 1859): 137; Sanborn to Higginson, January 19, 1859, Higginson-Brown Collection, Boston Public Library; Sanborn, *Life and Letters of Brown,* p. 492; Edelstein, *Strange Enthusiasm,* pp. 217–18.

Missouri." Instead, the man had freed eleven slaves at the expense of only one white life. Parker's defense was quite stirring, especially in view of the misgivings he had entertained about Brown's leadership abilities only a few months earlier.[14]

As it happened, Parker never got to discuss the Missouri escapade with Brown or to participate in the final planning for the Harpers Ferry raid. By late January 1859, his tuberculosis had become so severe that Howe and other Boston physicians advised him to leave New England and seek healthful rest in warmer climates. In early February, Parker began a yearlong journey with his wife, Lydia, which took him to the West Indies, London, Switzerland, and Rome, where he arrived in early fall.[15]

Realizing that Parker's tuberculosis would probably "spread rapidly and remove the foremost man of the continent," Samuel Gridley and Julia Howe decided to accompany the Parkers on the first leg of their journey. The two couples had lived near each other on Exeter Street in Boston for some years and were intimate friends. Lydia and Theodore Parker, childless throughout their marriage, considered themselves second parents to the Howe children. Both couples needed a few weeks together before they parted. In Samuel Gridley Howe's mind, there were other important reasons for the trip. Howe himself was very ill, again plagued by a physical reaction to the tension of his day-to-day existence. He and Julia discussed separation, worried about family finances, and continued their long-standing debate about Julia's desire for a literary career. Howe was certain a leisurely vacation would do them both some good.[16]

After a brief stopover in Nassau, the two couples headed for Cuba, where they toured together for a few weeks before separating. Theodore Parker was impatient to see Santa Cruz, so he and Lydia said their

14. Parker to Rebecca and Matilda Goddard, November 26, 1859, in Parker, *Correspondence,* 1: 382–83.

15. Ibid., 1: 270–75, 279, 289, 298–99; Commager, *Parker,* pp. 304–5; Howe to Charles Sumner, January 16, February 2, 1859, Howe Collection, Houghton Library.

16. Ibid.; Julia Howe to Anne Mailliard, October 2, December, 1857, Howe Collection, Houghton Library; Schwartz, *Howe,* pp. 321, 324, 327–28.

last good-byes and left. Samuel Gridley and Julia decided to remain in Havana a while longer before returning to Boston. During their stay, they met wealthy South Carolina plantation owner Frank Hampton and his wife. Despite different views on the institution of slavery, the two couples got along very well. Hampton respected Howes work with the blind, and Howe was intrigued by Hampton's acute analysis of southern politics. Before leaving Havana, the southern couple asked the Howes to visit their plantation on the way home to Boston. The idea was appealing to both. They liked the Hamptons, were very interested in viewing plantation life, and expected the visit to help resolve some serious differences of opinion they were having about the nature and role of the black man in American society.[17]

In late March the Howes arrived at Frank Hampton's prosperous Carolina plantation although, by this time, Samuel Gridley Howe had given up all notions that a vacation would alleviate his sickness. Throughout his stay at the Hampton's, the Boston doctor suffered from severe headaches and he was continually anxious about the state of Parker's health. Then, too, spending time on the plantation wasn't as rewarding as Howe had envisioned; indeed, it made him squeamish. Somewhat belatedly, it occurred to Howe that the Hamptons were the kind of people Brown might have to sacrifice while leading his attack. Howe now realized that it was one thing to talk about taking white lives for slave freedom and quite another to share the hospitality of the intended white victims. However, Howe's uneasiness, his tension and headaches, were due primarily to a new aggravation in his already strained relationship with Julia.[18]

Julia Howe had revised some of her abolitionist ideas. She had become irritated by the "calm satisfaction" with which some men divided the "national moral inheritance." She disliked the fact that because of slavery, the South had been given "all the vices" and the North "all the virtues." Julia was put off by the "habitual sneer, denunciation and malediction" which had become "consecrated forms

17. Ibid.; Howe to Parker, May 17, 1859, Howe Collection, Houghton Library.
18. Ibid.; Howe to Parker, January 22, 1860, Howe Collection, Houghton Library.

of piety in speaking of the South." Northerners should not be absolved from their "labor for amelioration" of slavery but should restrain themselves from the "infliction of wrong" and set bounds which "the wickedest dare not pass."[19]

Obviously impressed by the Hamptons' handling of their slaves as well as by a vivid recollection of blacks she had seen during the trip, Julia Howe felt she must be allowed "one heretical whisper—very small and low." She now believed the "negro of the North" was "an ideal negro" who was "refined by white culture" and "elevated by white blood." But the "negro among negroes" was something entirely different. He was "a coarse, grinning, flat-footed, thick skulled creature," who was ugly, lazy, and "chiefly ambitious to be of no use to any in the world." Even so, Julia contended that slavery must "gradually ameliorate" and "slowly die out." Admitting that anyone who gave a "mild . . . palliative view . . . of slavery" should be subject to "bitter censure," she further asserted that "intellectual justice" revolted from the "rhetorical straining, exaggeration and denunciation of facts" which northern abolitionists continually employed.[20]

Although Julia Howe was at once critical of inflated abolitionist rhetoric, underestimation of white southern virtue, and overestimation of black capabilities, she could still wonder why the negro was so despised in the South. In her view, his "gentle, attachable nature" should not have caused such hatred. But though she saw blacks as "gentle and attachable" and was mildly impressed with Cuban negroes (they were physically "fair"), she would not recant her general assumptions about blacks when she was confronted by her husband. She justified her position in a letter to Theodore Parker late in 1859 after she had published the revealing recollections of her journey in a small book entitled *A Trip to Cuba*. At that time she admitted that her "little spurt about blacks" had "caused some remark" but claimed that "without asking counsel of anyone," she would stick to her resolution to write what she thought, no matter whom it offended. To Julia Howe,

19. Julia Howe, *A Trip to Cuba* (Boston, 1860), pp. 213, 236.
20. Ibid., pp. 11–12, 236.

the aspiring writer, nothing was more vicious than to make "observation conform to theory." She was positive that her observations of the black man's nature were "genuine, clear and immediate." Abolitionist theory would just have to "make the best of it." After witnessing the "natural indolence" of blacks, her convictions about the advisability of "compulsory employment" were strengthened, though she said she was not arguing for slavery.[21]

There is no question that Samuel Gridley was deeply disturbed by his wife's views. He argued with Julia during the trip and during the months she prepared the publication of *A Trip to Cuba*. As he painfully noted at the time of publication, "Some things make me sad, e.g., the question of whether viewing the actual condition of the negro enforced labor is not best! As if anything would justify the perpetuation of such a wrong by the strongest race." His own view of blacks in Cuba led him to some other conclusions. According to Howe, "climatic influences" in Cuba were better for blacks, and as a result, blacks were "physically improving." Other influences did not help as much. Howe was particularly concerned that there was "no organized effort for their [the blacks'] improvement, no organized effort to keep them from going wrong." Mentally blacks were "rising," but morally they were "sinking." What Howe was suggesting by such comments is obvious. In a sense, he was making the same case that John Brown had been making for two years. Simply stated, both men believed that blacks, once freed, would need the firm discipline of a righteous and moral man. Brown had drawn up the provisional constitution for that reason. And hadn't he recruited "highly moral" men to help execute the raid?[22]

Howe attached himself to Brown's cause in the spring of 1859

21. Ibid., pp. 216–17; Julia Howe to Parker, May 18, 1859, Howe Collection, Houghton Library.

22. Howe to Parker, March 25, 1860; Howe to Charles Sumner, March 12, 1859, Howe Collection, Houghton Library. Howe, *Journals*, p. 467. As George Fredrickson suggests in his work *The Black Image in the White Mind*, Howe continued his quest to determine whether or not the black man could adapt to life in a free society when he examined black life in Canada for the American Freedman's Bureau (see Fredrickson, chaps. 5–6).

partially, at least, for the same reason that he separated his own racial views from Julia's. Both of the Howes accepted a romantic racialist image of the black man, but they were divided over the derivation of that nature. Julia tended to emphasize heredity over environment, though she never entirely dismissed the influence of white culture on the black man. The doctor placed greater importance on environmental causes of the black man's nature. It was because he stressed the impact of environment in his definition that Howe looked to Brown to lead an "organized effort" for slave "improvement." Getting slaves away from the institution through violence and exposing them to a person like John Brown was the same thing as moving the blind out of permanent residence at Perkins School and back into the "normal" community. Like Higginson, who looked for Brown to unleash slave violence by stimulating the "courage of emulation," Howe believed an insurrectionary strike by slaves would be their first step out of slavery as well as a "morally uplifting" stride into the "normal" community. Justified political violence and the willingness to fight for freedom were keystone virtues among righteous Anglo-American men. Parker, Howe, Higginson, and the rest of the secret committee, all knew that the essence of the American political experience had been the acquisition of personal freedom earned by virtuous men who were willing to fight for it. Brown's raid would acquaint the slaves with this virtue. Brown would demand that they struggle for their own freedom—something even Julia admitted was a prerequisite for black liberation. In so doing, Brown would break the circle of environmental debilitation and begin the slaves' assimilation of a "superior" culture—the culture of "normal" men who lived day to day in the freedom of the marketplace North. If exposure to nonhandicapped persons could help the handicapped, then exposure to Brown and violence could do much for the moral sensibilities, social outlooks, and political behavior of the slaves. John Brown and justified political violence would get the slaves "on the road to perfectibility." The slaves would be organized under the "proper influence."[23]

23. Howe to Parker, March 25, 1860; Howe to Charles Sumner, March 12, 1859, Howe Collection, Houghton Library.

When Howe arrived home in mid-April, he found a letter from Brown awaiting him. In it Brown advised him that all was going well and asked what was being done to raise the funds promised during the previous spring. The only thing hindering successful execution of the raid was a "trifling sum." Brown used the Missouri raid as a negotiating lever when he noted that the "entire success of our experiment ought (I think) to convince every 'capitalist.' . . ." The old man was ready to move, and Howe sensed that this time there would be no false starts or Forbes-like interruptions. Despite some uneasiness about reports that Brown had taken property as well as slaves during the Missouri venture, Howe again sought money for the "dash" south.[24]

A few days before Samuel Gridley Howe arrived in Boston, read Brown's letter, and started to search for money, the Kansas veteran launched his own fund-raising efforts at Gerrit Smith's home. He appeared at the landowner's Peterboro mansion on April 11 and immediately described the Missouri raid. Then he brought Smith up to date on the status of his plan and cautiously inquired about funds for the enterprise. At first Smith was reluctant to make any commitment. The only thing he seemed interested in was a religious discussion. The philanthropist wanted to continue the theological debate they had engaged in one year earlier, before Brown first revealed his scheme.[25]

For the past two and a half years Smith had felt a strong desire to reexamine his personal religious convictions. During this period the Peterboro squire wrote three discourses on the "religion of reason." Smith started his religious review in December 1857 while recuperating from a severe case of typhoid fever which had hospitalized him in New York City for over two months. His illness reinforced an ever-present notion that he was "ill and destined for an early grave." When this fear of death was coupled with the phenomenon of religious revival sweeping the Northeast in the spring of 1858, Smith was moved to continue his intense reconsideration of religious principle. Although

24. Brown to Howe, March 1, 1859, ibid.
25. Oates, Brown, pp. 268–69; Harlow, Smith, p. 403; Sanborn, Recollections, 1: 161–63.

he was gravely suspicious of theology (what was important was the practical application of Christian ethics), he began writing his first discourse on the "struggle for a religion of reason" in early January 1858 and had just finished the piece when Brown arrived at Peterboro in late February to unveil his project. Smith introduced his first discourse by suggesting that in America over the last half-century, nothing had contributed more to a religion of reason than the temperance and antislavery movements. They had "awakened a sense of human dignity and human rights." Both movements helped dispel the belief that salvation depended only on believing in doctrines, and both had shown the fallacy of believing that it was immeasurably more important "to have orthodox views in regard to the Trinity, the atonement, and future life than to imbibe in the spirit of Christ." Smith himself was searching for creeds that would "grow out of life," and as far as he was concerned, "true religion" would only prevail when men were "judged by their life and character rather than adoption or rejection of creeds." For Gerrit Smith reason under God was the final judge of all questions.[26]

Yet despite Smith's rational theological posture, a unique religious symbiosis took place between himself and Brown, the Old Testament Calvinist. Smith had never shed much of his own Calvinist training, and as a result, though he and Brown disagreed on the role of the Bible in a man's religious life, they could agree on many other fundamental spiritual principles. Smith's "manner of stating his argument was considerably more terrifying than his doctrine." Indeed, Smith, like Brown, believed in a God of Divine Providence and Inspiration; he believed in the necessity of conversion, baptism, communion, and the future life. Like Brown, he also read the Bible regularly and claimed the privilege of interpreting it as he saw fit. Gerrit Smith's religion was a blend of radical posturing and traditional content.[27]

26. Harlow, *Smith*, pp. 6, 37, 194–99, 204–6; Frothingham, *Smith*, pp. 54–59; Gerrit Smith, *Sermons and Speeches* (New York, 1861), pp. 17, 23, 25, 7; Harlow, *Smith*, p. 323; Frothingham, *Smith*, p. 73.

27. Ibid.; Smith, *Sermons*, pp. 9–10; Harlow, *Smith*, pp. 193–94, 388–89.

In addition, Smith's religious discourse was something more than an examination of sacred things. His discussion of religion with Brown allowed him to vent his laissez-faire, anti-institutional wrath. Smith used their spiritual debate as a vehicle to express certain social concerns. The debate appears to have been both an examination of religion and a rubric. Undoubtedly, it is for this reason that Brown was not worried when Smith diverted his first attempt to discuss the commitment of funds by turning instead to notions he was formulating for his third discourse. Brown acquiesced because he understood that the Peterboro squire was still caught up in feverish, pietistic speculation and that such concerns seemed to help him compose as much of his social theory as his religious. Brown must have realized that by listening closely to what Smith now said about "true religion," he would have as accurate an idea of Smith's willingness to finance insurrection as if Smith had spoken directly on the subject. Very soon after Smith had launched into his newest religious consideration, it became apparent to Brown that he would, indeed, be able to count on the New York landowner's support.

Smith initiated the discussion by asserting that he now believed every individual's religion "must stand in his own judgment" and that the one standard by which a man must test his religion lay within and not without. Not only must a man's conscience be his guide, but until it was, no legitimate religious community could be formed. Smith downplayed the significance of the Bible, feeling that the individual "deeply dishonored" God by surrendering his own judgment to Scripture or the church. Although both might surpass the individual in wisdom, the individual could not claim credit by simply adopting that wisdom. True wisdom (like "true courage" for Higginson and "true morality" for Howe) "became our own by being wrought into our convictions and made part of ourselves." One became truly religious by acting truly religious. Smith was calling for an age when men "scorned to work for party," when men should "identify themselves with all mankind and aspire to no other lot than their individual merits under Heaven's blessing can earn for them." Through a religious metaphor, Smith was propounding radical, individualist views that squared in all essentials with those of Brown. Indeed, Brown could hardly have misunderstood the implications for Smith's eventual support of the proposed "dash" at slavery.[28]

Brown's intuition about Smith was confirmed when the philanthropist developed a less abstract definition of the truly religious man. For Smith, the truly religious man was "one who kept all his passions, appetites and interests in subjugation to reason." Certainly Smith viewed Brown as such an individual. After all, Brown not only believed those views himself, but had labored for nearly two years to establish that image. And there was another "religious" reason for Brown's optimism about Smith's support. Smith believed that the "most barbarous people" could be Christianized if ministered to by a proper teacher. He, like his committee associates who were concerned about exposure of slaves to "normal persons," was certain that a true man of religion could impart that religion to others. At once Brown could be insurrectionist and secular missionary. The man who could pass the greatest test of religion could surely impart the greatest of all religious virtue: control of all "passions, appetites, and interest." Smith would assist Brown for the same reason the others did: Brown could exert a great moral and organizing influence on blacks.[29]

When Smith stopped talking and listened as Brown again outlined his plan, he expressed complete sympathy with the project. To Brown's repeated contention that slaves must be given the chance to strike for their own freedom, Smith must have responded affirmatively by religious analogy. He noted that when Jesus saw that men were "enslaved to authority," he realized the "experience of truth could alone set them free." Jesus himself "took men up out of bondage to superstition and out of . . . debasing . . . blinding submission to authority." He threw men "back upon their own consciences and councilors and demanded they should judge for themselves . . . what is right." Jesus' first rule had been to "individualize and insulate each man." Brown himself

28. Smith, *Sermons,* pp. 28–34, 19–20, 30, 36.
29. Ibid.

could not have made a more eloquent "religious" defense of his position.[30]

At the end of their second day of private discussions, ones which wove religion and insurrection into the same fabric, Smith asked Brown to speak before a group of abolitionists who lived in the area. At the gathering Brown made a stirring (though unspecific) appeal for funds to aid his "work." Edwin Morton attended the meeting and later said Brown's plea had moved Smith to tears. When Brown had finished speaking, Smith stood up and pledged $400 to him. Then Smith briefly addressed the group. According to Morton, Smith fervently stated that if he were asked "to point out the man in all the world I think most truly Christian, I would point out John Brown. I once doubted in my own mind as to Captain Brown's course. I now approve of it heartily having given my mind to it more of late."[31]

Brown left Peterboro appreciating Smith's contribution and knowing he could count on him for more in the future. He stopped at North Elba to visit his family and then hurried to Boston to promote his project, obtain funds, and bolster the committee's confidence. Once in Boston, Brown sought out Frank Sanborn, and the young secretary was again responsive.

From early January when Sanborn read of Brown's daring Missouri raid in the *New York Tribune*, he realized the days of discussing the feasibility of Brown's project were finished. He knew that as soon as Brown got back east, he would want the funds promised to him the previous spring. Brown had executed his part of the bargain to decoy Forbes and would now expect Boston members of the secret committee to honor their part of the arrangement. Sanborn also knew that it was unlikely any other incident similar to the Forbes disclosures would erupt. Higginson, Parker, and Howe had handled Spooner, and Forbes hadn't been heard from for months. Sanborn was sure of another thing:

30. Ibid., pp. 47, 69, 117.
31. Frothingham, *Smith*, p. 237; Edwin Morton to Sanborn, April 13, 1859, in Sanborn, *Recollections*, 1: 161.

He would temporarily bear major responsibility for gathering the "2000 to 3000" which had been promised Brown. Parker was leaving for Europe, Howe was going on vacation in February and March, and Stearns was absorbed in the financial problems of his friends. Because Higginson only responded to Brown, Sanborn understood the task would be his alone. He was very anxious.[32]

Throughout February, March, and the first three weeks of April, Sanborn frantically searched for funds but had little success. The secretary was hindered by the economic situation in Massachusetts, the relative quiet in Kansas, and the need for secrecy. In late March he was so desperate that he sought out George Cabot with the intention of opening the "whole matter" to him if that was what was called for to get funds. Cabot had contributed 100 Sharpe's rifles to the Massachusetts Kansas Committee during the early days of its existence. It seemed worth the risk to inform him of Brown's plan in exchange for support. At the last moment, however, Sanborn balked and, for some unknown reason, found it "not advisable" to enlist Cabot's aid. Finally, when the secretary visited Howe shortly after his return from the West Indies, he received some promising words about acquiring money for Brown. Howe said he could not be counted on for large sums but believed his friend John Murray Forbes, the wealthy Boston railroad magnate, would be willing to make a substantial contribution if Howe sent him a strong character reference for Brown. Sanborn breathed a short sigh of relief. At least he had some good news for Brown.[33]

On April 19, a few days after his visit with Howe, the committee secretary hurriedly scratched a brief note to Higginson which read: "Brown himself is in Boston." Though responses to his money-raising pleas had been poor, Sanborn was relieved to see Brown. Soliciting funds always seemed easier when Brown appeared in person to make the request. Sanborn told Brown of the difficulties he had encountered and though Brown claimed to understand, he was still angry. After all,

32. Oates, *Brown*, p. 269.

33. Sanborn to Higginson, March 4, April 6, 1859, Higginson-Brown Collection, Boston Public Library; Sanborn, *Life and Letters of John Brown*, p. 493.

the secret committee had promised to finance his work. Eventually the two men decided that Brown should seek money in other parts of New England for a few weeks. As Brown traveled, Sanborn would arrange speaking appearances for him in the Boston area.[34]

For the next three weeks Brown toured New England and began to realize the problems Sanborn had in acquiring contributions. Funds for the antislavery cause had dried up, and he was thoroughly disappointed. Two weeks after leaving Boston, Brown received word from Sanborn that he was to make a speaking appearance in Concord early in the second week of May. Brown greeted the news with enthusiasm; Massachusetts abolitionists had been generous in the past, and he hoped this would again be the case.[35]

Brown appeared in Concord with one of his recruits, Jeremiah Anderson, and spoke to virtually the same gathering that he had addressed two years earlier. Unfortunately, his much publicized visit was again a dramatic success and financial failure. He obtained only a small sum from his rapt Concord listeners. The reason Concord citizens received Brown so warmly and gave so little is difficult to determine. Certainly they were not exempt from the financial toll of economic panic. However, by the spring of 1859, the effects of panic had almost worn off; thus, a tight money supply isn't sufficient to explain their reluctance to give. Most likely Brown's Concord audience was uncertain about how he would use the money and about what he proposed to do to end slavery—Brown was unclear on both counts. Bronson Alcott expressed this sentiment best. He said Brown left his Concord friends "much in the dark concerning his destination and designs for the coming months" but "did not conceal his hatred for slavery nor his readiness to strike a blow for freedom." Brown's most perceptive listeners may have noticed that he was more excited and less controlled than during his first visit to Concord; perhaps for that reason they grew wary. Still, despite Brown's intensified tone, Alcott continued to regard Brown as

34. Sanborn to Higginson, Arpil 19, May 9, 1859, Higginson-Brown Collection, Boston Public Library; Sanborn, *Recollections,* 1: 163.
35. Oates, *Brown,* p. 269.

"the manliest man" he had ever seen. Brown was "the type and synonym for the Just."[36]

In view of the financial failure at Concord, Frank Sanborn was pleased that Samuel Gridley Howe made good on his promise to enlist the aid of John Murray Forbes. Very soon after the Concord visit, Brown was on his way to meet Forbes with a letter of reference from Howe. In the letter Howe described Brown as a man who could "deliver our land from the curse of slavery" and praised him for being "of the Puritan militant order." Howe recommended that Forbes assist Brown because he was "an enthusiast, yet cool, keen and cautious." Forbes should further bear in mind that Brown had a "martyr's spirit" and would ask "nothing but the pledge to keep to your self what he may say." The recommendation, combined with the short speech Brown gave to clergymen gathered at the Forbes home, impressed the railroad magnate, but he was judicious with his funds and gave only $100 to Brown for "travelling expenses." Before Brown left Forbes's home, however, a representative of the ministers approached him and pressed five twenty-dollar gold pieces into his palm.[37]

Despite Howe's favorable letter to Forbes and his desire to answer questions about slave capabilities, friction developed between the doctor and Brown soon after the Forbes meeting. It is possible that Howe never forgave Brown for the role he had been forced to play the previous spring. Brown's indiscretion had required Howe to lie to his friends and bear chief responsibility for putting Wilson and Sumner "off the track." For months Howe had been impressed by Brown's values and character, by his regard for discipline, control, and efficiency. Now, one year later, the doctor was upset by Brown's apparent failure to live by the very principles he had initially seemed to embody. Mistakes like the Forbes fiasco were unforgivable. At the same time,

36. Sanborn to Higginson, May 9, 1859, Higginson-Brown Collection, Boston Public Library; Sanborn *Recollections,* 1: 163.

37. Sarah Hughes Forbes, *The Letters and Recollections of John Murray Forbes* (Boston, 1899), 1: 178; John Murray Forbes to Howe, May 12, 1859; Howe to John Murray Forbes, May 25, 1859, Howe Collection, Massachusetts Historical Society; Schwartz, *Howe,* p. 232; Howe, *Journals,* p. 436.

Howe was made uneasy by a slight change he perceived in Brown's tone and temperament. The doctor sensed a subtle difference in the day-to-day manner of the "cool enthusiast" which irritated him further. Brown seemed overly excitable, exceptionally nervous, and unbearably imperious. He seemed absorbed by considerations quite apart from his immediate surroundings. He seemed too easily rattled by criticism and repeatedly, almost mechanically, quoted Scripture to quell any doubts expressed by his supporters. This kind of behavior disturbed Howe. The blind biblical spoutings and strange disembodied aura about Brown hinted at a loss of control. Because Howe was forever chastising himself for such behavior, he liked it less in a man who was about to incite a slave insurrection.[38]

The friction between these two men resulted in a minor confrontation over the tactics Brown used during his Missouri raid. Howe balked at Brown's seemingly cavalier attitude toward the theft of slaveholder's property during the raid. Stealing slaves was one thing; stealing the physical property of the slaveholder was entirely different. Howe kept remembering the Hamptons. The two men exchanged heated words over the issue. Brown said he was right to take property earned at the expense of slavery and muttered a scriptural justification for his acts. Howe responded by reasserting his own view and saying he was unmoved by men who quoted Scripture to cover unlawful activity. Theft was theft.[39]

Even though uncertainty and anger caused Howe to doubt Brown, the physician did not withdraw his support from the proposed insurrection. Nor did his concern about Brown's competence and his unresolved ambivalence about violence (masquerading as a worry about slaveholder's property) drive him away from the plan. There were too many new and unanswered questions growing in Howe about antislavery reform and the slave's behavior once he was freed from slavery. Brown's intended strike was one of the ways in which these and other questions could be answered.

38. Howe to Parker, January 22, 1860, Howe Collection, Houghton Library.
39. Ibid.

There were additional reasons for Howe's continued support of Brown. As Howe noted in a letter to Charles Sumner, it was important to give the "fullest and finest scope to individuals." Each man must be encouraged to "work with his own weapons in his own way." Such a belief implied a faith in God's providence. When Howe reflected on his experiences with Brown during the past two years, he realized that much of Brown's erratic behavior had been caused by not being allowed to fight for the freedom of the slave "with his own weapons" and "in his own way." Brown's imperiousness was a product of frustration. Perhaps if he were given "the fullest and finest scope" for his activities, slaves all over the South would rally to his banner. Howe may once again have reflected on the effect of political attempts to end slavery. They had all failed. Indeed, political currents seemed to be "drifting toward the destruction of the Republican Party." Much as he wanted to have faith in that party, by the spring of 1859, Howe believed strongly that it had contributed to its own demise. Any party "based on the principle of progress and reform" must die away when "it ceased to call for any progress." The antislavery movement had failed to extinguish slavery and so had the Republican Party. Where was one to turn except to a man like Brown?[40]

During the weeks Brown spent in Boston, he met with George Luther Stearns on a number of occasions. Their most memorable public exchange took place at the Bird Club, an informal gathering of Massachusetts politicians, literati, and businessmen, who regularly met at the Parker House. Here, before the many distinguished members of the club, Brown presented Stearns with the pearl-handled Bowie knife he had taken from Henry Clay Pate at Black Jack. The gesture moved Stearns, though he was mildly upset by Brown's presentation speech. When Brown gave him the knife, he said he did so with the thought that the two of them would probably "never meet again in this world." Brown hoped Stearns would accept the gift as a "token of his gratitude" and claimed that in the future the knife might have some "little

---

40. Howe to Charles Sumner, August 20, 1859; Howe to Martin Conway, September 15, 1859, Howe Collection, Houghton Library.

historic value." The obvious fatalism in Brown's words disturbed Stearns. For months he had been led to believe that, though there was a chance Brown would be killed, Brown expected to come away from his venture alive and ready to command a mountain fortress full of slaves. Stearns was also concerned by the angry exchange that took place between Brown and Henry Wilson after the presentation. Wilson was distressed by the Missouri raid and made it clear that he did not approve of it. His censure drew a sharp rebuff from Brown. Stearns was shocked by the vehemence of Wilson's comments and realized for the first time what his relationship with Brown might mean for his future standing in the political abolitionist community of Massachusetts. Still, Stearns's uneasiness did not prompt him to pull back from supporting Brown. When Brown left Boston, he did so with $1,200 which had been contributed by the Medford businessman.[41]

Whether by mere chance or Brown's careful planning, one incident that occurred in late May did much to bolster the confidence of Howe, Stearns, Higginson, and Sanborn. Harriet Tubman, the black woman whose underground railroad activities were legendary, appeared in Boston to support Brown. Tubman's visit seemed to buttress what other black leaders, Brown, and Redpath had said all along: Once the insurrection was started, southern slaves could depend on the support of their free northern brethren. Sanborn was particularly impressed by the imposing woman. He immediately notified Higginson of her presence and asked him to come to Boston. The minister would be "amazed" at the rescue stories she told. The secretary hoped Tubman's appearance would prompt Higginson to tap the Worcester County Committee funds, which both he and Brown had been pursuing for months.[42]

41. Henry Bowditch, Bowditch Letter, June 9, 1887, Brown Collection, Massachusetts Historical Society; Stearns, *Life of Stearns*, p. 181; Oates, *Brown*, pp. 270–72; "Wilson Testimony," *Mason Report*, p. 140; Villard, *Brown*, pp. 396–97; Sanborn, *Life and Letters of John Brown*, p. 523; Sanborn to Higginson, May 30, June 4, 1859, Higginson-Brown Collection, Boston Public Library.

42. Sanborn to Higginson, May 30, 1858, Higginson-Brown Collection, Boston Public Library.

Higginson did travel to Boston to speak with the powerful Canadian black woman, and after listening to her description of eight "railroad" trips to the South, he was indeed "amazed." Her "tales of adventure" were beyond anything in fiction, and her "ingenuity" was extraordinary. The trip to Boston did more than strengthen Higginson's belief in Brown's project. As he saw money being raised for Brown by Stearns, Sanborn, and Howe, the Worcester activist became less critical of their decision to postpone the plan during the previous May. Now they all seemed interested in keeping their promise to support Brown and showed some conviction that the plan would succeed. Higginson, in particular, was more charitable toward Sanborn, who was again playing a very active role in Brown's behalf. As a sign of this new-found respect for the young secretary's exertions, Higginson promised to stop in Concord during July to evaluate the progressive educational program Sanborn and his sister Sarah had devised for the children of the town.[43]

After collecting almost $2,000 from secret committee members and other New Englanders who knew little or nothing of his proposed venture, John Brown left Boston on June 3, 1859 for the last time. He was generally pleased by his fund-raising success and felt that "final arrangements" could be made for the Harpers Ferry raid. He confided to Sanborn (who surely conveyed the message to the other committee members) that he expected to be "on the ground" as soon as possible and wanted to begin operations "by July 4th." Brown was optimistic. He had funds, arms, a crew of fine men, and he was confident about

43. Higginson to Louisa Higginson, June 17, July 22, 1859, Higginson Collection, Houghton Library. In general, Higginson was pleased with the teaching methods Sanborn employed. He liked the informality of the classroom setup and the ease with which students moved around it. The "whole moral influence" of the school was "excellent." But one thing upset Higginson. He was afraid the relaxed routine of learning would bar students from "acquiring . . . or retaining habits of . . . application or regular discipline." Undoubtedly Higginson was prompted to reflect on the "school" which John Brown was preparing to start in the Virginia mountains. Certainly no such laxity would exist there. The routine Brown envisioned in his provisional constitution would definitely develop habits of "application" and "discipline."

"recruiting people from Harriet Tubman's ranks." On his way to New York City, Brown stopped at Collinsville, Connecticut, and made the last payment on the 1,000 steel pikes he had ordered from blacksmith Charles Blair two years earlier. Everything seemed ready.[44]

From his Peterboro mansion Gerrit Smith carefully followed the proceedings in Boston that spring. As he did, the intensity of his commitment to Brown and insurrection increased. Before Brown left Boston, the Peterboro squire forwarded an additional $200 for Brown's "Kansas work." But Smith's commitment is reflected by more than the allocation of funds. He had recently finished working on his third religious discourse, and the degree of influence Brown had on him is clearly evident in the tract. For three years Brown had been telling Smith that he felt a divine inspiration, a mission to free slaves and overthrow slavery. For the same length of time, Smith had just as vigorously advocated a "religion of reason" which emphasized man and conscience, not doctrine, the Bible, or God's providential manipulation of human events. In June 1859, Smith made a revealing theological concession to Brown. Before submitting his final discourse for publication, Smith incorporated the notion of divine inspiration into his own religious theory in a way which significantly departed from his previous treatments of the concept. In his third discourse he asked whether or not reason alone was sufficient to achieve "true religion" and answered that it was not. Smith asserted that "unless Divine influence" upon men was increasing, there could be no "true religion." Enlightened reason was vain unless there was also a "God-given spirit of submission to its control." Reason and will were vain unless man allowed "his Maker to work in him." Man must let heaven dispose him to put his physical, mental, and moral powers to "heavenly use." Certainly these notions about inspiration can be interpreted in many ways. They may be seen as another manifestation of Smith's desire to maintain certain well-established Calvinist concepts while advocating

44. Sanborn to Higginson, June 4, 1859, Higginson-Brown Collection, Boston Public Library; Oates, *Brown*, p. 272.

a radical religion of reason. It has already been shown that during Smith's religious perambulations, he always held to certain basic Calvinist tenets. And Smith was never one to worry about maintaining seemingly antithetical positions at the same time. Yet, it also appears that Smith's need to discuss inspiration, and the emphasis he accorded it, are reflective of both Brown's argumentation and Smith's view of him as the "greatest living Christian." Smith's support of Brown was based primarily on a regard for Brown's individualist values and his ability to "restrain passions and appetite." But, at least in part, it was also premised on a somewhat frail belief in Brown's assertions of his own providential instrumentality.[45]

Smith indicated the strength of his support for Brown more in the months ahead, particularly in the way he handled his annual invitation to speak at the Jerry rescue commemorative ceremonies on October 1 at Syracuse. When the invitation was submitted to Smith in late August, he declined to speak. The refusal was extraordinary. Smith had participated in the rescue and had always used the ceremony to elaborate his abolitionist views. The speeches he gave in the years following the attempt had been harbingers of his continually shifting thoughts on the direction in which abolitionism should be moving. In August 1859, however, Smith shocked and disappointed many who had shared the occasion with him previously by asserting that it was "unwise to repeat the farce any longer." The rescue had been a noble deed. Its participants had had their "humanity up," when they acted to resist Jerry's arrest. They understood there could be no law for slavery. But as far as Smith was concerned, it was again time to "let . . . professions make room for practice." People who talked well for slavery should stand aside for those who would vote well against it. Smith also pushed abolitionists to do more than vote because he went on to suggest that any declarations which were made against forcible resistance to the laws of slavery were "senseless." It was to instances of forcible resistance that nations were "indebted" for their "greatest progress." Ameri-

45. Smith to Brown, June 4, 1859, in Sanborn, *Recollections*, 1: 165; Smith, *Sermons*, pp. 80, 45–46.

can government was in rebellion against the "right of every innocent man to his personal liberty." Indeed, it was because of this rebellion against justice that the New York abolitionist believed it might be "too late to bring slavery to an end by peaceful means—too late to vote it down" because it must "go out in blood." In Smith's opinion there was not enough virtue left in white men for them to vote slavery down. Blacks had "come to despair accomplishment of this work by white people." The feeling among slaves was that they must deliver themselves, and it was a feeling that "gained strength with fearful rapidity." There was no resource left to slaves but "God and insurrection." Smith then promised that white Americans could look for insurrections "any year, any month, any day." Insurrection was a "terrible remedy," but it was necessary to overcome a "terrible wrong." Even an abortive uprising would have an effect because it would fill the South with horror and startle northern moral sensibilities. Smith closed his letter with a warning to all those who took his remarks lightly. He was "not a lying prophet—another Cassandra." Slaveholders' blood would be shed—soon.[46]

46. Frothingham, *Smith,* p. 228; Smith to John Thomas, August 27, 1859, Smith Collection, Syracuse University Library.

CHAPTER 8

The Harpers Ferry Raid

BEFORE JOHN BROWN LEFT Boston, he spoke of launching his insurrectionary strike by Independence Day, but the plan was predicated on such a range of variables that committee members were not surprised when the raid was temporarily put off and Brown missed his deadline. In early August Brown again pressed Sanborn for money so that his "operations" would not be delayed any further. He also sent John Jr. to seek more support from George Luther Stearns.[1]

Sanborn received Brown's request and immediately wrote to Higginson for assistance. Sanborn claimed to take great pleasure in learning that Brown had completed the first phase of his "business" and pleaded with Higginson to help him make up $300 so as not to thwart final execution of the plan. By the first week in September, the committee secretary hadn't come close to raising the amount Brown desired. Samuel Gridley Howe did send $50 south and then started scurrying around Boston looking for more money. Higginson could raise only $25. When Sanborn asked for more, the minister became infuriated by the implication that he was somehow shirking his duty.

While Sanborn looked for funds, Stearns listened to John Jr.'s pleas for assistance. Stearns told him that he had the "fullest confidence" in his father "no matter what the outcome of his efforts," but the Medford businessman refused to give any more money. Finally, in the third

---

1. Sanborn to Higginson, August 24, 1859, Higginson-Brown Collection, Boston Public Library; Sanborn to Brown, August 27, 1859, in *Mason Report,* p. 67.

week of September, Sanborn sent $50 to Chambersburg, Pennsylvania (Brown's backup base), along with an apologetic note explaining why he was unable to raise the full sum Brown had requested.[2]

For the next two weeks Sanborn continued to search for funds. On October 6, the search ended when Sanborn met and interviewed young Francis Merriam, the emotionally erratic nephew of the distinguished Boston abolitionist, Francis Jackson. Merriam was obsessed with the thought of joining Brown and asked Sanborn to give him specific information about Brown's plans. He already knew a good deal about the scheme because of his friendship with James Redpath. At first Sanborn balked. However, when Merriam offered to contribute $600 to the plan if he were allowed to participate in it, the committee secretary quickly reconsidered. Sanborn summoned George Luther Stearns and Lewis Hayden to Concord to assist him in making the decision. During the evening of October 6 and the early morning hours of October 7, all three men rigorously questioned Merriam about his motives for wanting to join with Brown and the personal qualifications he had for assisting the proposed raid. Merriam said he had traveled with Redpath in 1857 and 1858 as the journalist gathered information for his book *Talks with Slaves.* But in spite of these experiences, neither Sanborn, Stearns, nor Hayden was impressed with the unstable youth. Still, all of them knew of Brown's desperate need for cash. Merriam might not be qualified for the project, but the money he could contribute insured execution of the plan. Eventually, they all decided to send him to Chambersburg.[3]

---

2. Ibid.; "Stearns Testimony," *Mason Report,* pp. 233–35; Harry Stearns to Stearns, April 21, 1863, Stearns Collection, Massachusetts Historical Society; John Brown, Jr., to John Kagi, August 11, 17, 1859, *Mason Report,* p. 69. John Jr. also seems to have journeyed to Peterboro looking for aid from Gerrit Smith. Smith gave him $160, and Edwin Morton told him that the philanthropist had his "whole soul absorbed . . . in this matter."

3. Stearns to Higginson, September 8, 1859, Higginson-Brown Collection, Boston Public Library; Lewis Hayden to Mary Stearns, April 8, 1878, Memo on Francis Merriam, Boyd B. Stutler Collection; Stanley J. and Anita W. Robboy, "Lewis Hayden: From Fugitive Slave to Statesman," *New England Quarterly* 46 (December 1973): 591–613.

Within a few days Sanborn received a note from Merriam indicating that he had joined Brown, turned over the $600, and was patiently awaiting the "business operation" that was soon to commence. Sanborn was excited. Later, when he received a letter from Higginson complaining about Brown's delay and questioning the wisdom of sending Merriam south, he felt so confident that Brown was about to begin the venture that he boldly criticized Higginson's skepticism. Sanborn asked Higginson if they had "seen so little print" from Brown's labors "that we should distrust . . . his valor." Hadn't Brown "saved Kansas in '56 and wounded Missouri in '58?" There was absolutely no reason to doubt Brown. The secretary met Higginson's criticism of Merriam with a highly matured cynicism. Merriam had not been chosen because of any "great passion for Redpath" or belief in the youth's personal capacity. Sanborn agreed that Merriam was about "as fit to be in the enterprise as the Devil to keep a powder house." Merriam had been selected only because of the money he could contribute to the project. Sanborn reminded Higginson that "everything has its use and must be put to it if possible." Then, after informing Higginson that news could soon be expected from the site of Brown's activity, the secretary concluded his letter with a brief lecture on one of the most important lessons he had learned in the past few years. Sanborn told Higginson that he never expected much from anybody but believed there was "a grain of use in all persons and things." When "a plum" dropped in one's mouth, one shouldn't refuse to eat it because it wasn't "a peach or a pumpkin." Francis Merriam might not be "Divine property," but he was a "plum" and had his use.[4]

John Brown arrived at Harpers Ferry, Virginia, on July 3, 1859, with his sons Owen and Oliver. A third son, Watson, would join him in a few weeks. The town nestled on a small jetty of land near the confluence of the Shenandoah and Potomac Rivers, about eighty miles west of Baltimore and sixty miles northwest of Washington, D.C. It

4. Sanborn to Higginson, October 6, 13, 1859, Higginson-Brown Collection, Boston Public Library.

was a picturesque village surrounded by hilly terrain and small farms cut out of the pine and hardwood forest. Brown chose to launch his raid at Harpers Ferry because it housed a federal armory where firearms and munitions were manufactured for the army. He knew it would take more than Stearns's 200 revolvers, Massachusetts Kansas's 198 Sharpe's rifles, and the 1,000 pikes now being shipped to his backup base in Chambersburg, a few miles north, to properly supply the slaves who rallied to his banner.

Brown rented a small farmhouse north of town to serve as his headquarters and immediately began poring over maps and making final preparations. Brown consulted with John E. Cook, a recruit who had been living in the area for almost a year doing reconnaissance work at his request. In late July, Brown settled on his final plan of attack. He decided to storm the federal armory (a large multipurpose structure containing a fire engine house, forge, machine, and stocking shops, and an arsenal, or storehouse), then take over and loot the arsenal. The raiders would hold the entire complex briefly, while word went out to slaves in the surrounding area. When enough slaves had joined him, he would lead the entire group south, inciting further insurrection as he went. He would not, as he had often suggested, retreat to a mountain fortress.

Brown was surprised by the angry reaction which greeted his revelation of the plan's last feature. Threats of mutiny arose among his small cadre; tension mounted in the heat and confinement of his base. As he struggled to hold his tiny band together and prepare the assault, Brown faced other difficulties as great as his men's discontent. He was disappointed that so few men had joined him from the North. For over a year and a half he had partially revealed or, at least, vaguely alluded to his scheme among approximately eighty abolitionists, black and white. Few (except the Six) had done anything to finance the venture, but a number had promised to recruit raiders for the attack. By late August, it had become apparent that these promises were not to be fulfilled: Only sixteen men had trickled south to join him. Pleas sent to white abolitionist friends as well as hurried meetings with Frederick Douglass in Chambersburg and black leaders in Philadelphia did nothing to improve the situation. Brown was also plagued by dwindling finances. He had used all of the money given to him (over $2,000 raised by the Six that spring and $200 sent by Smith in June) to buy supplies, cover expenses, and pay for John Jr.'s travels throughout the Northeast in search of recruits. Without additional funds, Brown knew it would be impossible to launch his attack. There was also a bothersome delay in the shipment of the 1,000 pikes he had purchased from Connecticut blacksmith Charles Blair. Then, too, Brown's own behavior contributed to his problems. The men who assembled at the Kennedy farm watched skeptically as Brown seemed to show more concern for preparing "Vindication of the Invasion" (a justification of the raid written in the past tense) and "General Orders, No. 1" (which provided for the organization of his provisional army) than he did for examining possible escape routes out of Harpers Ferry.

Yet, somehow, in the midst of these troubles Brown prevailed. He quelled talk of mutiny with a threat to abandon the project entirely. He eventually resigned himself to the small size of the raiding party and even justified it to his men and himself on grounds of military efficiency. In late September, Brown rejoiced when he was notified by his second lieutenant, John Kagi, that the pikes had arrived at Chambersburg. Brown's final problem, the lack of money, was alleviated when Francis Merriam arrived in camp on October 15 with $600 in gold.

In the early evening of Sunday, October 16, John Brown gathered his twenty-one-man force together for a final discussion of the plan. He directed his son Owen, Barclay Coppoc, and Merriam to take control of the revolvers, rifles, and pikes and to store them in a small schoolhouse north of town. The group was to stay with the weapons and distribute them to slaves from Maryland and northwest Virginia who, Brown was sure, would stream toward Harpers Ferry when word of the raid spread. The rest of his men would follow him into town and be assigned special tasks once the armory was taken. After these instructions were given, a wagon was packed with arms and supplies, and each man prepared himself for the assault. Brown spent his last few moments in the farmhouse reviewing his insurrection documents and letters from northern sympathizers, all of which he placed in a carpet-bag and locked inside a trunk in the main room of the house. Shortly before eight o'clock, he signaled his men to move out.

After leaving Owen and his group at the schoolhouse, Brown and his cadre made their way toward Harpers Ferry. At the edge of town they cut telegraph lines, and Brown instructed John Kagi to hold the Shenandoah Bridge (a structure designed to transport both train and wagon traffic), which served as the main entrance to town. He took the rest of his men to the federal armory, seized it (taking a few hostages in the process), and then barricaded himself inside the arsenal. He then sent a few raiders under Osborne Anderson into the country-side south of town. They were to spread word of the raid among slaves and capture more hostages. (Anderson eventually returned with ten liberated slaves and three hostages, including Colonel Lewis W. Washington, a descendant of the nation's first president.) Brown and the remaining raiders sat still as the town exploded in panic. Men ran everywhere screaming insurrection, and a few unsuccessful attempts were made to drive Kagi off the bridge. In the midst of this uproar, Brown was patient, even allowing a train coming in from the West to pass across the bridge on the theory that the news it bore would hasten slave revolt. Unfortunately for Brown, by eleven o'clock Monday morning the only people who had flocked to Harpers Ferry were Virginia militiamen and armed farmers. They moved so rapidly that they effectively barred escape and then refused Brown's bid to negotiate his way out of the armory during the afternoon and early evening. In the meantime, Brown and his men skirmished with everyone who tried to retake the building. By the early morning hours of Tuesday, only Brown and four raiders were alive, holed up with a few hostages inside the engine house. The rest of his men, including John Kagi and his sons, Oliver and Watson, were either dead or mortally wounded. Late in the morning, federal troops under the command of Brevet Colonel Robert E. Lee and Lieutenant J. E. B. Stuart arrived from Washington, D.C., and were stationed in front of the armory. Stuart requested Brown to release the remaining hostages and give up. Brown said he would do so only if guaranteed safe passage out of town. Stuart replied by sending troops into the engine house. In the melee that followed, Brown was wounded, Dauphin Thompson and Jeremiah Anderson were killed, and the raid intended to instigate wholesale slave insurrection was over.

Tuesday afternoon Stuart and some of his men inspected Brown's headquarters at the Kennedy farm and found the carpetbag filled with insurrection documents and incriminating letters. The information was turned over to Governor Henry Wise, and United States Senator James Mason of Virginia, and Ohio Representative Clement Vallandingham who had traveled to Harpers Ferry to interrogate Brown. When Mason asked how the raid had been financed, Brown claimed to have furnished most of the money himself. Brown told Vallandingham that he had corresponded with northerners about the raid, but no one had participated in its planning. When Vallandingham asked him if he had read Gerrit Smith's letter to the Jerry Rescue committee, he said he had not but that he certainly agreed with Smith's sentiment that "moral suasion is hopeless."[5]

On Monday, October 17, a few days after he received Sanborn's note, Higginson was forced to agree with its contentions. Merriam had been useful. His money had primed an explosion at Harpers Ferry, Virginia. Reports were circulating in Worcester about an attack on the federal armory in that small southern town, and Higginson was thrilled. In fact, he thought of rushing south to assist Brown and said he would have done so if it hadn't been for his wife's poor health. He considered Brown's escapade the "most formidable insurrection" that ever occurred, believed there was "great capacity and skill" behind it, and was sure it would weaken the Slave Power. In the past nothing had so strengthened slavery as the slave's "timid submission."[6]

As Higginson heard the first, sketchy reports of the raid, he was confident that such submissiveness was ended. If this new assertive attitude were coupled with "constant communication with Canada,"

5. Oates, *Brown,* pp. 274–306.
6. Higginson to Louisa Higginson, October 1859, Higginson Collection, Houghton Library.

it would teach blacks "self-importance and resistance." Higginson
eagerly awaited Brown's retreat to the mountains, where he would
establish a "Maroon colony" like those in Jamaica. Hoping to publicize
the positive effect that such a fortress community would have on slaves
and at the same time discreetly link himself to Brown among those
abolitionists who were not already aware of the connection, Higginson
wrote James Russell Lowell at the *Atlantic Monthly* asking if he could
do an article about the Maroons of Surinam and Jamaica—"suggested
by the late Virginia affair."[7]

The minister's initial optimism, however, was soon replaced by
dejection. Further reports from Virginia indicated the raid had failed.
After joining Howe, John A. Andrew, and others in forming a defense
committee for Brown, Higginson spent the next week reading newspaper accounts of the attack and carefully gauging the impact it had
on northern public opinion. In a speech given at Brimley Hall in
Worcester on October 25, the day Brown's trial began, Higginson
stated that "nine out of ten" in Worcester sympathized with the
insurrection and "only regretted that Captain Brown was not successful." Despite this bold assertion, Higginson knew that in Worcester
there was less enthusiasm for insurrection than for the man who had
attempted it. People were unsure about the act; however, they had a
strong, personal sympathy for Brown. This situation forced a predica-
ment upon the minister. On one hand, he knew that, given such
tremendous popular sympathy, Brown's martyrdom would be a powerful spur to antislavery sentiment. On the other hand, Higginson had
strong feelings that he should make some effort at rescue. His quandry
is reflected in an emotional response to his mother's scoldings about
the failure of Massachusetts abolitionists to do anything to secure
Brown's release. Higginson told his mother that he thought about
Brown's plight but said he didn't feel certain Brown's "acquittal or
rescue would do half as much as his being executed." He assured his
mother that a defense committee was doing all it could for Brown.

7. Ibid.; Higginson to James Russell Lowell, October 27, 1859, Higginson Collection, Houghton Library.

They had provided counsel and had sent a young lawyer, George Hoyt, from Athol, Massachusetts, to assist Brown and to act as a liaison with his supporters. Beyond such help, there seemed no way open for anything. There was "no chance for forcible assistance and next to none for strategem." The minister had never seen a situation more impractical for rescue.[8]

Higginson was torn between the desire to make a rescue attempt, in spite of its impracticality, and the desire to exploit Brown's death for the cause of abolition. No doubt he remembered the advice of Wendell Phillips and Albert Browne in the wake of the Burns rescue attempt. At that time the two men told him to shake off any despair about the failure—Burns's rendition was a secondary matter. Higginson's effective use of the issue to influence popular opinion against the Fugitive Slave Law was the important thing. Higginson understood abolitionist tactics enough to know what effect Brown's death would have on northern minds—abolitionist and nonabolitionist alike. Though no specific documentation exists to prove the contention, it seems certain that at least a small portion of Higginson's willingness to finance Brown was based on this realization. Certainly after the Burns affair there can be no question that Higginson understood that a failed abolitionist act often did as much for the cause as a successful one. He said as much in a letter to John Jr. shortly after the raid aborted. Higginson told young Brown that his father *had failed in his original effort only to succeed in a greater result.*[9]

It has been suggested that Thomas Wentworth Higginson denied John Brown by never again admitting what he had when first reports of the attack filtered into Worcester—namely, that Brown meant to incite the "most formidable slave insurrection ever." He has also been criticized for waiting too long to explain the absence of a slave

8. Thomas Wentworth Higginson, Speech at Brimley Hall [October 25, 1859], in *New York Herald,* October 28, 1859; Higginson to Louisa Higginson, October 27, 1859, Higginson Collection, Houghton Library; Edelstein, *Strange Enthusiasm,* pp. 225, 231; Higginson, *Journals,* pp. 86–87; Schwartz, *Howe,* p. 235.

9. Higginson to John Brown, Jr., November 10, December 2, 1859, Higginson-Huntington Collection, Huntington Library; Edelstein, *Strange Enthusiasm,* p. 231.

uprising at Harpers Ferry. But his so-called denial becomes more understandable as we examine Higginson's awareness of the way in which northern public opinion responded to Brown. Higginson's major concern in the days after Harpers Ferry was to exploit the personal sympathy that welled up for Brown. As Higginson saw it, his primary task and that of other northern abolitionists was to promote Brown's character and play down the act of insurrection. Tactically this was simply a variation on the same theme used by Howe, Parker, and Phillips when they attempted to remove Edward Loring from his probate judgeship after the Burns rendition. Higginson knew that most northerners did not accept the legitimacy of insurrection. Thus, it was necessary to justify Harpers Ferry by defining it in personal terms. It was not insurrection, but Brown's character which had to be legitimized. In this way Brown could do "more than Sumner or Kansas to re-awaken antislavery agitation." John A. Andrew, the abolitionist lawyer and state representative, made the point clearly in an address to abolitionists who gathered at Tremont Temple shortly after Brown's sentencing in early November. Andrew said he had not considered "whether the enterprise of John Brown and his associates in Virginia was wise or foolish, right or wrong." He only knew that "whether the enterprise was one or the other, John Brown himself was right." Like Higginson and other noted abolitionists, Andrew said he revered the man because he believed in "eternal right." Andrew did not sympathize with insurrection.[10]

Julia Howe read about Brown's raid in the *Boston Transcript*. When she told her husband, he is said to have casually replied, "Brown has got to work." That simple assertion belied Howe's emotional turmoil about the disastrous results of the attack—a turmoil which flared into panic on Wednesday, October 19, when an investigation at the Kennedy farmhouse uncovered letters written to Brown by Howe and the other members of the secret committee. Although Howe said he

10. Ibid., pp. 224–25; Higginson to Louisa Higginson, November 5, 1859, Higginson Collection, Houghton Library; Henry Greenleaf Pearson, *The Life of John A. Andrew* (Boston, 1904), 2: 160.

was confident that Brown would not compromise himself or those dealing with him, he may have had some uneasy recollections of the Forbes fiasco. In the weeks following Brown's arrest, the doctor became paralyzed by the fear of being implicated in the venture. When he joined Higginson, John A. Andrew, and others in setting up a defense committee for Brown, this apprehension prompted Howe's vehement opposition to any discussion about using extralegal efforts to gain Brown's release. Howe's fear forced him to become excessively dependent on the advice of Frank Sanborn, who was, ironically, quite as unnerved by the whole episode as the doctor.[11]

Twenty months earlier, in February 1858, shortly after first hearing Brown's plan at Gerrit Smith's home, Frank Sanborn received a note from his Harvard classmate Edwin Morton. In it, Morton recounted a curious experience with Brown. It seems that after Sanborn left Peterboro, Brown asked Morton whether he would mind accompanying him on a short evening walk. Morton said he'd be happy to do so. After walking side by side through drifts of freshly fallen snow for some time, Morton lapsed into a daydream and forgot that Brown was walking with him. When he realized what he had done and turned to apologize to Brown for allowing his mind to wander, Morton found that he was indeed walking alone. He turned around to look for his companion and saw Brown a few yards behind him. Brown was looking alternately at the imprints his boots made in the snow and the untrodden expanse that lay before him. After a few moments of silence, Brown looked thoughtfully backward, where his and Morton's footprints lay uncovered in the snow. He turned to Morton and said slowly, "I like to see my tracks behind me." Morton felt like he was in the presence of a man who would "leave tracks in the snows of centuries." And Sanborn heartily concurred. After Harpers Ferry, however, Sanborn was considerably less sentimental about the "tracks" Brown left behind. Those "tracks" were incriminating letters from

11. Julia Ward Howe, *Reminiscences* (Boston, 1899), p. 233; Schwartz, *Howe*, pp. 235–37; Howe to Amos A. Lawrence, October 24, 1859, Amos A. Lawrence Collection, Massachusetts Historical Society.

Sanborn, Howe, Stearns, and Smith, which had been left in a carpet-bag at the Virginia farmhouse Brown had used as his base of operations. They led all the way back to Boston, Peterboro, and the Secret Committee of Six.[12]

On October 19 many newspapers carried the first full account of the bag's contents. In it there were two letters from Sanborn, a note from Gerrit Smith, and an envelope addressed to Brown from Howe. The two letters from Sanborn were dated September 4 and 23 and contained drafts for $50 and $55, respectively. In the letter sent on September 23, Sanborn told Brown he was "glad to hear all goes well and is so ready for business." More disheartening to Sanborn and the other committee members was the *New York Herald*'s published report on the questioning of Brown's men about northern assistance. The *Herald* noted that all of the prisoners' stories were the same, except for that of "Young Brown" (most likely the dying Watson). He answered a question about whether or not his father had received support from radical northern abolitionists by saying there were "parties in the North connected with this movement."[13]

Sanborn was unnerved when he read these reports. Late in the afternoon on Wednesday (the same day the account was printed), he rushed to Stearns's home in Medford to decide what action he should take to prevent the inevitability of arrest. After consultations which lasted into the early morning hours on Thursday, October 20, the two conspirators decided to seek the assistance of Stearns's legal counsel, John A. Andrew. In their meeting with Andrew both men asked if they were liable to arrest in Massachusetts for their complicity with Brown. They did not, however, give Andrew the "full particulars" of what that complicity involved. Because Andrew was uncertain about what the two men had done, he was only able to give general answers to their questions. Stearns and Sanborn grew more upset. As a precautionary measure against arrest, they decided to run to Canada for safety.

12. Edwin Morton to Sanborn, February 1884, Sanborn-Brown Collection, Houghton Library; *Boston Traveller,* October 21, 25, 1859; *New York Herald,* October 25, 1859.

13. Ibid.

Late Thursday afternoon they boarded a cargo ship bound for Quebec and arrived there one day later.[14]

Once in Canada, the two secret committee members had second thoughts about their flight. Both Sanborn and Stearns feared arrest and had fled Boston hoping to avoid it, but during their stay they saw how their panic had intensified the threat. At the same time they attempted to rationalize their behavior by claiming that they had left Massachusetts to keep the size of Brown's effort concealed. By this action, both the reach and character of the raid would be "exaggerated." While in Quebec the two conspirators received further disheartening news about their legal position. Wendell Phillips sent a detailed analysis of Andrew's views. According to Phillips, the lawyer now believed Stearns's and Sanborn's complicity could be regarded as treason. These words shattered both men. A year earlier they had been certain that such treason would be considered patriotism by most northerners. Now they were confused about where they should be, uncertain about what they should do, and doubtful about support from the citizens of Massachusetts. It seemed that "treason" would not be considered "patriotism" after all.[15]

Phillips's letter did contain some information that gave them hope. Andrew thought that if they were arrested for treasonous activity, they could only be "tried in the district where the acts had been committed." This advice, coupled with Higginson's urging that they come home immediately, a note from Emerson suggesting the same thing, and their own worries about running away, prompted their return to Boston on October 26, six days after their panic-stricken flight. They came home in time to read newspaper accounts of Brown's stoic behavior at his trial. Unquestionably, their guilt was compounded by Brown's heroic posture. But that guilt was not enough to prevent either man from further flights, further denials of complicity, further

14. Sanborn to Higginson, October 21, 1859, Higginson-Brown Collection, Boston Public Library; Villard, *Brown,* p. 530; Sanborn, *Recollections,* 1: 187–89.

15. Sanborn to Parker, November 22, 1859, Sanborn-Brown Collection, Houghton Library; Sanborn, *Recollections,* 1: 192, 196.

rationalizations, and further panicked discussions about the possibility of arrest.[16]

In Worcester Thomas Wentworth Higginson was shamed and angered by the disparity between Brown's behavior and that of his fellow conspirators. He saw their actions as nothing more than a shabby reenactment of their activities during the Forbes disclosures. The same patterns of moral self-righteousness combined with physical cowardice were appearing once again, and Higginson didn't like it. In fact, he was so outraged that he reenacted some of his own previous behavior. This time he decided to do more than boycott a few meetings to show his displeasure. He tried to dissociate himself completely from his fellow committee members. Though he understood the importance of Brown's death to the antislavery movement and though he knew the logistical impracticality of a rescue, Higginson toyed with the idea of freeing Brown. It was his way of divorcing himself from Sanborn and Stearns and atoning for the dishonor he thought their acts brought to the committee. Years later, Higginson said he acted because he would have been "ashamed of doing nothing for Brown." During the last days of October, as Brown's trial proceeded to its inevitable conclusion, the minister considered rescue less out of shame for having done nothing to help Brown, than out of shame at being associated with the other members of the Secret Committee of Six.[17]

As Brown's trial ended on November 2 and he was sentenced to hang one month later, Higginson initiated a "mock" attempt to free Brown—a symbolic gesture of dissociation. He traveled to North Elba ostensibly to pick up Mary Brown and bring her back to Boston where she was to begin the journey to her husband's side in Charlestown. In reality, Higginson made his trip to the Brown homestead for a far different reason. He hoped to persuade Mary Brown to argue the case for rescue with her husband, who had steadfastly spurned all such

16. Ibid.

17. Higginson to Sanborn, January 6, 1875, in Some Verdicts and Trials, Higginson-Barney Collection, Houghton Library; Higginson, *Cheerful Yesterdays,* p. 226.

suggestions. The minister was counting on a plea from Mary to change Brown's mind and to convince him that escape was still desirable. If Brown refused Mary's request, Higginson knew her visit wouldn't be wasted because it was sure to "evoke sympathy."[18]

On November 4 Mary Brown arrived in Boston with Higginson. She was warmly greeted by many prominent members of the Massachusetts abolitionist community at a reception in the American House hotel arranged by Sanborn, Stearns, and Howe. Early the next day she departed for New York City accompanied by George Hoyt, who had recently returned from Virginia, Thomas R. Russell, and Higginson. When the group reached the city, Higginson turned around and headed back to Worcester. The others continued on to Philadelphia, where Higginson had arranged for Mary to be met by J. Miller McKim who was to accompany her to Charlestown. Soon after his return, Higginson received a telegram from George Sennot, another young Massachusetts lawyer sent to Virginia by Brown's Boston defense committee. Sennot told Higginson that Brown had been informed of his wife's pending visit and did not want to see her. Brown was certain the meeting would only distract Mary's mind and add to his own "affliction." Higginson immediately notified McKim, explained Brown's reluctance to see his wife, and asked that Mary not be taken south.[19]

Higginson doubted that Brown's desire not to see Mary was merely a "matter of sentiment." It occurred to the minister that Brown might be worried about her being called as a witness in the pending trials of others caught in the raid. It is also possible that Higginson felt something other than concern for Mary's well-being prompted Brown's refusal. Mary Brown might not only be distracted, she might distract.

18. Higginson to Louisa Higginson, November 5, 1859, Higginson Collection, Houghton Library; Edelstein, *Strange Enthusiasm,* pp. 227–28.

19. Higginson to Brown Family, November 4, 1859, Boyd B. Stutler Collection; Higginson to J. Miller McKim, November 3, 5, 1859, McKim Collection, Cornell University, Ithaca, N.Y.; Edelstein, *Strange Enthusiasm,* p. 228; George Sennot to Higginson, November 5, 1859, Higginson-Brown Collection, Boston Public Library; Higginson to J. Miller McKim, November 5, 1859, McKim Collection, Cornell University.

Mary's appearance might disrupt the image of Brown as a solitary warrior struggling against the institution of slavery. Higginson sensed that Brown knew (better than anyone) the implication of his own martyrdom. Brown's composure at the trial and his consistent refusal to save himself by pleading insanity or contemplating rescue, all led Higginson to suspect the "mysteriously inept" handling of the raid. Brown's veto of Mary's visit increased that suspicion. Higginson was certain that Brown understood how much a failed attempt at insurrection meant to abolition and his own historical identity. It meant that others would see Brown's "tracks" in the "snows of centuries," that the further inscriptions on the Brown family gravestone would have meaning, and that there would be no speculation about the significance of his gift of Pate's knife to Stearns. For a failed ex-businessman, martyrdom at Harpers Ferry was a form of success in the wake of an inglorious string of failures.[20]

When Mary Brown's trip to Charlestown was cancelled, Higginson wrote a short note to the Brown children explaining what had happened. He told them of their father's reluctance to consider escape but suggested that something might still be done for him. Higginson said that there was always a possibility their father would change his mind once he realized his sentence would not be commuted. There can be little doubt, however, that Higginson made such remarks only to bolster the children's spirits. By early November the minister knew Brown would not change his mind. He never mentioned it to the children, but Higginson was aware their father had chosen to die.[21]

In addition to the minister's sensing of Brown's wish, two letters further reinforced his conviction about the pointlessness of rescue. On November 7 Higginson received a note from John LeBarnes, a former Kansas freedom fighter, who had traveled to Charlestown to check on the feasibility of rescue. LeBarnes told Higginson that the whole idea of escape was the furthest thing from Brown's mind—he would not listen to it. Six days after receiving the LeBarnes letter, Higginson

20. Ibid.
21. Higginson to Brown Family, November 4, 1859, Boyd B. Stutler Collection.

heard from James Redpath. The journalist's note proved to Higginson that his assumptions about Brown and martyrdom were correct. Redpath wrote from Baltimore, where he had traveled in search of members of the raiding party who had not been captured. He told Higginson that he had heard rumors about a planned rescue attempt and expressed surprise that anyone would undertake such a scheme. Redpath didn't want Brown freed. He hadn't the faintest desire for Brown to escape martyrdom because Brown's death meant too much to abolition. Redpath himself had already begun to exploit that death. As soon as "Old B was in heaven," the journalist intended to publish a biography which would glorify Brown and repudiate "the notion that his wrongs in Kansas had any influence on his present movements," because such notions cheapened the Harpers Ferry attack and degraded Brown "from the position of Puritan (warring for his Lord) to a guerrilla chief of vindictive manner."[22]

Higginson understood the implication of "Old B's" martyrdom. He understood the catalytic effect Brown's death would have on northern antislavery sentiment. He understood that Brown's repeated refusal to cooperate with rescue efforts was based on a full awareness of his martyrdom's effect. He knew the strategic impossibility of trying to break Brown out of jail. Yet he continued planning, doing so in direct response to his fellow conspirators, who continued to behave in ways which angered him. Making such plans (although they were ritualistic) provided a dramatic way to separate himself from their acts.

Higginson's anger wasn't directed only at Sanborn, Howe, and Stearns. He also felt Gerrit Smith squandered his reputation by the way he acted after Harpers Ferry. In August, Smith had predicted insurrection "any month, any week, any day," but Brown's capture had shocked and unnerved him. Fearing his own implication in the scheme (especially when some of his letters to Brown were found at the Kennedy farmhouse), Smith immediately sent his son-in-law Charles Miller to Boston to collect all other letters that might link him to

22. James Redpath to Higginson, November 13, 1859, Higginson-Brown Collection, Boston Public Library.

Harpers Ferry. Smith's Peterboro mansion was guarded day and night, and parcels arriving for the landowner were inspected for bombs. During Brown's trial and while he awaited the gallows, Smith became distraught and spoke of going to Virginia himself to assist Brown, but what he intended to do by such action remains a mystery.[23]

Smith's biographer suggests that these feelings of shock, anger, fear, and guilt put an enormous strain on the philanthropist in the weeks following the raid and argues that when this strain is coupled with the residual effects of Smith's bout with typhoid in 1857, the exertions of the gubernatorial campaign in 1858, and Smith's arduous religious research in 1859, the reformer's breakdown in the second week of November is understandable. Smith is said to have gone "down under a troop of hallucinations." He supposedly stalked around the Peterboro mansion ranting about his responsibility to Brown and claiming he ought to go south and join him. Because his family believed he might try to convert these fantasies into reality, they had him committed to Utica Asylum under the "humoring notion" that he was, indeed, going south to share Brown's fate. During the next four weeks at Utica, Smith was attended by Dr. John P. Gray. Then, shortly after Brown went to the gallows, Smith was released from the asylum, spent a few weeks recuperating at Gray's home, and returned to Peterboro on December 29, seemingly recovered.[24]

It is difficult to say whether or not Smith did break down only to recover miraculously in four weeks. There is no doubt that Smith had previously become distraught in the face of extreme tension. On other occasions his breakdowns had been treated by isolation, rest, and relaxation. It is possible the trauma caused by Brown's capture and his own implication in the plan demanded repetition of the therapy. It is also possible that Smith's retreat to Utica was an elaborate attempt to avoid arrest. But to suggest that Smith went "temporarily insane" is another matter. No accurate medical analysis of his collapse exists, and a breakdown under pressure is a far cry from insanity. What is certain

23. Frothingham, Smith, p. 241.
24. Ibid., pp. 242–43; Harlow, Smith, p. 222.

about this whole episode is that Smith, like his coconspirators in Boston, had contemplated Brown's failure, but had not prepared himself to face it or the possibility of his own public implication in the affair. Neither Smith nor his committee associates dreamed that Brown would leave letters behind in Harpers Ferry. That Brown had been mistaken in his evaluation of Forbes's character was one thing; the idea that he did not have enough sense to burn correspondence before beginning the raid was quite another. Nor did Smith understand the seeming ineptitude which trapped Brown's cadre inside the federal armory. Given such occurrences, Smith's nervous breakdown is plausible. In any case, Smith and his family must have known that a brief stay at Utica made sense whatever his condition. The asylum was the perfect sanctuary in which to avoid any proslavery retribution and to await the conclusions of those who were investigating the possibility of conspiracy. By mid-December, when it looked as though the only prolonged examination of the raid would be handled by a United States Senate committee chaired by James Mason of Virginia, Smith felt he could relax a bit. Word had it that Mason was more intent on playing down the notion of conspiracy than exposing the existence of one.[25]

The prolonged drama of Smith's so-called insanity compounded Thomas Wentworth Higginson's continued disappointment with the behavior of Stearns and Sanborn. During Mary Brown's visit to Boston, for instance, the two men incessantly discussed the possibility of arrest and what to do about it. Rumors circulated that Stearns had asked George Sennot to retrieve the supplies Brown used during the raid in order to recoup some of the money he had invested in the project. Sanborn continued to contemplate another flight to Canada. He said he had "no intention of going to Canada to avoid arrest *as a criminal* nor for any cause," but he rested that assertion on the stipulation that he could be "reasonably sure" of being protected by his Concord townsmen. And although he often stated he would "hate to leave" Massachusetts, he also said he wouldn't hesitate to flee if it

25. Frothingham, *Smith,* p. 242.

would prevent him from going to jail for six months or a year.[26]

In the first two weeks of November, the overwrought committee secretary frequently huddled with John A. Andrew for advice but still held back "full particulars" of his participation in the conspiracy. Andrew's counsel wasn't pleasing to hear. Andrew believed that under an 1846 law, a material witness could be arrested by warrant from a U.S. judge without any previous summons. While there was some possibility for a writ of *habeas corpus* in the procedure, the lawyer knew that unless a state judge was willing to rule the law unconstitutional, the only way a witness could be released was "by tumult." When Higginson wrote to Sanborn asking him to reconsider fleeing to Canada, the secretary angrily insisted that if he, Howe, and Stearns had the same assurance of citizen protection which Higginson had, there would be no need to flee. At the same time, Sanborn lectured Higginson on the undesirability of Brown's rescue, and said he agreed with Bronson Alcott that the "spectacle of martyrdom" would be of "greater service to the country than years of agitation by Press and voices of partisans." Higginson didn't need the lecture because he was now certain Sanborn was more concerned with Brown's deathly silence than his deathly service.[27]

The minister was further upset by the poor counsel Sanborn seemed to be giving Howe and Stearns. Prompted by Sanborn's views on the reasonableness of flight and Andrew's assessment of their legal position, both men fled to Canada shortly after Mary Brown's visit. They were reluctant to leave Massachusetts but decided that, unless a resolution was introduced in the Massachusetts legislature to protect them, they should stay in Canada as long as it was necessary. Howe's rationale sounded remarkably like Sanborn's. The doctor asserted that Brown's "best chance" was "the appearance of acting upon his own motive and

26. "Stearns Testimony" in *Mason Report,* pp. 225–50; Sanborn to Higginson, November 10, 1859, Higginson-Brown Collection, Boston Public Library; George Sennot to Howe, November 15, 1859, Howe Collection, Massachusetts Historical Society.

27. Sanborn to Higginson, November 13, 1859, Higginson-Brown Collection, Boston Public Library; Sanborn, *Recollections,* 1: 210.

responsibility . . . without the active cooperation of organized Committees or from . . . individuals of the North."[28]

In Higginson's view, flight only added more evidence that the men had been involved in the conspiracy. In his anger at the activities of Howe, Sanborn, Stearns, and Smith, Higginson continued to consider rescue, but only perfunctorily, and had virtually abandoned the scheme by the second week of November because he understood the importance of Brown's martyrdom. He abandoned the idea, that is, until November 15, when he picked up a copy of the *Worcester Telegram*. That day the *Telegram* and other newspapers around the state contained a disclaimer card from Samuel Gridley Howe. In the card Howe attempted to justify his flight to Canada and disavowed any responsibility for John Brown's actions. He insisted that he had no specific knowledge of the Harpers Ferry raid, implied he had no general knowledge either, and suggested that his expatriation should "draw attention to the infamous act by which slaveholders throw a lasso over northern citizens."[29]

When Thomas Wentworth Higginson read the denial card, he immediately roughed out a response. He thought it was one thing to rationalize flight, quite another to begin believing in one's own rationale. In fact, Higginson thought it was "extreme baseness" for Howe to deny complicity with Brown. He reminded Howe of his suggestion that secret committee members make no statements about their relationship to Brown. The minister understood the impropriety of judging other men's acts but said he could not help feeling that Smith's "insanity" and Howe's card were the "only two bad results of the whole affair." It would be the "universal" opinion of all "intelligent" people that the doctor denied "all knowledge" of the raid, "not merely the precise time and place." Higginson knew this was false.[30]

28. Howe to Higginson, November 9, 1859, Higginson-Brown Collection, Boston Public Library; Villard, *Brown,* p. 513; Howe to Charles Sumner, November 21, 1859, Howe Collection, Houghton Library.

29. Samuel Gridley Howe, "Disclaimer Card," in *Worcester Telegram* and *Boston Transcript,* November 15, 1859.

30. Higginson to Howe, November 15, 1859, Higginson-Brown Collection, Boston Public Library.

Surprisingly, Higginson did not send his rebuke to Howe. Instead, he drafted a second protest note and sent it to Sanborn, whose advice he suspected was behind Howe's act. In the brief letter to the secretary, Higginson asked if there was "no such thing as *honor* among confederates." Sanborn replied by apologizing for Howe's card, but he rejected the minister's conclusion that it was the "height of baseness." Sanborn said he saw good reason to prevent southerners from knowing about Brown's accomplices. Then he made what Higginson must have regarded as a ridiculous assertion. Sanborn said that if the names of the conspirators were kept secret, they might "work in the same way" again. As far as Sanborn was concerned, it wasn't "any worse to conceal the facts now than before the outbreak."[31]

What worried Sanborn much more than Howe's card was the possibility of erratic behavior by the volatile Higginson. Any testimony by the minister about the secret committee's activities would be disastrous, and Sanborn knew Higginson was capable of speaking, if only as a gesture of disdain for the "dishonorable" acts of his fellow conspirators. The minister's testimony threatened Sanborn far more than Smith's "insanity," a few burnt letters, some trips to Canada, or a denial card, so Sanborn tried to head off any such action. In his reply to Higginson, he suggested that the minister could recoup his own "honor" by declaring himself in Brown's plot, but he had no right to implicate anyone else. Such implications, declared the petulant committee secretary, would constitute the definition of "baseness." Maybe Howe hadn't "acted well in all ways," but neither had Higginson. Sanborn concluded his note by suggesting that "so long as each person acts for *himself* we must allow some diversities."[32]

The efforts of Sanborn, Stearns, Smith, and Howe to deny their relationship with Brown prompted Higginson again to seriously contemplate a rescue attempt. Until Howe's card and Sanborn's reply to his remonstrance, Higginson had only been playing with the notion

31. Higginson to Sanborn, November 17, 1859; Sanborn to Higginson, November 17, 1859, ibid.; Edelstein, *Strange Enthusiasm,* p. 226.

32. Sanborn to Higginson, November 17, 1859, Higginson-Brown Collection, Boston Public Library.

of rescue. His efforts had been more ritualistic than real. But, in the face of Sanborn's rejection of the scheme and Howe's contention that Brown's death would be "holy and glorious," the minister made a more serious, if still somewhat ritualistic, effort to gain Brown's freedom. He would not allow men who were lacking in physical courage to dictate his actions. Ironically, it was just as Howe wrote to Andrew from Canada and confessed that he had "come away from Boston on a fools errand," that Higginson began his last attempt to separate himself psychologically from the other committee members by returning to his rescue scheme.[33]

The minister first wrote to Sanborn. He assured the secretary that he would not "expose the whole matter" and he would not reveal the names of the other secret committee members if he decided to testify about his own role in the affair. Next, he contacted John LeBarnes and resumed rescue discussions. LeBarnes seemed a bit more optimistic about an attempt than he had been a few days earlier. He now felt such a project might have a chance and believed assistance could be obtained in Kansas. Finally, Higginson considered specific proposals. Lysander Spooner suggested chartering a boat, sailing up Chesapeake Bay, kidnapping Virginia's governor, Henry Wise, and then exchanging him for Brown. When LeBarnes heard of this, he applauded its audacity but was not sure it would work. He and Higginson thought in more conventional terms. They debated a variety of infantry assaults on Charlestown, though both were aware that 1,000 soldiers guarded the town and a direct infantry attack would require at least 200 to 300 men. The two men also discussed the possibility of sneaking a handful of well-trained mercenaries into Charlestown.[34]

Five days after LeBarnes and Higginson began their debate, Lysander Spooner contacted the minister and notified him that LeBarnes had recruited men, a pilot, and a boat for the "Richmond expedition." Spooner expressed full confidence that the plan would work if some-

33. Julia Howe to Anne Mailiard, November 6, 1859, Howe Collection, Houghton Library; Schwartz, *Howe,* p. 236.

34. Sanborn to Higginson, November 19, 1859; John LeBarnes to Higginson, November 7, 14, 15, 1859, Higginson-Brown Collection, Boston Public Library.

one would furnish the money. On November 22 Higginson received another report from LeBarnes in which the freedom fighter assured him that one of the plans they had discussed could be managed; only the money was "uncertain."[35]

That same day Higginson heard from Brown, and the letter dampened any remaining enthusiasm he had for rescue. Brown tried to explain more fully why he had refused to see his wife and wanted to let everyone know that, though he was unable to write, he had not forgotten their love and kindness. Brown's heroic resignation to his own death stunned Higginson and made his planning seem foolish. When Higginson coupled this feeling with the pessimistic tone of a report LeBarnes sent him on November 24, his momentary sense of foolishness grew into a decision to finally abandon the rescue project. LeBarnes wrote about the progress he was having in recruiting men and, in the process, signaled his skepticism about Spooner's Richmond plan. He said that he did not feel well enough about it to take part in it in anything other than a supervisory capacity, and he agreed with Wendell Phillips that "success would be brilliant—defeat fatally inglorious."[36]

Although both Higginson and LeBarnes had given up on the idea, they played out the charade during the course of the next few days for the sake of appearance. On November 27 LeBarnes notified Higginson that 15 to 25 men had been assembled and were ready to attack Charlestown or to execute Spooner's Richmond scheme. The men were resolute and confident of success, though LeBarnes himself thought that under the circumstances such confidence was unwarranted, even "strange." If $1,500 to $2,000 could be raised, the *desperate chance* could begin; if not, the whole matter must be forgotten. LeBarnes did not have to wait long for an answer. One day later Higginson notified him that the money could not be raised. Within

35. Lysander Spooner to Higginson, November 20, 1859; John LeBarnes to Higginson, November 22, 1859, ibid.

36. Brown to Higginson, November 22, 1859, Brown Collection, Boston Public Library; John LeBarnes to Higginson, November 24, 1859, Higginson-Brown Collection, Boston Public Library.

hours the minister received a simple reply from his confederate: "Objects abandoned."[37]

Soon after receiving this confirmation from LeBarnes, Higginson wrote to Lysander Spooner to explain the reasons for failing to carry out a plan. There were several objections to an advance on Charlestown. It was "absurd" to assume that money could induce the "worst men in the country to a desperate act." Any one of them could have made twice as much by betraying the effort. The same held true for Spooner's Richmond plan. Near the end of his note Higginson said he felt "most unwillingly compelled to abandon the hope of redeeming the honor of the Free States in the only way open—by the rescue of John Brown."[38]

At one level, Higginson was sincere in his consideration of a rescue attempt. He had the natural and laudable desire to save Brown from what he thought to be an unjust execution. If Higginson could have saved him, he would have; but to suggest this does not mitigate Higginson's equally strong impulse to see Brown martyred. Higginson knew quite well the significance Brown's death would have for the abolitionist movement: It would inflame popular indignation in the North. If most northerners were as horrified by the idea of insurrection as southern slaveholders, Brown could be portrayed as a man of the highest Puritan virtue, "warring for the Lord." The intense personal sympathy which went out to him could eventually be converted to the cause of abolition. What is more, Higginson knew perfectly well that Brown himself understood and relished this fact. Thus, in examining the correspondence between Higginson and those who helped develop rescue plans, one senses an underlying reluctance to carry out the plans. Not only were these schemes practically impossible, they were also at odds with abolitionist attempts to exploit popular sentiment. It is in this context, then, that Higginson's remarks about "Free State honor" and "honor" among confederates should be interpreted. Higginson's action was less of an attempt to redeem northern integrity than an

37. John LeBarnes to Higginson, November 27, 28, 1859, ibid.
38. Higginson to Lysander Spooner, November 28, 1859, Spooner Collection, Boston Public Library.

attempt to redeem the integrity which he believed had been forfeited by the other members of the secret committee. In the wake of Canadian flights, Smith's retreat to Utica, Howe's disclaimer card, and Sanborn's repeated denials of complicity with Brown, Higginson was compelled to dramatize his contempt for such behavior by a mock rescue effort. It was his way of counterposing the actions of the secret committee; his way of dissociating himself from his coconspirators' lack of probity. Perhaps the most poignant symbol of the way in which Higginson used the rescue attempt is his caution to LeBarnes at the end of one of his letters. While other members of the committee were making exertions to destroy all incriminating evidence, Higginson warned LeBarnes not to burn any of their correspondence.

CHAPTER 9

Testimony

I N ROME, THEODORE PARKER read about Harpers Ferry in letters written by his many Massachusetts friends. As he did, he grew more confident that the money contributed to Brown by the secret committee had not been thrown away or "wasted." Over three thousand miles from America, separated by a vast ocean from threats of arrest or trial, Parker was free to speak calmly and rationally about the whole affair. He thought Harpers Ferry marked a beginning to the end of slavery, however, "many acorns must be sown before one comes up." But if Parker could remain dispassionate about the episode, such was not the case with his longtime friend and fellow secret committee member Samuel Gridley Howe. The doctor was confused, and his panic-stricken behavior from the time he was notified of the raid's failure until Brown's hanging in the first week of December underscored that confusion. Howe was terrified by the possibility of his implication with Brown and looked to other men to make decisions for him. When John A. Andrew told him that he might be indicted or imprisoned and Sanborn justified any action to prevent arrest, Howe guiltily ran to Canada. It was not until shortly before Brown went to the gallows that the doctor regained control of himself.[1]

Soon after Brown's execution, Howe asked Andrew for a reevaluation of his legal status and an estimate of public sentiment in eastern Massachusetts toward those who might have assisted Brown. Andrew

1. Parker to Francis Jackson, November 24, 1859, in Parker, *Correspondence,* 1: 170–71; Howe to Charles Sumner, December 3, 1859, Howe Collection, Houghton Library.

did not give him encouraging news. Efforts to change the law of 1846, by which those implicated with Brown could be forced to give testimony, had bogged down in the Massachusetts legislature, and though Andrew had written numerous letters to newspapers assuring Massachusetts citizenry of Howe's innocence, he did not feel that people had become aroused enough about the issue to prevent the doctor from being taken outside of the state. In addition, Andrew told Howe about rumors circulating around Boston that a special United States Senate committee would be selected to investigate the raid. The lawyer felt that if these rumors were true, Howe, Stearns, and Sanborn would surely be summoned to testify. He speculated that once they were in Washington anything could happen. They might be "spirited over the river to Virginia and lynched; or taken by V[irgini]a authorities and proceeded against as accessories before the fact if they gave Brown aid and comfort for general purposes even if they were ignorant of special purposes."[2]

Despite Andrew's dire prediction, Howe did not lose his composure. He was awaiting an opinion from Charles Sumner about the state of affairs in the nation's capital and was confident that Sumner's views would be more accurate than Andrew's. Besides, Howe wanted to testify. He thought that it would be a better way to alleviate his concern than continued flights to Canada. He wanted to atone for his behavior during the past two months and knew that the only person outside of the secret committee who could give *prima facie* evidence against him was dead.[3]

In the middle of December rumor became fact. A special investigating committee was appointed under the chairmanship of Senator James Mason of Virginia. As soon as news of the committee's appointment reached Boston, Howe, Stearns, and Sanborn met and debated their course of action. Sanborn refused to consider the possibility of going to Washington when Howe suggested it. Stearns was less adamant.

2. Howe to Parker, January 22, 1860, ibid.; John A. Andrew to Howe, December 3, 1859, Andrew Papers, Massachusetts Historical Society, Boston, Mass.
3. Howe to Charles Sumner, December 3, 1859, Howe Collection, Houghton Library.

Sanborn was certain Andrew's assessment of their fate was accurate: A trap was being set for all who were suspected of assisting Brown. When Howe disputed this view but could not prove otherwise (he hadn't received a reply from Sumner yet), he and Sanborn argued. Howe wanted to testify. He felt guilty for having issued the disclaimer, felt a need to redeem himself in public, and was tired of panicky trips north. Just as important, Julia was expecting their fourth child at the end of the month, and he wanted to be with her.[4]

Sanborn would not budge. He would not testify just to "avoid a conflict." He would not honor a summons because he was sure that was what the South wanted. And there were other reasons for resisting Howe's arguments—reasons Sanborn kept to himself. Unlike Howe, who had only received secondhand information about Brown's movements in the last few weeks before Harpers Ferry, Sanborn was directly linked to Brown in the days prior to the raid. If the committee ever found Francis Merriam and persuaded him to talk, Sanborn knew he would be in serious trouble. Furthermore, Sanborn believed he could count on Concord citizenry's protection against arrest should he ignore the summons. Above all, Sanborn resisted testifying because he thought his own contentions about the hearings were correct: They were an elaborate pretext to lure Brown's friends into prison. And the notion of a jail sentence terrified him.[5]

The intensity of his fear is reflected in his treatment of Francis Merriam. A few days after Sanborn met with Howe and Stearns, Merriam appeared at his Concord home looking for help as he dodged arrest by Virginia authorities. He was heading toward Canada and needed food, shelter, and funds before continuing his journey. Sanborn refused to see him, refused to have anything to do with the "plum" who only a few weeks earlier had been of such great "use" to the cause of freedom. The secretary later claimed that his inaction had been governed by "a regard for his [Merriam's] safety," that Merriam was

4. Howe to Parker, January 22, 1860; Howe to Charles Sumner, January 18, 1860, ibid.; Schwartz, *Howe*, p. 246.

5. Sanborn to Higginson, November 28, 1859, Higginson-Brown Collection, Boston Public Library; Villard, *Brown*, p. 517; Sanborn, *Recollections*, 1: 203–4.

"wholly crazy," and that to have been seen with him would have jeopardized the entire secret committee. There is, however, little question about whose safety most concerned Sanborn. He did send his sister Sarah to speak to Merriam, and Sarah, in turn, sought Henry David Thoreau's help. Thoreau introduced himself to Merriam as "Mr. Lockwood," took the young man to the Concord train station, and gave him a ticket to Canada.[6]

Because Howe had not received word from Sumner about the political climate in Washington, he grudgingly conceded that Sanborn might be correct about the possibility of a trap. Both he and Stearns went back to Canada to await Sumner's assessment and continued the debate about their course of action. They remained in Canada for a little over a week and then returned to Boston ready to give evidence as long as they didn't have to "give their bodies." Howe was determined to "own up" to his part in the affair, and he told Andrew this in a letter written from Canada before his return. When Andrew received the letter, he immediately informed Sanborn and the young secretary again tried to blunt Howe's desire. Writing the doctor on December 19 (a few days before Howe and Stearns came back), he assured Howe that his reasons for going to Canada had been "righteous," that he should not be upset at Higginson's criticism of the disclaimer card, and that such criticism by no means reflected popular opinion about his behavior. According to Sanborn, Howe should not feel pressed to testify in order to regain his reputation. He had never lost that reputation and should understand that Higginson's remarks were "extravagant." Sanborn desperately tried to head off Howe's testimony by convincing the doctor that he had no reason to atone for his behavior. The secretary also sought to hold Howe in place by suggesting that once information came in from Washington on the nature of the investigation, they could all act publicly. He seemed to hint at a willingness to speak out in some forum other than a Washington hearing room.[7]

6. Ibid.; Edelstein, *Strange Enthusiasm*, p. 222; Sanborn interview by Katherine Mayo, January 19, 1909, Villard Collection, Columbia University, New York, N.Y.
7. Howe to John A. Andrew, December 17, 1859, Howe Collection, Houghton

Clearly Sanborn's hint was only a ploy. He had no intention of testifying anywhere. About the time he wrote Howe indicating a desire to act in public, he also wrote to Higginson and scolded him for leaving incriminating letters in John A. Andrew's possession. Sanborn was bent on destroying every piece of evidence that could possibly tie him or any other committee member to Brown. He told Higginson that he believed Boston abolitionists should direct all their attention toward challenging the federal government's right to compel individuals to leave their own state in order to give testimony before a committee like Mason's. Sanborn thought that repeal of the 1846 statute was a good issue for reformers to stand on and said he hoped Henry Wilson could be persuaded to lead the fight. No matter what anyone said, Sanborn knew that abolitionists didn't "stand a chance" in Washington, D.C. How could they? It was a place that could not protect its own senators, an absurd sanctuary for "creeping things" called office-seekers.[8]

As already suggested, the attempt to prevent Howe from returning failed. The doctor and George Luther Stearns came back to Boston intending to appear before the Mason Committee. Both men were buoyed by Sumner's contention that they had "nothing to fear from Virginia's menaces." They called for a meeting at Henry Wilson's offices on the day before Christmas and asked that Sanborn and Martin Conway, a former Kansas Committee agent, attend. When the group convened, they first had to endure an outburst by the tempestuous Wilson. The senator, who was furious about the whole Harpers Ferry episode, said he would do nothing to block summonses from the Mason Committee and insisted that anyone called to Washington to testify ought to do so. Wilson believed that any attempt to avoid testimony would endanger Republican Party chances in the coming fall elections. If it was not made clear to the public that the party had

---

Library; Sanborn to Howe, December 19, 1859, Howe Collection, Massachusetts Historical Society.

8. Sanborn to Higginson, December 20, 1859, Higginson-Brown Collection, Boston Public Library; Franklin Benjamin Sanborn, *Samuel Gridley Howe, The Philanthropist* (New York, 1891), p. 273.

had nothing to do with Brown and had not sanctioned his violent, illegal activity, then all hopes of increasing party strength in Congress were doomed. Wilson assured the group that they would be perfectly safe in the capital. Howe was angered by Wilson's outburst and defended Brown by saying that the raid was only an attempt to carry certain "currents of antislavery thought to their logical sequence in action." When tempers finally settled, Howe, Stearns, and Conway reaffirmed their desire to face Mason and the other members of his committee.[9]

Frank Sanborn did not agree to honor a committee summons. He believed that Howe and Stearns were mistaken in their decision and condemned Wilson for acting like "a craven and a blockhead." As far as the secretary was concerned, there were "a thousand better ways of spending a year in warfare against slavery than by lying in a Washington prison." By the time he received his summons in early January, he was so upset that not even assurances of protection could keep him in Concord; he fled to Canada. Once there, he explained that friends and family had urged him to go away and sought to legitimize his flight further by writing Mason and making a request he knew the senator could not honor. Sanborn said that he was willing to give testimony, but only in Massachusetts. What Sanborn really wanted to do was "go abroad" and join Edwin Morton who had fled to England at the first news of Harpers Ferry. Sanborn even toyed with the idea of taking up permanent residence in Canada, where he could "go down among the fugitives and explore their condition with a view to some better organization of them."[10]

9. Charles Sumner to Howe, December 15, 1859, Sumner Collection, Houghton Library, Harvard University, Cambridge, Mass.; Sanborn to Parker, January 2, 1860, Sanborn-Brown Collection, Houghton Library; Richard Abbot, "Cobbler in Congress: The Life of Henry Wilson, 1812–1875" (Ph.D. diss., University of Wisconsin, 1965); Howe to Charles Sumner, December 18, 1859; Howe to Henry Wilson, January 23, 1860, Howe Collection, Massachusetts Historical Society; Sanborn to Higginson, January 2, 1860, Higginson-Brown Collection, Boston Public Library.

10. Sanborn to Parker, January 2, 1860, Sanborn-Brown Collection, Houghton Library; Sanborn to Higginson, January 29, 1860, Higginson-Brown Collection, Boston Public Library.

In addition to being afraid of arrest and at odds with those who disagreed with his refusal to testify (they were all "wholly crazy," "extravagant," or "blockheads"), Sanborn now became as concerned about his public reputation as Howe had been. He wanted to avoid jail and still maintain the respect of those who applauded his activity for Brown. To do so, he wrote the one man who would most likely criticize his behavior—Thomas Wentworth Higginson. In the letter to Higginson, written only a few days after arriving in Canada, Sanborn explained that he would be "glad to give Massachusetts a chance to keep her citizens at home" but didn't "have much faith in her people in the capacity of defenders against the law." Indeed, the *"keeping back of evidence"* was much "too important to leave to chance." Without testimony, Sanborn was certain "no new light could be thrown on the matter." The South would exaggerate the raid, and the North would extenuate it. The committee secretary believed the North's silence would likely foster similar schemes, and he said he wanted to "reserve" himself for that time. A few weeks earlier he had attempted to alleviate Howe's guilt in order to keep the doctor in Canada, but now he tried to create guilt. At the end of his letter to Higginson, Sanborn scolded the minister for "rushing upon" his friends and implied that any harsh words about his flight to Canada would not do. Sanborn also pleaded with Higginson; he "implored" the minister not to tell what he knew to the "enemies of the cause."[11]

The meeting with Wilson and his eventual summons drove Sanborn to Canada, but they had a far different effect on Samuel Gridley Howe. The doctor stood by his decision to go to Washington. He was finished with running and finished with taking Sanborn's advice. Henry Wilson wanted to use the hearings to exonerate himself and the Republican Party, and Howe wanted to use them to recapture his reputation. A few years earlier, in the midst of a crisis of character, the doctor had admitted his feelings of cowardliness in "dangerous situations," but at

---

11. Ibid.; Sanborn, *Recollections,* 1: 206–7, 222; Sanborn to Parker, January 26, 1860, Sanborn-Brown Collection, Houghton Library.

the time he remarked that he was proud of his ability to seem "cool" in such instances. Between October 16 and December 24, 1859, he had failed to act coolly. He had failed to maintain a calm pose for public consumption, and he was both embarrassed and upset with himself. His concern about the judgment he would make of his own behavior in the future and his worries about lost "public approbation" in the present far outweighed his fears of arrest. He had once been wary of being lured into prison if he set foot in Washington. At the moment he wanted to go there, correct his "missteps," set himself *"in rectus curia,"* and "express the admiration and respect" he had for John Brown.[12]

Even though Howe wanted to redeem himself and his reputation, he was decidedly against revealing his true relationship with Brown. He wanted to exonerate himself, avoid imprisonment, and "express his admiration" for Brown, but he intended to divorce himself from Brown's "special purposes." He would testify that his hands and those of other abolitionists who supported Brown were "clean." He intended to use Massachusetts Kansas Committee records to prove this contention before a public tribunal. And, obviously, he never thought of mentioning the Secret Committee of Six. If questions were asked about the arms distributed in Kansas, he would say that they were to be used only as the subscribers had intended. Stearns had instructed Brown about this, but Brown had disobeyed orders. Howe thought of suggesting that Brown was "already *tete exalte:* not mad but intensified to the

12. Howe to Horace Mann, 1856; Howe to Charles Sumner, April 25, 1852, Howe Collection, Houghton Library; Howe, *Journals,* pp. 370–71; Howe to Charles Sumner, January 18, 1860; Howe to Parker, January 22, 1860, Howe Collection, Houghton Library. In 1848 Howe was wary of running for public office because he feared having to eventually face people as a defeated candidate. While he claimed to fully understand that this attitude implied "little faith in God's arrangements," he nonetheless refused to run. And when he did not run for office he also reproached himself for "want of faith and courage in my past," but he admitted that his need for "approbation" outweighed this concern. Indeed the need for public approbation was the "rock" on which "most of my hopes have split" (Howe, *Journals,* pp. 370–71).

verge of madness." This monomania took "the form of the love of arms," but these weapons "had only been entrusted to him for the defense of Kansas."[13]

Howe also stood by his decision to testify because he heard stories from Washington that cast some doubt on James Mason's willingness to fully document conspiracy. The doctor had suggested this in a letter to Charles Sumner in mid-January. Howe said he wanted to "clear up" the matter of his relationship to Brown but was sure that by the time he testified Mason would "have got so much of what he did not want that he will hardly press me into service." To make certain this was the case, Howe asked that the date of his testimony be moved from January 24 to the first week in February. The more Mason heard about the depth of support for Brown, the less likely he was to pressure those most closely associated with the martyr. Thus, with evidence assembled to separate himself from Brown's "special purposes," a strong possibility Mason didn't want to document the conspiracy anyway, and the assurances of Sumner and Wilson that he need not fear coming to Washington, Howe was prepared to correct his "missteps." He was relieved by his decision to go on, relieved that he had stopped yielding "too much to others." The thought of evading testimony had always been "repugnant" to him. However, he admitted having some misgivings about a trap when he was first notified of the committee's formation. Now he wanted to stand boldly before the Senate investigators.[14]

One man in Massachusetts watched Howe's newfound courage with curiosity, confusion, and some disdain. In fact, Thomas Wentworth Higginson was so upset with Howe, Sanborn, and Stearns that he refused to "expostulate" on their motives. In November, long before the Mason Committee was set up, Higginson had decided not to volunteer testimony because, though he did not fear proclaiming his relationship to Brown, he was worried about implicating other secret committee members. However, in time he saw that none of the other

13. Ibid.; Howe to Henry Wilson, January 23, 1860, Howe Collection, Massachusetts Historical Society.

14. Howe to Charles Sumner, January 24, 25, 26, 1860, Howe Collection, Houghton Library; Schwartz, *Howe*, pp. 243–46.

members were hindered by such consideration for him. Each had offered his "own confession" on his "own terms," after urging him to hold back evidence. The minister wondered what Sanborn hoped to accomplish by running to Canada or what Howe thought he would prove by consenting to testify after twice fleeing there. Howe and Stearns couldn't accomplish a thing by going in front of investigators who didn't want to fully probe the alleged conspiracy anyway. Higginson had recently discussed the matter with Vermont's Senator Jacob Collamer and knew, as he was sure Howe did, that Mason's determination to uncover wrongdoing was weakening. According to Collamer, all the Virginia senator wanted to do was say he had tried to expose the conspiracy but had failed because he "could not obtain the necessary information." Collamer speculated that Mason took this new approach to the investigation because he was very fearful of "the effect on the country of witnesses who shall defend John Brown."[15]

Higginson suspected that personal considerations controlled the actions of his confederates, and he was offended. The only thing he was certain of was why he had not been called to the Mason hearings. He had always openly refused to go to Canada and refused to disavow his support of Brown. If Collamer was correct, the committee chairman wasn't willing to take a chance on examining a witness who would speak the whole truth.

Jacob Collamer's comments to Higginson about James Mason's fears were astute. The Virginia senator was worried that popular emotions would be inflamed by men willing to defend Brown; however, he had not always been afraid of such a result. As early as October 21, only a few days after the discovery of documents hinting at the possibility of an organization behind Brown's raid, Mason had been eager to start a thoroughgoing investigation. He was convinced that enough evidence existed to warrant belief in conspiracy and was determined to expose it. Mason knew Brown "acted from the impression made upon

15. Higginson to Sanborn, February 3, 1860, Higginson-Brown Collection, Boston Public Library.

him by abolitionist tracts" which implied that all one had to do was put arms in the reach of slaves to incite immediate insurrection. The Virginian wanted an inquiry made to discover the source of funds for this "military expedition," and by mid-December 1859, Mason had his wish. He was appointed chairman of a special Senate committee charged with investigating the Harpers Ferry incident, and he was empowered to ask questions that bore directly on the issue of conspiracy. Mason and his fellow committeemen, G. N. Fitch, Jefferson Davis, James R. Doolittle, and Jacob Collamer, were asked to find out whether or not Brown had worked with any organization which "intended to subvert the government of any of the states," whether any citizen of the United States was implicated as an "accessory to [the raid] by contributions of money, arms, munitions or otherwise," and what the character of such an organization might be if it did exist.[16]

Mason's initial desire to prove conspiracy dismayed Brown's Boston friends. At first it seemed to them that their only hope for sympathy lay with the two Republicans on the committee, Doolittle and Collamer. Collamer's attitude toward the whole investigation was particularly heartening and is best exemplified by his statements to Amos A. Lawrence in late December. The Vermont senator said that any "fair investigation" would show that the number of Brown's accomplices, beyond those caught at Harpers Ferry, was "extremely small." Collamer seriously doubted whether anyone who contributed to Brown "knew his purpose to be of the criminal proportions and insane expedition it turned out." Though the senator was very disturbed by people furnishing arms "to carry violence into the Slavery States" (he termed such acts as "criminal"), his hints were obvious: The committee lacked enough evidence to build its case, Brown was dead, and those called to the witness stand would determine the direction of the investigation. If they handled themselves properly, the inquiry might prove to be a blessing in disguise. They (Brown's supporters) could prove that he had not

16. James Mason, article on conspiracy in the *New York Herald,* October 21, 1859; *Worcester Spy,* November 14, 1859; [Governor] Henry Wise to (?), November 6, 1859, Brown Collection, Massachusetts Historical Society; *Mason Report,* p. 1; Oates, *Brown,* p. 359.

received arms "for the purposes to which they were eventually put."[17]

Surprisingly, in view of the respective positions taken by Mason and Collamer previous to the hearings, one of Brown's friends, George Luther Stearns, found he had more to fear from the Vermont sympathizer than from the Virginia enemy. Mason gradually developed misgivings about the investigation's potential as a catalyst for northern antislavery sentiment and slowly moved away from his commitment to expose conspiracy. On the other hand, Collamer, by the time he interrogated Stearns, had begun to sense that Brown's Boston supporters might not have been as ignorant of Brown's "criminal" intent as he had originally supposed. Collamer would end up pressing witnesses to speak fully and truthfully about their attitude toward Brown and his violent acts. At times it seemed he was much more concerned about the possibility of conspiracy than Mason had originally been. Mason pressured witnesses—but never too much. Collamer defended them—but not entirely.

When subpoenas went out in early January, some men refused to comply. For one reason or another, Gerrit Smith, James Redpath, Hugh Forbes, Frank Sanborn, and John Brown, Jr., would not go to Washington to testify. But the younger Brown used the occasion to separate himself from certain of his father's supporters. John Jr. claimed he would not appear to testify, but he let it be known that his "business" didn't call him to Canada. If he visited that temporary home for "American exiles," it would be from "other considerations than personal safety." Most men subpoenaed by the Mason Committee, however, did consent to make an appearance. During late January, February, and early March, they paraded through the hearing room and answered numerous questions about their knowledge of Brown, his antislavery activities, and his Harpers Ferry plans.[18]

At the start of the hearings, when Henry Wilson was asked about his relationship with Brown, he answered by describing Hugh Forbes's

17. Jacob Collamer to Amos A. Lawrence, December 29, 1859, Amos A. Lawrence Collection, Massachusetts Historical Society.

18. John Brown, Jr., to (?), 1860(?), Boyd B. Stutler Collection.

revelations, discussing his exchange of letters with Howe, speaking of his own (and the Republican Party's) disdain for violence, and documenting this position by telling the committee of his confrontation with Brown at the Parker House hotel the previous spring. When John A. Andrew testified, he was asked why he did not defend Brown during his trial. Andrew answered that, as a Republican, a Massachusetts man, and an abolitionist, he would have been on trial quite as much as his client. He was also unfamiliar with Virginia jurisprudence. Andrew's testimony is significant because it represents the basic defense agreed upon by Brown's Boston supporters in meetings held previous to their testimony. Andrew emphasized what most impressed him about Brown, as well as what he thought would enhance the dead man's reputation in the eyes of northern people. At the same time, he depicted Brown as one who would never have shared his Harpers Ferry plan with anyone. Who was John Brown? According to this abolitionist lawyer, Brown was a controlled enthusiast, one who spoke in tones "perfectly level without emphasis and exultation of feeling." Brown was a rugged individualist, a man who "scarcely regarded other people," who was entirely "self-possessed and unto himself." He "appeared to have no emotion of any sort but to be entirely absorbed in an idea."[19]

Andrew's statement continued the theme of secrecy originated by Brown's Kansas associate Richard Realf. In testimony given on January 21, Realf, who had participated in Boston meetings intended to orchestrate the statements of all those who were summoned, denied knowledge of where Brown had procured funds for his venture. He said Brown had been cautious and uncommunicative about the particulars of his plan. Brown hadn't trusted anyone with anything more than what was "barely sufficient" to "secure cooperation and support." Realf did admit that Brown had told him Gerrit Smith "promised to assist him in his further enterprises against slav-

19. "Wilson Testimony," February 1, 1960, *Mason Report,* pp. 140–45; "Andrew Testimony," February 9, 1860, ibid., pp. 186–92.

ery." But Realf did not know if this meant assistance against the South.[20]

On January 11 Samuel Gridley Howe was summoned to appear before the committee thirteen days later. As planned, the doctor asked to postpone his testimony until the first week of February, saying he had previously scheduled an exhibition of blind children before the Canadian Parliament. Howe's request was approved and he was resummoned for early February.[21]

From the outset of his testimony, Howe moved quickly to close the door on any attempt to link him to Brown. To Mason's question about who controlled guns purchased by Massachusetts for Kansas, he replied that he could not answer "with precision." From that moment on, he qualified his answers by claiming that he could "not recall," or had "no definite knowledge of," or "could not say for certain." Asked how Brown had regained possession of weapons supposedly confiscated by the Massachusetts Kansas Committee in May 1858, the doctor deftly noted that he had "no means of knowing" that the arms used at Harpers Ferry were the same donated for Brown's defense of Kansas. Unsatisfied with this reply, Mason asked Howe to produce letters which proved that Brown had been given the guns only for defensive purposes in Kansas. Howe balked, saying he could only speak for himself; correspondence with Brown had been the responsibility of the committee chairman, George Luther Stearns. Howe admitted that he had seen Brown in the spring of 1858, but said that Brown "gave no definite information" about his plans. When Collamer interrupted and asked Howe what he meant when he suggested that Brown sought arms and funds for the "defense of Freedom in Kansas," the physician answered revealingly. Howe asserted that when Brown used such terms, he (the doctor) had not thought about "anything but the freedom of Kansas, as such, without any thought of colored men at all." Further on in the questioning, Collamer returned to the issue of

20. "Realf Testimony," January 21, 1860, ibid., pp. 98–107.
21. Howe to Parker, January 22, 1860; Howe to Charles Sumner, January 21, 1860, Howe Collection, Houghton Library; *Mason Report,* p. 21.

Brown's plans in 1858 and the funds he had collected in Boston during that spring. Again Howe hedged; Brown had given him "no definite statement of any plan or purpose" and had only appealed to him as an antislavery man.[22]

Until that point in the testimony the committee had no evidence to dispute Howe's denials. When questioned about his relations with Brown in 1859, however, the doctor found himself under more pressure. The committeemen had enough information to partially rebut his denials, and they proceeded to rattle the forgetful physician. Furthermore, Collamer suspected that Howe and the other men who supported Brown had taken no clear stand against him when he advocated the use of violence. Collamer opened a series of questions about 1859 by asking Howe to comment on a note found at Brown's Virginia headquarters. It read: "Dear Friend, Our friend from Concord called with your note. I began the investment with fifty dollars enclosed and will try to do more through friends. Doctor."

Collamer: Will you say to whom it was addressed?
Howe: I presume it was addressed to Captain Brown.
Collamer: Do you remember the fact of time?
Howe: I do not remember the time.[23]

James Mason was disturbed by Howe's failure to answer the question and so prodded the doctor by asking him if he recalled sending a telegraphic dispatch to John Kagi, a friend of Brown, in June 1859.

Mason: Will you be good enough to inform the committee whether you were acquainted with a man named J. H. Kagi?
Howe: I never saw him.
Mason: Did you have any correspondence with him?
Howe: I never corresponded with him that I recollect.

22. "Howe Testimony," February 3, 1860, ibid., pp. 157–78.
23. Ibid., pp. 163–64.

Mason then exhibited the telegram sent by Howe to Kagi on June 6, 1859, which read: "He got the needful and left three days ago, direction unknown. S.G.H."

Mason: Will you say if you have any recall of this telegraphic dispatch?
Howe: I have not the slightest idea.[24]

Howe was then questioned about a note John Brown, Jr., sent to John Kagi on August 17, 1859 after his Boston visit. The note read: "First called on Dr. H– though I had no letter of introduction he received me cordially. He gave me a letter to a friend who does business on Milk Street. Went with him to his house in Medford and took dinner. The last word he said to me was, 'Tell friend (Issac) that we have the *fullest confidence in his endeavor,* whatever may be the result.' "

Mason: Did he tell you the object of his visit?
Howe: He did not.
Mason: Did he apply to you for money?
Howe: He did not.
Mason: Did you learn it [the object of his visit] from any other source?
Howe: I did not.[25]

After Howe admitted that he had given money to Brown in 1857 and 1858 but that he did not know "what disposition" was made of the funds, Collamer interrupted.

Collamer: To prevent any misunderstanding about these contributions I desire to ask a question. Were not the contributions re-

24. Ibid., p. 164.
25. Ibid., p. 168.

ceived by the committees which were made by the people of Boston and Massachusetts for and during the Kansas troubles?

Howe: For that definite purpose.

Collamer: Was any money of these contributions ever sent to Brown in 1858?

Howe: Not that I know of.

Mason: But there were other contributions that were sent to him after the fall of 1858 . . . to be used at his discretion.

Howe: I had personal knowledge of several small sums.

Mason: What were the limits imposed on his discretion?

Howe: No further than the confidence he inspired among his friends by two opinions entertained by him, one of which was that he was opposed to promoting insurrection among slaves, and another that he was opposed to shedding human blood except in self-defense.

Mason: Do you know of any plan he had . . . for . . . promoting insurrection?

Howe: I know of no definite plan; he was secretive.

Doolittle: In all your conversation or communication with Brown had you ever . . . any intimation . . . of an organized effort, on his part, to produce an insurrection among slaves?

Howe: Never.[26]

Most certainly the committee members—Democratic and Republican—were not pleased with Howe's responses; yet, they dismissed him after he answered Doolittle's question because they realized they did not have enough evidence to contravert his story. It is also possible they believed more information could be obtained from the individual in charge of Massachusetts Kansas Committee funds, George Luther Stearns.

In mid-January, while the first sessions of the Mason Committee were being held, Stearns traveled to North Elba to visit the Brown

26. Ibid., pp. 177–78.

family. He wanted to assure them that Massachusetts abolitionists would continue their financial assistance. While he presented the family with money already contributed for their support, Stearns inquired about the possibility of Ann Brown attending Sanborn's school at Concord, tuition-free. While in North Elba, he mentioned his forthcoming testimony but said he was not worried about it. Like Samuel Gridley Howe, the Medford businessman knew that if he maintained his composure during questioning, nothing illegal could be proved against him. The evidence in the committee's possession was scanty and inconclusive. Only his own admission of guilt would give investigators enough material to recommend prosecution. And Stearns was not about to make that kind of slip. He carefully prepared an opening statement for the committee, attended meetings with Howe and others in order to coordinate his story with theirs, and closely followed the committee proceedings in the newspapers. When he returned home from North Elba, he found his summons waiting. He was to appear on February 24 before Mason, Collamer, and the others.[27]

Stearns began his testimony by reading the prepared statement about his relations with John Brown. In it he said he knew nothing about Brown's Chatham meetings or the remarks attributed to him by John Brown, Jr., after their August meeting. The younger Brown's visit to his Medford home had been only a pleasure call, and no money had been given for his father's use. Stearns reiterated the theme which ran through all previous discussions of Brown by those testifying: He had not known much of John Brown's plans because of Brown's extreme secretiveness. Brown had repeatedly told Stearns that "it was the worst possible policy for a man to reveal his plans." Surprisingly, Stearns did admit to having had contact with Francis Merriam, but only after the raid. The Medford businessman stated that while he was in Canada during December, Merriam came to his hotel room and introduced himself as a Mr. Lockwood. Merriam tried to discuss Harpers Ferry,

27. Ruth Brown Thompson to Mary Stearns, January 17, 1860, Boyd B. Stutler Collection; Stearns, *Life of Stearns,* p. 199; "Stearns Testimony," February 24, 1860, *Mason Report,* pp. 225–51.

but Stearns promptly cut him off by saying that he was "very busy and could not attend him."[28]

After he finished his statement, Stearns was questioned. Mason asked him whether or not it was true that he had attempted to recover the weapons taken from Brown during his capture. Stearns denied having done so, saying that he presumed "in the confusion of Harpers Ferry everything was distributed." Stearns did admit that George Sennot came to him and asked what was to be done with such equipment. At the same time Sennot exhibited a letter from Brown authorizing him (Sennot) to take possession of the property for the benefit of the Brown family.[29]

Like Howe, Stearns never gave his questioners much satisfaction. He was able to deny knowledge of Brown's plans, deny knowledge of funds being raised to support insurrection, and not worry about rebuttal. Circumstantial evidence like the letter from John Brown, Jr., pointed to Stearns's assistance of Brown and indicated he knew more than he admitted, but the committee lacked the will and conclusive evidence to establish such a connection. Indeed, Stearns handled himself with ease before their barrage of questions and relaxed. Unfortunately, it was the confidence he gained in dealing with Mason, Fitch, and Davis that led him to make an unintended admission to the increasingly suspicious Collamer.

Collamer: Did you at any time before the transaction at Harpers Ferry, in any way directly or indirectly, understand that there was any purpose on the part of Brown to make an inroad upon the subject of slavery in any of the states?

Stearns: No sir . . . I did not suppose he had any organized plan.

Collamer: My idea is, making any forcible entry upon Virginia, or any other state.

Stearns: No sir.

Collamer: Had you ever any intimation of that kind, any idea of it?

28. Ibid., pp. 232, 234–35, 236; Howe also refused to see Merriam while he was staying in Canada.
29. Ibid., p. 237.

Stearns: No sir. Perhaps I do not understand you. I did suppose he
would go into Virginia . . . and relieve slaves.

Collamer: In what way?

Stearns: In any way he could, give them liberty.

Collamer: Did you understand he contemplated doing it by force?

Stearns: Yes sir, by force if necessary.

Collamer: Will you explain in what manner by force you understood
he contemplated doing it?

Stearns: I cannot explain any manner because . . . I never talked with
him on the subject.

Collamer: Had you any idea that these arms were to be used for any
such purpose as making an inroad into any State?

Stearns: I think I do not understand you.

Collamer: John Brown has made an inroad into Virginia, with force
and arms to relieve slaves; you understand that!

Stearns: Yes sir.

Collamer: Now, did you ever before that took place, have any intimation that that was . . . intended . . . by him?

Stearns: No sir. I never supposed that he contemplated anything like
what occurred at Harpers Ferry.

Collamer: Then I ask you do you disapprove of such a transaction as
that at Harpers Ferry?

Stearns: I should have disapproved of it if I had known it.[30]

Despite his previous admission that Brown contemplated the use of
force, Stearns's final denial of Brown satisfied Collamer enough to end
his questioning. Undoubtedly the Vermont senator no longer saw the
inquiry as a way to exonerate Brown's Massachusetts supporters. Collamer had learned too much during the hearings to continue holding
that view. Yet, like his committee colleagues, Collamer was handicapped by a lack of substantial factual evidence to support any further
action against certain witnesses. He knew it, and Brown's Boston
friends knew it. They had come to Washington believing there was

30. Ibid., pp. 240–41.

very little chance a case could be made against them, and they had been right. Stearns, like those who had preceded him, was dismissed from the witness stand only superficially bruised by the experience.

As he traveled back to Boston, Stearns realized that he was as nervous about the way in which the Massachusetts public would react to his Mason Committee testimony as he had been about going to Washington to give that testimony. He had denied Brown and had claimed disapproval of his tactics before the Senate investigators, and, as he returned home to face the men and women before whom he had defended Brown in the months preceding Harpers Ferry, he wondered if they would condemn him as a hypocrite. When he arrived in Medford he was happily surprised to find that people were not only satisfied, but praised him heartily for his "bold speech." This reaction persuaded him that Harpers Ferry had sunk "deep into the hearts of our people" and would greatly influence forthcoming elections.[31]

Unquestionably, George Luther Stearns was also thankful he had had the wit to make certain additions to his Mason Committee testimony after that testimony had ended. As has been suggested, Stearns was fearful of defending Brown once he had inadvertently admitted that he had known Brown contemplated the use of force. He answered Collamer's most important query by asserting that he would not have approved of the Harpers Ferry scheme if he had known of it in advance. But when Stearns had completed his testimony and all of the committeemen (except Mason) had left the hearing room, the Medford businessman had asked the committee stenographer if he could add another sentence to that answer. In the addition, Stearns said that disapproval of Brown's act had been only his first reaction to it and that since then he had "changed" his opinion. Instead of disapproving of the raid had he known of it, he now believed John Brown to be the "most representative man of this century" and regarded Harpers Ferry as an event that would free America. Mason must have smiled knowingly as Stearns finished the statement and left the room. Once

---

31. Stearns to Charles Sumner, March 10, 1860, Sumner Collection, Houghton Library, Harvard University, Cambridge, Mass.; Stearns, *Life of Stearns,* pp. 207–10.

home, Stearns was relieved to find that all newspaper accounts of his testimony included the addenda. He had expunged his most blatant denial of Brown, and it appeared that, of all those who testified, he had made the firmest commitment to Brown.[32]

Samuel Gridley Howe, too, was concerned with public reaction to his testimony. After all, he went to Washington primarily to set himself *"in rectus curia,"* to correct "missteps," and to recapture public "approbation." Howe was particularly hopeful that his testimony would dissolve the animosity of Thomas Wentworth Higginson. When the doctor came home from Washington, he tried to rehabilitate himself with the minister. Howe wrote Higginson and told him that during the time Brown had been in Boston the previous spring, the two of them had argued about the morality of stealing slaveholders' property in slave rescue attempts. Howe said that as a result of this disagreement, he and Brown had not conversed about future plans. Brown's appearance at Harpers Ferry had been "astonishing." Howe did have some trouble explaining why he had sent money to Brown in September 1859 and how he had known where to send it. He claimed he had sent funds only to show sympathy for Brown, but did so "without cognizance of his purposes." Howe did admit to something he failed to say before the Mason Committee. He told Higginson that if he had known that Brown intended to steal nothing but slaves, he would have given him "aid and encouragement." Unquestionably, Higginson wondered how the doctor had managed to avoid discussion of Brown's plan during his numerous conversations with Sanborn and Stearns between June and October. Was it possible he had sent the money to Chambersburg without knowing of its proximity to Harpers Ferry? Was it possible that Howe didn't know of Sanborn and Stearns's all-night meeting with Francis Merriam? Higginson hardly thought so. The minister wondered if Howe seriously believed he could separate himself from Brown's "special purposes."[33]

Howe was apologetic about the disclaimer card. He told Higginson

32. Stearns to Howe, February 27, 1860, in Stearns, *Life of Stearns,* p. 213.

33. Howe to Higginson, February 16, 1860, Higginson-Brown Collection, Boston Public Library.

it would not have been published if the two of them had been able to speak to each other before it was submitted to the newspapers. Howe explained that he had doubted the "expediency" of the card all along. He had, however, shown it to "an honorable man" who "knew about Brown's movements and a great deal more" and that man had approved of it, so Howe had submitted the card. At the end of his letter Howe returned to his introductory theme. He told Higginson that he had assisted Brown with his plans because he had had "confidence" in him, but he said he had never expected "anything like what happened or anything more than a stampede."[34]

It is doubtful that Higginson's attitude toward Howe was changed by the letter. None of the members of the secret committee had expected what had happened at Harpers Ferry. For one thing, Brown wasn't supposed to get caught in the arsenal. Brown had said he hoped to obtain additional weapons there, but he certainly had not said he expected to get trapped inside. All committee members had been stunned by that occurrence, so Howe could not divorce himself from the project by saying that Brown's entrapment surprised him. Nor could Howe dismiss his role in the whole affair by claiming that he had expected only "a stampede" and no violence. They had all expected a stampede, but they had been prepared for bloodshed if that was necessary to make the stampede a success. Maybe Howe had argued with Brown about stealing slaveholders' property, but Higginson remembered that at the time of the Missouri raid a year earlier, Howe had accepted the death of a white slaveholder without comment. Howe

34. Ibid. It is difficult to say who Howe's "honorable man" was. Three different men made key judgments about what Howe should do in the wake of Harpers Ferry. John A. Andrew, his legal counsel, encouraged Howe to go to Canada and wrote a number of letters to newspapers in early December defending Howe's character. It is possible that these letters were partially motivated by a desire to recompense Howe for having given him poor advice about the disclaimer, although Andrew knew little, if anything, about Brown's movements. Frank Sanborn also exerted a good deal of influence over Howe that fall, and his defense of the card to Higginson suggests that he was not nearly as offended by it as the minister. Sanborn also "knew about Brown's movements and a great deal more." Another candidate is George Luther Stearns. Stearns knew of Brown's movements and was with Howe in Canada when the card was submitted.

had agreed with Parker's estimate of the episode and had been more than willing to trade one white life for the lives of eleven slaves. No, Howe could not remove himself from responsibility for Brown's acts in the eyes of Thomas Wentworth Higginson.

When Samuel Gridley Howe and George Luther Stearns met after the hearings, both agreed that the investigation had been conducted "unskillfully." They had not been forced to make incriminating revelations because the questions had been poorly conceived. The failure of the committee to uncover conspiracy had, however, nothing to do with a lack of skill. It resulted from a combination of half-truthful answers, a minimum of evidence, Mason's reluctance to fully establish conspiracy, and Collamer's initial wish that the hearings exonerate all those called to testify. These factors, not poorly conceived questions, produced a less-than-probing analysis of the money and men behind John Brown. When the committee's report was issued in June 1860, these elements were reflected on virtually every page of the testimony.[35]

Mason's misgivings are particularly noticeable in the majority report of the investigation. Mason concluded that Brown's purpose in Kansas was to keep the public mind inflamed on the subject of slavery "with a view to effecting such organization as might enable him to bring about servile insurrection in the slave states." Mason stressed that testimony before his committee indicated the "utter insecurity of peace and safety, in some states of the Union, in the existing condition of the public mind and its purposes in the non-slaveholding States." He was convinced that northern public opinion had become a tinderbox that could easily be set off by the committee hearings, and this view is pervasive in the majority report. Despite obvious flaws in the testimony of Howe and Stearns, despite Realf's implication of Smith, and despite the refusal of certain of Brown's associates to testify, the report carefully avoided any accusation of direct complicity with Brown.

35. Howe to Higginson, February 16, 1860, Higginson-Brown Collection, Boston Public Library.

Admittedly, the committee lacked the necessary hard evidence to make such an accusation, but what evidence did exist was handled in a remarkably discreet fashion by the chairman.[36]

On the whole issue of accessories "not present" who might have given Brown arms, money, or munitions, the majority report held that it appeared such contributions had not been made with "actual knowledge of use for which they were intended by Brown." Money had been freely contributed by those who considered themselves Brown's friends "without inquiry" about how it was to be used. Mason accepted the conspirators' own definition of the way Brown obtained funds. By doing so, he walled them away from the very thing he suspected: that they believed in the appropriateness of violent means to end slavery. Mason described Brown as one who "successfully impressed himself and his capacity . . . upon the sickly . . . depraved sensibilities of his allies." In the process, Brown commanded their confidence "if he did not altogether bill their suspicions."[37]

Mason's analysis was not an "unskillful" one. Indeed, anyone who reads the report can recognize it as a piece of master craftsmanship. The Virginia senator implied a full understanding of how and why the conspiracy took place. Yet he succeeded in doing to the general public what the conspirators tried to do to him. In the report he successfully obscured the relationships of Brown and his supporters so as to prevent the public from learning of their tacit agreement on the principles of justified political violence. Mason accepted statements about Brown's "remarkable reticence" and his "secretiveness," not so much because he believed that this was the case, but because he wanted to turn these claims to his own advantage. Brown's friends might escape prosecution by pleading that they were not informed of his intentions, but Mason then used the same argument to prove they did not condone Brown's acts at Harpers Ferry. Mason was able to demonstrate that the men who supported Brown did so because they lacked knowledge, not because they believed in the "cause of insurrection." There was no need to

36. "Majority Conclusions," *Mason Report*, p. 13.
37. Ibid., pp. 7–8, 10.

suggest legislation on the matter because the invasion was "simply the act of lawless ruffians under the sanction of no public or political authority." Mason had beaten Howe and Stearns at their own game.[38]

In their minority report, Collamer and Doolittle were less interested than Mason in portraying the raid as an "act of lawless ruffians." Consequently they tended to focus more attention on Brown's friends. In the end the minority report came down much harder on Brown's supporters than the majority report did. Both Senators Doolittle and Collamer accepted the premise that Brown's Boston friends "placed too much implicit confidence in him." Although they saw no conclusive evidence of conspiracy, they were angered that the Bostonians had acquiesced in the use of forceful means. They believed it was "astonishing" that there should "still be found large bodies of men laboring under the infatuation that . . . a good object can be effected by lawlessness and violence."[39]

Thomas Wentworth Higginson ended his immediate connection to the Harpers Ferry episode when he decided not to proceed with his rescue scheme. Gerrit Smith severed his attachment to the affair by being committed to the Utica Asylum. When the *Mason Report* was published in the late spring of 1860, it officially ended Howe's and Stearns's connection to the raid—although they considered their February testimony as the termination date. In the first week of April 1860, Frank Sanborn came full circle.

Early in the evening of April 3 a group of deputies under the direction of Silas Carlton rode into Concord, inquired where the young committee secretary lived, deployed themselves around his home on Sudbury Road, and then quietly waited until darkness enveloped the town. At about nine o'clock, Carlton, accompanied by five deputies, walked up the front steps of Sanborn's home and knocked on the door. When Sanborn answered, he was informed that Carlton had been deputized by the sergeant at arms of the United States Senate,

38. Ibid., pp. 17–18.
39. Ibid., p. 23.

Dunning R. McNair, to arrest him for failure to heed a Mason Committee summons. Carlton and his men then burst into the house, grabbed Sanborn, and pulled him toward their carriage in the road. Sanborn struggled violently against the group, first pinning his long legs against the doorway, then hooking them on the railing of the front porch. As he struggled, he called to his sister Sarah, told her he was being arrested without warrant, and asked her to warn the neighbors. Sarah ran from the house screaming. She managed to awaken a friend named Colonel Whiting and then returned to her front yard where Frank was still struggling against Carlton and the others. Sarah ran to the deputy's carriage, grabbed the whip, cracked it, and sent the horses bolting down the street.[40]

The commotion caused by the arrest attempt wakened people in the area. Colonel Whiting and many others came out of their homes to see what was happening and soon found themselves grappling with the deputies in an attempt to release Sanborn. John Keyes had the presence of mind to go to the nearby home of Judge Rockwell Hoar, obtain a writ of *habeas corpus,* and then seek out the town constable, John Moore. When Moore and Keyes arrived at the scene, they temporarily called a halt to the melee and tried to discuss the situation with Carlton. Moore asked Carlton on what authority he was arresting Sanborn. Carlton told Moore he had been deputized by McNair. Moore then showed Carlton the writ and asked him to give up Sanborn. When Carlton refused, Moore deputized the Concord residents who were present and asked them to take Sanborn into custody. During the night of protective custody he spent at George Prescott's home, the secretary hastily penned an open letter to the Massachusetts legislature censuring that body for allowing laws to persist which encouraged the "kidnapping" of "white men" by federal authorities.[41]

40. John Clarkson, Jr., "Wanted in Concord," *Yankee Magazine,* April 1969, pp. 128–32; Sarah Sanborn's Account of the Arrest, Sanborn-Brown Collection, Houghton Library; Sanborn, *Recollections,* 1: 208–18.

41. Clarkson, "Wanted in Concord," pp. 128–32; Betty L. Mitchell, "Realities Not Shadows, Franklin Benjamin Sanborn, the Early Years," *Civil War History* 20 (June 1974): 115–17; Franklin Benjamin Sanborn, "Petition to the Massachusetts Legislature," *Boston Transcript,* April 4, 1860.

Early the next morning, Sanborn traveled to Boston where a hearing had been called in the chambers of the chief justice of the Massachusetts Supreme Court, Lemuel Shaw. Appearing with lawyers Robert Treat Paine, Samuel Sewall, and John A. Andrew, Sanborn patiently endured the legal arguments and then waited for Shaw's decision. Shaw did not think Sanborn should be taken to Washington, but in his ruling he refused to challenge the constitutionality of the law of 1846 or the right of a congressional committee to arrest witnesses who disregarded a summons. Instead, Shaw based his decision against the government on the premise that "the warrant returned the power to arrest the respondent in terms limited to McNair . . . and could not be executed by a deputy." In short, McNair could not legally delegate the authority to arrest Sanborn. The young secretary was free.[42]

During the hearing a large crowd gathered outside the Court House. George Luther Stearns, fearing an unpleasant confrontation when his young friend left Shaw's chambers, had a carriage waiting by a side door of the building. After the hearing ended he hustled Sanborn to the carriage, and the two of them then rode out to Concord. Upon arriving there, Sanborn was greeted by a cheering crowd and saluted by a cannon as people screamed insults at Colonel Joseph Holbrook and Postmaster Charles Davis, the two townsmen who had provided Carlton with information the night before. Soon Sanborn learned that a town meeting had been called in his honor. That evening he was to share the platform with Emerson, Thoreau, and Higginson. In less than twenty-four hours he had been arrested, tried, found innocent and become Concord's "hero of the hour." He was dazed and overwhelmed.[43]

At eight o'clock that evening his triumphant moment began. He strode briskly to the speaker's platform, thanked Emerson and Thoreau for their introductory remarks, turned to the assemblage, and launched into a brief but dramatic tirade against the Slave Power. Sanborn

42. Sanborn, *Recollections,* 1: 212.
43. "The New Martyr," *New York Herald,* April 7, 1860; Sanborn, *Recollections,* 1: 217.

started by describing the arrest attempt. He acknowledged the heroism of those who had assisted him and spoke of Shaw's decision. Sanborn firmly believed the judgment "agreed with the sentiments of two-thirds of the people of Massachusetts." Then he lashed out at the men who had tried to arrest him: They were "ruffians." Furthermore, he was certain that, had they been killed during the rescue, the deed would not have been judged unlawful. In fact, Sanborn said he believed the deputies "ought to have been killed." Finally, in a dramatic gesture, Sanborn held up the handcuffs used to bind him during the arrest attempt. He asked the crowd what they symbolized. "Tyranny!" came the resounding cry. Sanborn had learned many lessons during the course of his relationship with Brown. He had shown Francis Merriam one of them in early October. Concord was receiving a demonstration of another.[44]

After holding the handcuffs aloft, Sanborn continued to excite the emotions of the crowd. He shouted that dealing with southerners was like "dealing with demons" and said that slavery must be opposed by force. But as always, Sanborn was careful not to push the idea of justifiable political violence too far in public. He did not counsel attacking slavery. Rather, he suggested that northerners prepare to meet the encroachments of slavery with force because that was the "only argument some people can understand." Sanborn then concluded his remarks with a Brown-like nod to the Almighty and to practical abolition. He swore that "so help him God," he would "put in practice the teachings of the last twenty-four hours." The secret committeeman received a thunderous ovation, waved to the audience, walked off the platform, and strode out of the building into the cool night air. He was much too excited to listen to the remaining speakers and undoubtedly realized that he might never again receive such a powerful acclamation of popular favor. It was something to be savored in solitude.[45]

The kidnapping incident and Sanborn's reaction to it suggest one dimension of his motives for committing himself to full-time work in

44. "The New Martyr," *New York Herald,* April 7, 1860.
45. Ibid.

the abolitionist movement and for attaching himself to John Brown. From the time he first moved to Concord in the spring of 1855 Sanborn had felt alone, estranged from the community and still wounded by the loss of Ariana. Of course, he had his schoolteaching, Sarah's company, and a superficial acquaintance with some of the famous personages of the town. But these things did not sustain him, did not create in him a feeling of acceptance. Indeed, he was dismayed by the aloofness of both Emerson and Thoreau—they liked him, but kept their distance. For all of Sanborn's transcendental ardor, he could not make the famous men and women of Concord his intimates. At the same time, his identification with these men and women closed him off from many other Concord citizens. As he noted years later, in peaceable times the "Concord majority sided with itself and did not approve of people like abolitionists and Transcendentalists who would turn the world upside down." This Concord majority disliked the "enemies of constituted authorities" and turned "all the weapons of exhortation, gossip and Pharisaic aloofness" against them. So there he was, a schoolteacher and second-generation transcendentalist, spurned by the Concord majority and not yet fully sustained or accepted by those he longed to emulate. Even during the six months after Harpers Ferry when he received repeated hints that he would be protected by the community, Sanborn had not trusted Concord's citizens. Then, in little over a day, he had experienced a dramatic and intoxicating change of status. He had been rescued, feted, saluted by cannon, and confirmed by those whose friendship he had so long sought. The "people" had "defended" him and "vowed" to protect him.[46]

In the next few days the young man had a chance to reflect on his newfound station and decided to write to Theodore Parker about it. In the letter, Sanborn strained to define the essential meaning of the whole episode, managing to do so in two revealing sentences. Sanborn told Parker that "everything is going on as favorably for me as it can." The tyranny of "the other side has put all good citizens with me of all parties." The kidnap attempt and, indirectly, his relationship to

46. Sanborn, *Recollections*, 2: 452, 347, 447.

abolition and Brown had won him acceptance. He was, as he noted years later, made "popular in quarters where I was not known before." Frank Sanborn, the bright young son of a New Hampshire clerk, who found that a Harvard education did not automatically provide one with a niche in Boston society, had finally found his place.[47]

47. Sanborn to Parker, April 9, 1860, Sanborn Collection, Concord Free Public Library.

CHAPTER 10

The "Superadded" Conspiracy

T HE EFFORT TO RECONSTRUCT historical motive is
a difficult one and cannot help but leave those who undertake it with feelings of humility and a tinge of resignation. It is
sometimes a search for reasons which people at the time could not fully
comprehend and which may never completely explain what actually
happened. But it is a search that must be made because it is here that
past and present meet and redefine each other. It is in the study of past
motive that the subtle differences between one era and another reveal
themselves. And it is here that historians begin to comprehend how
societies move and are moved by the individuals who comprise them.
Furthermore, motives can and often do prefigure results—allowing us
a more accurate understanding of historical events.

Armed with an awareness of both the limitations and rewards of the
search, this analysis of the Secret Committee of Six seeks as much to
provide a meaningful context for motive as it does to describe the
particular reasons for individual and group acts. I undertook the work
with a number of guiding assumptions. First, I thought that to understand why men subsidize political violence required asking what they
hoped to accomplish by that subsidy and how they hoped to justify
it. It seemed reasonable, as well, to ask whether or not their choice of
an insurrectionary leader was in any way linked to the answers of the
first two questions. Finally, since men are more often moved by their
society than they are society's moving agents, it seemed as important
to understand the general demands of mid-nineteenth-century northern

life on the conspirators as it did to consider them in their particular roles as "practical" abolitionists.

Initially I tried to discover what political acts the Six were able to justify in the name of Higher Law. I was disappointed to find that the principles of Higher Law were insufficient justification for political violence for all of the group members, except Higginson, because those principles failed to take them beyond belief and into action. I thought the reasons for the group's support of John Brown's plan had to be reexamined. Simultaneously, I looked for any new theories of political violence that they might have developed during the conspiracy. I found that the Six decided to finance a slave insurrection as a way of expressing their moral outrage at an institution which had afflicted black men and women in America for two hundred and fifty years. Their commitment was further prompted by a growing concern that abolitionism, both political and moral suasionist, had failed and would continue to fail to undo the wrong of slavery. Equally significant, the Six decided to back a white-led slave assault on slaveholders in order to answer deep-seated questions about the effect of slavery on the Afro-American character. The conspirators hoped that the act of insurrection would destroy their own and white America's preconceptions about the docile slave nature. But their subsidy of slave revolt was meant to do more than vent moral outrage, answer questions about racial makeup, or change racial images: It was meant to *alter* what the Six considered to be a plantation-induced slave temperament. By June 1859 these men had become persuaded that violent acts would shock slaves out of submissiveness and into the first stage of a process which would instill in them new beliefs and new behaviors. The act of insurrection would inculcate a system of values suited to the demands of the democratic, industrial North. The Six theorized that northern free society was based on their forefathers' willingness to take up arms and fight for freedom, that such a willingness was a dominant Anglo-American racial trait, and that it was the basis of northern institutional life. If slaves struck a blow for their own freedom, they would acquire social, economic, and political perspectives suited to life in the northern marketplace. Whether the slaves were persons who were environmentally debilitated by plantation life (a consuming interest of all members of the group, but particularly of Samuel Gridley Howe) or persons who were innately inferior, it was essential that they be brought to insurrection in order to spark the inner potential (Higginson called it the "courage of emulation") which would lead to a rebirth of character. Here, the theorizations of Higginson in his article "Physical Courage," Theodore Parker, Samuel Gridley Howe, and the journalist James Redpath as well as the assertions of key black men in Boston and black abolitionists in general were crucial: They momentarily satisfied the committeemen that slaves did have the inner potential, the "superadded something," to rise up and strike for freedom. For an instant, the Six convinced themselves that, by the act of insurrection, slaves would exchange docility and group consciousness for a more assertive and individualist outlook. Violent acts were first steps to responsible participation in a democratic, wage-labor society, first steps to assimilation of Anglo-American culture, and first steps to a respected place in northern social life.

Helping the secret committee to formulate and act upon these notions was the man they chose to subsidize—John Brown. Brown desperately sought to spark the violent moment when slaves would take up arms. He wanted to spread revolt to areas surrounding Harpers Ferry and then erect a colony in the Virginia mountains, where further attacks against slaveholders could be prepared. In the minds of the Six, this mountain retreat would serve as a testing ground for their speculations about violence and values. Brown would act as a model for the newly liberated black men.

John Brown appealed to the members of the secret committee for many reasons. All of them admired his moral contempt for slavery, his intense religiosity, his thoroughgoing belief in the principles of Higher Law, his almost reckless physical valor, and his complete willingness to sacrifice family and friends to the cause of abolition. The group also based their support of Brown, at least initially, on the presumption that his experiences in the northern marketplace were not only similar to their own, but had elicited a value system that they believed was most suited to an emerging urban-oriented class of men and the entire society that spawned such a class. Brown was self-controlled, ambitious, concerned with his civic reputation, and committed to the nuclear family. He was a business failure but, in failure, seemed to cling more resolutely to the values which the Six revered. And, in failure, he had learned to effectively convey the image of a determined, competent decision-maker—a man who was experienced, professional, organized, and cautiously bold.

Still, in spite of all Brown's positive qualities and the way he reinforced the Six's developing theories of political violence, the group committed themselves to insurrection only tentatively when they gave funds to Brown in June 1859. There are many reasons for their hesitancy. For all of their personal successes, the Six were very uncertain men in a rapidly changing society. Their theory arose as much from their own precarious psychological participation in northern life as it did from their analysis of black character. These men believed they understood the requirements of life in a "free" society, and they looked for a way to prepare blacks for its demands: People new to freedom must assimilate its values. They also searched for their theory out of self-interest and seemed to feel that, in defining the values necessary for black survival, they would acquire a clearer understanding of the values they needed (or thought they needed) to survive in that society. Nor was it ever lost on the Six that in setting criteria for the behavior of another group, they were exercising control over that group. As a result, their theory was born, at least partially, out of self-doubt. Although it took the group beyond Higher Law, it remained a fragile speculation.

And there were other reasons for their misgivings. Brown's behavior during the conspiracy grew increasingly flawed. The elements of his personality which had so often cost him favor in previous business transactions surfaced in his negotiations with the Six. His tantrum during the North Elba land purchase gave Sanborn, Stearns, and Smith pause. When the Hugh Forbes fiasco erupted, it alienated everyone on the committee except Higginson. Thus, committeemen found discordant elements in both their theory of violence and their commitment to Brown. And they were reminded of what Higginson had noted at the time of the Burns rescue: There was an array of experiences in all of their lives that led to abhorrence of violence, whether it could be justified or not. Man was man precisely because he had rational faculties and could bring them to bear in solving human problems.

Personal motives also produced the Six's ambivalent commitment to insurrection. Members of the committee attached themselves to Brown for an array of secondary reasons. These reasons, like the group's theory of violence and their confidence in Brown, contained ingredients which could both prompt and diminish desires to instigate the use of forceful means. A brief look at these secondary motives suggests that, in at least three of the committeemen, concerns about their place in Boston reform society acted alternately as stimulus and obstruction to their support of slave violence.

Sanborn's elation over the welcome he received in Concord after the attempt to arrest him best makes the point. I believe it indicates that his commitment to abolitionism, Brown, and slave revolt was to a degree conditioned by his hunger for recognition from that segment of Boston-area society which most appealed to him. Sanborn's commitment cannot be divorced from considerations of career and status. At the same time, he feared that his support for Brown's insurrectionary act could bring disfavor from those he wanted to impress—not to mention the possibility of a jail sentence. Perhaps "treason" would not be construed as "patriotism" by either transcendentalists or the vast majority of abolitionists who continued to believe that moral suasion and political action were still the best ways to end slavery. His flight to Canada, his denial of a relationship with Brown, and his refusal to testify before the Mason Committee, all show his concern at having acted too rashly in financing slave violence. When he was rescued by Concord citizens, feted by transcendentalists, and applauded by abolitionists, he was uplifted.

George Luther Stearns, too, was a relative newcomer to abolition and, as such, was highly sensitive to the opinions of those who had been in the movement a long time. He took heart when Higginson, Smith, Howe, and Parker supported Brown but was unsettled when he saw the hostility which Henry Wilson and others displayed at Brown's

Kansas activity and violent utterances. Like Sanborn, Stearns was pushed and pulled by his desire for acceptance in the respectable abolitionist community. Like Howe, Stearns tried to make his Mason committee testimony prove that he both did and did not condone Brown's insurrectionary act. But more than any of the committeemen, Stearns had based his attachment to Brown on an intimate knowledge of Brown's experiences in the marketplace. Stearns had exerted great efforts to succeed in mid-nineteenth-century America, and his experiences were most reminiscent of Brown's. Hard work, a fortuitous marriage, and the assistance of wealthy friends during his disastrous lead-pipe venture kept Stearns from suffering Brown's failures and undoubtedly revealed to him that the distance between his palatial Medford home and Brown's humble wood-frame farmhouse in North Elba was not great. Stearns had grounded his faith, to a greater extent than any of the others, on Brown's competence and businesslike manner. When Brown acted erratically, Stearns was shocked and his confidence was shaken.

For some time before meeting John Brown, Samuel Gridley Howe had searched for a cause that would give him a chance to justify his reputation to himself—a reputation that he believed he had undeservedly acquired. He looked for a cause that would help him throw off the crisis of confidence that engulfed him throughout the late 1850s. In the wake of his Canadian flight, disclaimer note, and Mason testimony, he must have thought that the same elements of character he had hoped to purge by his commitment to Brown were forcing him to deny his relationship to the martyr and to the validity of political violence. Furthermore, the whole question of black capabilities made Howe pause. He desperately wanted Brown's raid to prove that slaves had been corrupted by the environment of slavery and were not innately inferior human beings. He believed that the exposure of slaves to Brown in a "normal" community established in the Virginia mountains would redeem their pliant personalities. Yet, Howe was also repelled by his gamble on slave revolt. What if the raid failed? What if the mountain community failed? Such failure might deepen white

America's contention that black men were innately inferior. There seemed as much to be lost in failure as gained in success.

Gerrit Smith, Thomas Wentworth Higginson, and Theodore Parker, all grappled with the problem of their role in northern society. For the most part, however, they had resolved their doubts and were less prone to the social and psychological anxieties of their fellow committeemen. Nevertheless, both Smith and Parker balked at conspiracy. Gerrit Smith's entire abolitionist career suggests that he was subject to a continuing inner debate about the use of violent means and the character of Afro-Americans. These doubts plagued him before, during, and after the raid. His ambivalence abated only briefly with a new theory of violence and an enthusiastic belief in Brown's personal virtue. It is fortunate for Brown that the wealthy New York landowner found himself in a period of turbulent religious reassessment. The reassessment perfectly suited the Bible-quoting Brown because it acted as the medium through which he could promote his scheme, reveal his personal value system, and sketch out, in the roughest of terms, his contentions about slave capacities. Paradoxical thought and erratic behavior were commonplace in the life of the enigmatic Smith, and it is no wonder that he behaved so fitfully when Brown was caught. Whether that behavior was a ploy to put off the federal authorities or a genuine nervous breakdown precipitated by Brown's capture is difficult to determine. What is clear, however, is that such actions perfectly express the ambivalence Smith felt about his commitment to a slave uprising at Harpers Ferry.

Theodore Parker and Thomas Wentworth Higginson exhibited much greater constancy in their attachment to John Brown and slave violence. To begin with, both men played essential roles in formulating the rationale for violence. They did much of the thinking and arguing about the interconnection of violence and value assimilation, and they moved the other committeemen with their conceptions. Parker briefly stepped back from the scheme in May 1858, and it is likely that his enthusiastic response to Harpers Ferry was somewhat conditioned by the realization of his impending death and his residence in Rome on that fateful day in October 1859.

On the other hand, Thomas Wentworth Higginson never wavered in his support of Brown once he had committed himself to the plan. From the moment he broke down the Court House door in the attempt to rescue Anthony Burns to his days as a colonel in a South Carolina black regiment during the Civil War, Higginson believed that violence, and particularly black violence, was necessary to end slavery. Perhaps years of personal reflection on his societal role—one waged between the contemplative and active sides of his character—helped him to resolve any personal doubts about his course and better prepared him for his radical abolitionist stance. He had concerns about his reputation and questions about the Afro-American character, but at the same time he had the confidence to move forward without hesitation. As a result he played a vital role, perhaps the key role, in coaxing the Secret Committee of Six to support John Brown's raid, and he provides the only example of unambivalent behavior for the entire group.

Bibliography

This is a selected bibliography. It contains all the sources consulted as well as those secondary works that were helpful in developing this study.

PRIMARY SOURCES

Manuscripts

Agassiz, Louis. Papers. Houghton Library, Harvard University. Cambridge, Mass.

Andrew, John A. Papers. Massachusetts Historical Society. Boston, Mass.

Black Abolitionist Papers. Florida State University. Tallahassee, Fla.

Brown, John. Boyd B. Stutler Collection. Charleston, W.Va.

―――. Brown Collection. Boston Public Library. Boston, Mass.

―――. Brown Collection. Library of Congress. Washington, D.C.

―――. Brown Collection. Massachusetts Historical Society. Boston, Mass.

―――. Papers. Kansas State Historical Society. Topeka, Kans.

Dana, Richard Henry, Jr. Dana Journal. Massachusetts Historical Society. Boston, Mass.

Garrison, William Lloyd. Garrison Collection. Boston Public Library. Boston, Mass.

Higginson, Thomas Wentworth. Higginson Collection. Houghton Library, Harvard University. Cambridge, Mass.

―――. Higginson–Barney Collection. Houghton Library, Harvard University. Cambridge, Mass.

―――. Higginson–Brown Collection. Boston Public Library. Boston, Mass.

―――. Higginson–Burns Collection. Boston Public Library. Boston, Mass.

―――. Higginson–Huntington Collection. Huntington Library. San Marino, Calif.

————. Higginson-Kansas Collection. Kansas State Historical Society. Topeka, Kans.

Howe, Samuel Gridley. Howe Collection. Houghton Library, Harvard University. Cambridge, Mass.

————. Howe Collection. Massachusetts Historical Society. Boston, Mass.

Jackson, Francis T. Papers. Massachusetts Historical Society. Boston, Mass.

Lawrence, Amos A. Lawrence Collection. Massachusetts Historical Society. Boston, Mass.

McKim, J. Miller. McKim Collection. Cornell University Library. Ithaca, N.Y.

Massachusetts Kansas Committee. Records. Massachusetts Historical Society. Boston, Mass.

May, Samuel, Jr. May Collection. Boston Public Library. Boston, Mass.

Parker, Theodore. Letterbooks. Massachusetts Historical Society. Boston, Mass.

————. Letters. Harvard-Andover Theological Library, Harvard University. Cambridge, Mass.

————. Parker Collection. Boston Public Library. Boston, Mass.

————. Sermons, 1850–1859. Widener Library, Harvard University. Cambridge, Mass.

Sanborn, Franklin Benjamin. Letters. Atlanta University Library. Atlanta, Ga.

————. Sanborn Collection. Concord Free Public Library. Concord, Mass.

————. Sanborn Collection. Kansas State Historical Society. Topeka, Kans.

————. Sanborn-Brown Collection. Houghton Library, Harvard University. Cambridge, Mass.

Smith, Gerrit. Smith Collection. Houghton Library, Harvard University. Cambridge, Mass.

————. Smith Collection. Syracuse University Library. Syracuse, N.Y.

Spooner, Lysander. Spooner Collection. Boston Public Library. Boston, Mass.

Stearns, George Luther. Letters. New York Historical Society. New York, N.Y.

————. Papers. Cornell University Library. Ithaca, N.Y.

————. Stearns Collection. Houghton Library, Harvard University. Cambridge, Mass.

————. Stearns Collection. Kansas State Historical Society. Topeka, Kans.

————. Stearns Collection. Massachusetts Historical Society. Boston, Mass.

Sumner, Charles. Sumner Collection. Houghton Library, Harvard University. Cambridge, Mass.

Villard, Oswald Garrison. Villard Collection. Columbia University. New York, N.Y.

Newspapers

Boston Atlas & Daily Bee (Boston, Mass.). October 1859.

Boston Transcript (Boston, Mass.). October 1859–June 1860.

Liberator. (Boston, Mass.). January 1854–June 1860.

National Anti-Slavery Standard. (New York, N.Y.). January 1854–June 1860.
New York Herald (New York, N.Y.). October 1859–November 1859.
New York Tribune (New York, N.Y.). October 1859–June 1860.
Syracuse Journal. (Syracuse, N.Y.). May 1856.
Worcester Daily Spy (Worcester, Mass.). January 1857–June 1860.

Magazines

Atlantic Monthly Magazine. 1858–1861.

Books, Articles, Reports

Bearse, Austin. *Reminiscences of Fugitive Slave Days in Boston.* Boston: Warren
    Richardson, 1880.
Brown, William Wells. *Narrative of William Wells Brown, a Fugitive Slave.*
    Boston: Bela Marsh Co., 1848.
————. *Santo Domingo: Its Revolution and Its Patriots.* Boston: Bela Marsh Co.,
    1855.
Burns, Anthony. *Boston Slave Riot and the Trial of Anthony Burns.* Boston:
    Fetridge and Co., 1854.
Clarke, James Freeman. *Anti-Slavery Days.* New York: R. Worthington, 1884.
Dana, Richard Henry, Jr. "How We Met John Brown." *Atlantic Monthly* 28
    (July 1871): 5–14.
Drayton, Daniel. *Personel Memoir.* Boston: Bela Marsh Co., 1855.
Emerson, Ralph Waldo. "Remarks on the Character of George Luther Stearns
    at Medford" (eulogy), April 14, 1867. American Antiquarian Society.
    Worcester, Mass.
Forbes, Sarah Hughes. *The Letters and Recollections of John Murray Forbes.* 2 vols.
    Boston: Houghton Mifflin Co., 1899.
Garrison, W. P., and Garrison, F. J. *William Lloyd Garrison, 1805–1879: The Story
    of His Life. . . .* 4 vols. London: T. Fisher Unwin, 1885–1889.
Hayden, Lewis. "War of Races" (an address before Prince Hall Grand Lodge of
    Free Masons). Boston: Edward S. Coombs, 1868.
Higginson, Thomas Wentworth. *Army Life in a Black Regiment.* Boston:
    Houghton Mifflin Co., 1900.
————. *Black Rebellion.* Reprint of portions of the work *Travellers and
    Outlaws.* New York: Arno Press, 1969.
————. *Cheerful Yesterdays.* Boston: Houghton Mifflin Co., 1896.
————. *Contemporaries.* Boston: Houghton Mifflin Co., 1900.
————. *The Letters and Journals of Thomas Wentworth Higginson, 1846–1909.*
    Edited by Mary Thacher Higginson. Boston: Houghton Mifflin Co., 1921.
Howe, Julia Ward. *Julia Ward Howe, 1819–1910.* Edited by Laura Richards and
    Maud Elliot Howe. 2 vols. Boston: Houghton Mifflin Co., 1916.

————. *Reminiscences*. Boston: Houghton Mifflin Co., 1899.

————. *Samuel Gridley Howe, a Memoir*. Boston: Howe Memorial Committee, 1886.

————. *A Trip to Cuba*. Boston: Ticknor and Fields Co., 1860.

Howe, Samuel Gridley. *The Collected Writings of Samuel Gridley Howe*. Boston: Ticknor and Fields Co., 1857.

————. *Discourse on the Social Relations of Man*. Boston: Marsh, Capon and Lyon Co., 1837.

————. *The Letters and Journals of Samuel Gridley Howe*. Edited by Laura E. Richards. 2 vols. Boston: Dana, Estes and Co., 1906.

————. "The Refugees from Slavery in Canada West," *Report to the American Freedman's Inquiry Commission*. Boston: Wright and Potter Printers, 1864.

————. *Slavery at Washington: A Narrative of the Heroic Adventures of Drayton, an American Trader*. London: Ward and Co., 1848.

————, et al. *American Freedman's Inquiry Commission Preliminary Report*. New York: John F. Trow, 1863.

Loguen, Jermain Wesley. *The Reverand J. W. Loguen, as a Slave and as a Freeman*. 1859. Reprint. New York: Negro Universities Press, 1968.

Mason, James M. *Public Life and Diplomatic Correspondence*. Edited by Sarah Mason. Roanoke: The Stone Co., 1903.

May, Samuel. *The Fugitive Slave Law and Its Victims*. New York: American Antislavery Society, 1861.

Nell, William C. *Colored Patriots of the American Revolution*. Boston: Bela Marsh Co., 1855.

————. *Services of Colored Americans in the Wars of 1776 and 1812*. Boston: Bela Marsh Co., 1852.

Parker, Theodore. *The Boston Kidnapping*. 1852. Reprint. New York: Arno Press, 1969.

————. *The Collected Works of Theodore Parker*. Centenary Edition. 15 vols. Boston: American Unitarian Association, 1910.

————. *The Collected Works of Theodore Parker*. Edited by Francis P. Cobbe. 14 vols. London: Trubner and Co., 1863–1874.

————. *The Life and Correspondence of Theodore Parker*. Edited by John Weiss. 2 vols. Boston: Bergman Publishers, 1864.

————. *Social Classes in a Republic*. Edited by Samuel E. Eliot. Boston: American Unitarian Society, 1941.

————. *The Trial of Theodore Parker*. Boston: Published for the author, 1855.

Proceedings of the Convention of Radical Political Abolitionists. New York: Central Abolition Board, 1856.

Proceedings of the Worcester Disunion Convention, January 15–17, 1857. Boston: Printed for the State Disunion Committee, 1857.

Redpath, James. *Hand-book to Kansas Territory*. New York: J. H. Colton, 1859.

————. "Notes on the Insurrection or Reminiscences of the Insurrection." *Boston Atlas & Daily Bee*. October 21, 24, 29, 1859.

————. *The Public Life of Capt. John Brown.* Boston: Thayer and Eldridge, 1860.

————. *The Roving Editor: or Talks with Slaves in the Southern States.* New York: Burdich Co., 1859.

————, ed. *Echoes of Harpers Ferry.* Boston: Thayer and Eldridge, 1860.

————, ed. *A Guide to Hayti.* 1861. Reprint. Westport: Negro Universities Press, 1970.

Sanborn, Franklin Benjamin. *The Life and Letters of John Brown.* Boston: Roberts Bros., 1885.

————. *Recollections of Seventy Years.* 2 vols. Boston: Richard G. Badger, The Gorham Press, 1909.

————. *Samuel Gridley Howe, the Philanthropist.* New York: Funk and Wagnalls, 1891.

Smith, Gerrit. "Peace Better Than War" (pamphlet of a speech delivered in May 1858). Boston: American Peace Society, 1858.

————. *The Religion of Reason.* Peterboro: Hammond Company, 1864.

————. *Sermons and Speeches.* New York: Ross and Tausey, 1861.

————. *Speeches of Gerrit Smith in Congress.* New York: Mason Brothers, 1855.

————. *The True Office of Civil Government.* New York: S. W. Benedict Co., 1851.

Stevens, Charles Emery. *Anthony Burns: A History.* Boston: John P. Jewett and Co., 1856.

Thayer, Eli. *A History of the Kansas Crusade.* New York: Harper Brothers, 1889.

————. *The New England Emigrant Aid Company.* Worcester: F. P. Rice, 1887.

U.S. Senate. Mason Committee. *Report on the Invasion of Harpers Ferry.* 36th Cong., 1st sess., 1860, I. Rept. 278.

SECONDARY SOURCES

Books

Abels, Jules. *Man on Fire: John Brown and the Cause of Liberty.* New York: Oxford University Press, 1971.

Aptheker, Herbert. *The Negro in the Abolitionist Movement.* New York: International Publishers, 1941.

Barnes, Gilbert. *Antislavery Impulse.* New York: Harcourt, Brace and World, 1964.

Bartlett, Irving H. *Wendell Phillips, Brahmin Radical.* Boston: Beacon Press, 1961.

Berwanger, Eugene. *The Frontier Against Slavery.* Urbana: University of Illinois Press, 1967.

Boyer, Richard O. *The Legend of John Brown: A Biography and a History.* New York: Alfred Knopf Co., 1973.

Brauer, Kinley J. *Cotton Versus Conscience; Massachusetts Whig Politics, 1843–1848.* Lexington: University of Kentucky Press, 1967.

Brock, Peter. *Radical Pacifists in Antebellum America.* Princeton: Princeton University Press, 1968.

Campbell, Stanley W. *The Slave Catchers: Enforcement of the Fugitive Slave Law, 1850–1860.* New York: Norton and Co., 1968.

Commager, Henry Steele. *Theodore Parker, Yankee Crusader.* Boston: Beacon Press, 1960.

———, ed. *Theodore Parker: An Anthology.* Boston: Beacon Press, 1960.

Craven, Avery. *The Coming of the Civil War.* Chicago: Chicago University Press, 1957.

Daniels, John. *In Freedom's Birthplace: A Study of the Boston Negro.* Boston: Houghton Mifflin Co., 1914.

Davis, David Brion. *Homicide in American Fiction, 1798–1860: A Study in Social Values.* Ithaca: Cornell University Press, 1957.

———. *The Problem of Slavery in Western Culture.* Ithaca: Cornell University Press, 1966.

———. *The Slave Power Conspiracy and the Paranoid Style.* Baton Rouge: Louisiana State University Press, 1969.

Dillon, Merton L. *The Abolitionists: The Growth of a Dissenting Minority.* DeKalb: Northern Illinois University Press, 1974.

Donald, David. *Charles Sumner and the Coming of the Civil War.* New York: Harper and Row, 1961.

———. *Charles Sumner and the Rights of Man.* New York: Knopf, 1970.

Duberman, Martin. *Charles Francis Adams, 1807–1886.* Stanford: Stanford University Press, 1968.

———. *James Russell Lowell.* Boston: Houghton Mifflin Co., 1966.

———, ed. *The Antislavery Vanguard: New Essays on Abolitionists.* Princeton: Princeton University Press, 1965.

DuBois, W. E. B. *John Brown.* Philadelphia: G. W. Jacobs and Co., 1909.

Dumond, Dwight L. *Antislavery Origins of the Civil War.* Ann Arbor: University of Michigan Press, 1959.

Duncan, Jeffrey L., ed. *Thoreau: The Major Essays.* New York: E. P. Dutton and Co., 1972.

Edelstein, Tilden G. *Strange Enthusiasm: A Life of Thomas Wentworth Higginson.* New York: Atheneum, 1970.

Elkins, Stanley M. *Slavery: A Problem in American Institutional and Intellectual Life.* 2d edition. Chicago: University of Chicago Press, 1968.

Farrison, William Edward. *William Wells Brown, Author and Reformer.* Chicago: University of Chicago Press, 1969.

Foner, Eric. *Free Soil, Free Labor, Free Men: The Ideology of the Republican Party Before the Civil War.* New York: Oxford University Press, 1970.

Foner, Phillip. *Frederick Douglass: A Biography.* New York: Citadel Press, 1964.

Fredrickson, George M. *The Black Image in the White Mind: The Debate on*

Afro-American Character and Destiny, 1817–1914. New York: Harper and Row, 1971.

————. *The Inner Civil War: Northern Intellectuals and the Crisis of the Union.* New York: Harper and Row, 1965.

Friedman, Lawrence J. *Gregarious Saints: Self and Community in American Abolitionism, 1830–1870.* New York: Cambridge University Press, 1982.

Frothingham, O. B. *Gerrit Smith.* New York: G. P. Putnam's Sons, 1877.

————. *Theodore Parker.* Boston: J. R. Osgood and Co., 1874.

————. *Transcendentalism in New England.* Reprint 1876 edition. Gloucester, Mass.: Peter Smith Co., 1965.

Furnas, J. C. *The Road to Harpers Ferry.* New York: William Sloane Associates, 1959.

Gara, Larry. *The Liberty Line: The Legend of the Underground Railway.* Lexington: Kentucky University Press, 1961.

Harlow, Ralph V. *Gerrit Smith, Philanthropist and Reformer.* New York: Henry Holt and Co., 1939.

Helper, Hinton Rowan. *The Impending Crisis of the South.* Cambridge, Mass.: Harvard University Press, 1968.

Higginson, Mary Thacher. *Thomas Wentworth Higginson: The Story of His Life.* Boston: Houghton Mifflin Co., 1914.

Hosmer, Charles F. *The Life of James Redpath and the Development of the Modern Lyceum.* New York: Barse and Hopkins Publishers, 1926.

Kraditor, Aileen S. *Means and Ends in American Abolitionism: Garrison and His Critics on Strategy and Tactics.* New York: Pantheon Books, 1969.

Krasner, David. *John Brown, Terrible Saint.* New York: Dodd, Mead and Co., 1934.

Lader, Lawrence. *The Bold Brahims: New England's War Against Slavery, 1831–1863.* New York: Dutton Publishers, 1961.

Litwack, Leon. *North of Slavery: The Negro in the Free States.* Chicago: The University of Chicago Press, 1961.

Lutz, Alma. *Crusade for Freedom: Women of the Antislavery Movement.* Boston: Beacon Press, 1968.

McLaughlin, William G. *The Meaning of Henry Ward Beecher: An Essay on the Shifting Values of Mid-Victorian America, 1840–1870.* New York: Alfred Knopf, 1971.

McPherson, James M. *The Struggle for Equality.* Princeton: Princeton University Press, 1964.

Mabee, Carleton. *Black Freedom: The Nonviolent Abolitionists from 1830 through the Civil War.* New York: Macmillan Co., 1970.

Madden, Edward H. *Civil Disobedience and Moral Law in Nineteenth Century American Philosophy.* Seattle: University of Washington Press, 1968.

Malin, James. *John Brown and the Legend of Fifty-Six.* Philadelphia: The American Philosophical Society, 1942.

Meyer, Howard N. *Colonel of the Black Regiment: The Life of Thomas Wentworth Higginson.* New York: Norton and Co., 1967.

Nevins, Allan. *The Emergence of Lincoln.* 2 vols. New York: Charles Scribner's Sons, 1950.

Newton, John. *Captain John Brown of Harpers Ferry.* New York: A. Wessels Co., 1902.

Nye, Russel B. *Fettered Freedom: Civil Liberties and the Slavery Controversy.* East Lansing: Michigan State University Press, 1964.

Oates, Stephen B. *To Purge This Land in Blood: A Biography of John Brown.* New York: Harper and Row, 1970.

Pearson, Henry Greenleaf. *The Life of John A. Andrew.* 2 vols. Boston: Houghton Mifflin Co., 1904.

Pease, William H., and Pease, Jane H. *Bound with Them in Chains: A Biographical History of the Antislavery Movement.* Westport: Greenwood Press, 1972.

————. *The Fugitive Slave Law and Anthony Burns: A Problem in Law Enforcement.* Philadelphia: J. B. Lippincott Co., 1975.

————. *They Who Would Be Free: Blacks' Search for Freedom, 1830–1861.* New York: Atheneum, 1974.

Perry, Lewis. *Radical Abolitionism: Anarchy and the Government of God in Antislavery Thought.* Ithaca: Cornell University Press, 1973.

Pond, J. B. *The Eccentricities of Genius.* New York: G. W. Dillingham Co., 1900.

Quarles, Benjamin. *Allies for Freedom: Blacks and John Brown.* New York: Oxford University Press, 1974.

————. *Black Abolitionists.* New York: Oxford University Press, 1969.

————. *Frederick Douglass.* Englewood Cliffs: Prentice Hall, 1968.

————. *The Negro in the Civil War.* Boston: Little Brown and Co., 1953.

————, comp. *Blacks on John Brown.* Urbana: University of Illinois Press, 1972.

Ratner, Lorman. *Powder Keg: Northern Opposition to the Antislavery Movement.* New York: Basic Books, 1968.

————. *Pre-Civil War Reform.* Englewood Cliffs: Prentice Hall, 1967.

Rawley, James A. *Race and Politics: "Bleeding Kansas" and the Coming of the Civil War.* Philadelphia: J. B. Lippincott Co., 1969.

Richards, Leonard L. *Gentlemen of Property and Standing, Anti-Abolition Mobs in Jacksonian America.* New York: Oxford University Press, 1970.

Rothman, David J. *The Discovery of the Asylum: Social Order and Disorder in the New Republic.* Boston: Little, Brown and Co., 1971.

Ruchames, Louis, ed. *A John Brown Reader.* New York: Oxford University Press, 1959.

Schultz, Stanley K. *The Culture Factory: Boston Public Schools, 1789–1860.* New York: Oxford University Press, 1973.

Schwartz, Harold. *Samuel Gridley Howe: Social Reformer, 1801–1876.* Cambridge, Mass.: Harvard University Press, 1956.

Shapiro, Samuel. *Richard Henry Dana, Jr., 1815–1882.* East Lansing: Michigan
    State University Press, 1961.
Siebert, Wilbur H. *The Underground Railroad in Massachusetts.* Worcester:
    American Antiquarian Society, 1936.
————. *The Underground Railroad from Slavery to Freedom.* New York:
    Macmillan Co., 1898.
Smith, Timothy. *Revivalism and Social Reform: American Protestantism on the Eve
    of Civil War.* New York: Abington Press, 1957.
Sorin, Gerald. *Abolitionism: A New Perspective.* New York: Praeger, 1972.
————. *The New York Abolitionists: A Case Study of Political Radicalism.*
    Westport: Greenwood, 1970.
Sperry, Earl E. *The Jerry Rescue.* Syracuse: Onondiaga Historical Association, 1924.
Stanton, William R. *The Leopard's Spots: Scientific Attitudes Toward Race in
    America, 1815–1859.* Chicago: Chicago University Press, 1960.
Stearns, Frank Preston. *Cambridge Sketches.* Philadelphia: J. B. Lippincott Co.,
    1905.
————. *The Life and Public Services of George Luther Stearns.* Philadelphia: J. B.
    Lippincott Co., 1907.
Stewart, James Brewer. *Holy Warriors: The Abolitionists and American Slavery.*
    New York: Hill and Wang, 1976.
Thomas, John L. *The Liberator: William Lloyd Garrison.* Boston: Little Brown
    Co., 1963.
Trevelyan, G. M. *Garibaldi and the Making of Italy.* London: Longmans, Green
    and Co., 1914.
————. *Garibaldi's Defense of the Roman Republic.* London: Longmans, Green
    and Co., 1907.
Turner, Lorenzo Dow. *Antislavery Sentiment in American Literature prior to 1865.*
    Port Washington: Kennikat Press, 1966.
Villard, Oswald Garrison. *John Brown, 1800–1859: A Biography Fifty Years After.*
    Boston: Houghton Mifflin Co., 1910.
Walters, Ronald G. *The Antislavery Appeal: American Abolitionists after 1830.*
    Baltimore: The Johns Hopkins University Press, 1976.
Warren, Robert Penn. *John Brown: The Making of a Martyr.* New York: Payson
    and Clark, 1929.
Wells, Anne Mary. *Dear Preceptor: The Life and Times of Thomas Wentworth
    Higginson.* Boston: Houghton Mifflin Co., 1963.
Wilson, R. Jackson. *In Quest of Community, 1860–1920.* New York: John Wiley
    and Sons, 1968.
Wishy, Bernard. *The Child and the Republic.* Philadelphia: University of
    Pennsylvania Press, 1968.
Wolf, Hazel C. *On Freedom's Alter: The Martyr Complex in the Abolitionist
    Movement.* Madison: University of Wisconsin Press, 1952.
Wyatt-Brown, Bertram. *Lewis Tappan and the Evangelical War Against Slavery.*
    Cleveland: Press of Case Western Reserve University, 1969.

Articles

Alexander, John A. "The Ideas of Lysander Spooner." *New England Quarterly* 23 (June 1950): 200–217.

Andrews, Horace, Jr. "Kansas Crusade: Eli Thayer and the New England Emigrant Aid Society." *New England Quarterly* 35 (December 1962): 497–514.

Aptheker, Herbert. "Militant Abolitionism." *Journal of Negro History* 26 (October 1941): 438–84.

Bell, Howard. "Expressions of Negro Militancy." *Journal of Negro History* 45 (January 1960): 11–20.

Brown, Ina. "Miller McKim and Pennsylvania Abolitionism." *Pennsylvania History* 30 (January 1963): 56–72.

Clarkson, John, Jr. "Wanted in Concord." *Yankee Magazine* (April 1969): 128–32.

Connelly, William E. "Personal Reminiscences of Franklin Benjamin Sanborn." *Collections of the Kansas State Historical Society* 14 (April 1918): 59–69.

Curti, Merle. "Non-Resistance in New England." *New England Quarterly* 2 (January 1929): 34–57.

Demos, John. "The Antislavery Movement and the Problem of Violent Means." *New England Quarterly* 37 (December 1964): 501–26.

Dyson, Zita. "Gerrit Smith's Effort in Behalf of Negroes in New York." *Journal of Negro History* 3 (October 1918): 354–59.

Edelstein, Tilden. "John Brown and His Friends," in *The Abolitionists: Immediation and the Question of Means,* edited by Hugh Hawkins, pp. 11–19. Boston: D. C. Heath Co., 1964.

Farrison, William Edward. "A Flight Across Ohio: The Escape of William Wells Brown from Slavery." *Ohio State Historical Quarterly* 11 (July 1952): 273–83.

———. "William Wells Brown in Buffalo." *Journal of Negro History* 60 (October 1954): 299–14.

———. "William Wells Brown, Social Reformer." *Journal of Negro Education* 5 (December–March 1949): 29–39.

Fellman, Michael. "Theodore Parker and the Abolitionist Role in the 1850's." *Journal of American History* 61 (December 1974): 666–84.

Friedman, Lawrence J. "Antebellum American Abolitionism and the Problem of Violent Means." *The Psychohistory Review* 9 (Fall 1980): 23–58.

———. "The Gerrit Smith Circle: Abolitionism in the Burned-Over District." *Civil War History* 26 (March 1980): 18–38.

Harlow, Ralph V. "Gerrit Smith and the John Brown Raid." *American Historical Review* 38 (October 1932): 35–57.

Haynes, George H. "The Causes of Know-Nothing Success in Massachusetts." *American Historical Review* 3 (October 1897): 67–82.

Hickman, R. F. "Speculative Activities of the Emigrant Aid Company." *Kansas Historical Quarterly* 15 (June 1918): 33–41.

Johnson, S. A. "The Genesis of the New England Emigrant Aid Company." *New England Quarterly* 3 (January 1930): 95–122.

Klinger, Samuel. "Emerson and the Usable Anglo-Saxon Past." *Journal of the History of Ideas* 16 (June 1955): 476–93.

Levy, Leonard. "The 'Abolition Riot': Boston's First Slave Rescue." *New England Quarterly* 25 (March 1952): 85–92.

———. "Sims Case: The Fugitive Slave Law in Boston." *Journal of Negro History* 35 (January 1950): 49–74.

McPherson, James M. "A Brief for Equality: The Abolitionist Reply to the Racist Myth, 1860–1865," in *The Antislavery Vanguard: New Essays on the Abolitionists,* edited by Martin Duberman, pp. 155–77. Princeton: Princeton University Press, 1965.

Maginnes, David R. "The Case of the Court House Rioters in the Rendition of Fugitive Slave Anthony Burns, 1854." *Journal of Negro History* 61 (January 1971): 31–43.

Mitchell, Betty L. "Realities not Shadows, Franklin Benjamin Sanborn, the Early Years." *Civil War History* 20 (June 1974): 105–17.

Moody, R. E. "The First Year of the Emigrant Aid Company." *New England Quarterly* 4 (January 1931): 148–55.

Oates, Stephen B. "John Brown and His Judges: A Critique of the Historical Literature." *Civil War History* 17 (March 1971): 5–23.

Ostander, Gillman. "Emerson, Thoreau and John Brown." *Mississippi Valley Historical Review* 34 (March 1953): 713–26.

Pease, William H., and Pease, Jane H. "Antislavery Ambivalence: Immediatism, Expediency, Race." *American Quarterly* 27 (Winter 1965): 682–95.

———. "Confrontation and Abolition in the 1850s." *Journal of American History* 58 (March 1972): 923–37.

Potter, David M. "John Brown and the Paradox of Leadership Among American Negroes," in *The South and the Sectional Conflict,* pp. 200–218. Baton Rouge: Louisiana State University Press, 1968.

Quarles, Benjamin. "John Brown Writes to Blacks." *Kansas Historical Quarterly* 41 (Winter 1975): 454–67.

———. "Letters from Negro Leaders to Gerrit Smith." *Journal of Negro History* 27 (October 1942): 432–54.

Robboy, Stanley J., and Robboy, Anita W. "Lewis Hayden: From Fugitive Slave to Statesman." *New England Quarterly* 46 (December 1973): 591–613.

Salter, William M. "Emerson's View of Society and Reform." *International Journal of Ethics* 13 (1903): 13–35.

Sanborn, Franklin Benjamin. "A Concord Notebook." *The Critic* 47 (October 1905): 76–81.

————. "The Early History of Kansas, 1854–1961." *Proceedings of Massachusetts Historical Society* 41 (February 1907): 331–57.

————. "Gerrit Smith and John Brown." *The Critic* 47 (October 1905): 349–56.

————. "Guesswork History." *Outlook* (April 29, 1911), pp. 983–85.

————. "John Brown and His Friends." *Atlantic Monthly* 28 (July 1872): 122–35.

————. "John Brown in Massachusetts." *Atlantic Monthly* 27 (April 1872): 400–415.

————. "The Real John Brown." *Sunday Magazine* 35 (July 1906): 192–201.

————. "The Virginia Campaign of John Brown." *Atlantic Monthly* 34 (December 1875): 713–30.

Schwartz, Harold. "Fugitive Slave Days in Boston." *New England Quarterly* 27 (June 1954): 191–212.

Shapiro, Samuel. "The Rendition of Anthony Burns." *Journal of Negro History* 44 (January 1959): 34–49.

[Shoemaker, Floyd C.] "John Brown's Missouri Raid: A Tale of the Kansas-Missouri Border Retold with Some New Facts." *Missouri Historical Review* 26 (October 1931): 78–83.

Siebert, Wilbur H. "The Underground Railroad in Massachusetts." *Proceedings of the American Antiquarian Society* 45 (April 1935): 25–100.

Smith, Robert P. "William Cooper Nell: Crusading Black Abolitionist." *Journal of Negro History* 55 (July 1970): 185–99.

Stearns, Frank Preston. "John Brown and His Eastern Friends." *New England Magazine* 42 (July 1910): 589–99.

Stern, M. B. "James Redpath and His Books for the Times." *Publishers Weekly* 147 (December 1945): 2649–53.

————. "Trial of Anthony Burns." *Proceedings of the Massachusetts Historical Society* 44 (1910–1911): 322–34.

Stephenson, Wendell H. "The Political Career of James Lane." *Kansas State Historical Society Publications* 3 (1930): 59–82.

Stewart, James Brewer. "Peaceful Hopes and Violent Experiences: The Evolution of Reforming and Radical, 1831–1837." *Civil War History* 17 (December 1971): 293–309.

Story, Ronald. "Black, Brown and Blood: The Hourglass Pattern." *Reviews in American History* 3 (June 1975): 213–18.

Tomkins, Sylvan S. "The Psychology of Commitment: The Constructive Role of Violence and Suffering for the Individual and for His Society," in *The Antislavery Vanguard: New Essays on the Abolitionists,* edited by Martin Duberman, pp. 419–51. Princeton: Princeton University Press, 1965.

Turner, L. D. "Antislavery Sentiment in Literature: The Second Period of Militant Abolitionism, 1850–1861." *Journal of Negro History* 14 (October 1929): 440–75.

Woodward, C. Vann. "John Brown's Private War," in *The Burden of Southern History,* pp. 41–63. Baton Rouge: Louisiana State University Press, 1960.

Wyatt-Brown, Bertram. "John Brown, Weatherman and the Psychology of Antinomian Violence." *Soundings* 58 (Winter 1975): 425–41.

Dissertations

Abbot, Richard. "Cobbler in Congress: The Life of Henry Wilson, 1812–1875." Ph.D. dissertation, University of Wisconsin, 1965.

Anderson, Godfrey T. "The Slavery Issue as a Factor in Massachusetts Politics from the Compromise of 1850 to the Outbreak of Civil War." Ph.D. dissertation, University of Chicago, 1944.

Bean, William G. "Party Transformation in Massachusetts with Special Reference to the Antecedants of Republicanism, 1848–1860." Ph.D. dissertation, Harvard University, 1922.

Clarkson, John W. "An Annotated Checklist of the Letters of Franklin Benjamin Sanborn." Ph.D. dissertation, Columbia University, 1971.

Davis, Stuart. "Massachusetts in the Secession Crisis, 1859–1961." Ph.D. dissertation, University of Massachusetts, 1975.

Levesque, George August. "Black Boston: Negro Life in Garrison's Boston, 1800–1860." Ph.D. dissertation, State University of New York at Binghamton, 1976.

Story, Ronald. "Class Development and Cultural Institutions in Boston, 1800–1870: Harvard, The Anthenaeum, and the Lowell Institute." Ph.D. dissertation, University of Wisconsin, 1970.

Unpublished Papers

Newbold, Mary Crocker. "Franklin Benjamin Sanborn, 1831–1917: The Unknown Concord Transcendentalist." Unpublished honors essay, Harvard University, 1970.

Sanborn, Franklin Benjamin. "Reminiscences of John Brown and His Friends." Unpublished address to the Mendon Historical Society, June 22, 1911.

Story, Ronald. "John Brown and the Injuries of Class." Paper read before the Department of History at the University of Massachusetts, Amherst, Spring 1973.

Index